GETCHA ROCKS OFF

Sex & Excess. Bust-Ups & Binges.
Life & Death on the Rock 'n' Roll Road

MICK WALL

Copyright © Wallwrite 2015

The right of Mick Wall to be identified as the author
of this work has been asserted in accordance with the
Copyright, Designs and Patents Act 1988.

This edition first published in Great Britain in 2015 by
Orion
an imprint of the Orion Publishing Group Ltd
Carmelite House
50 Victoria Embankment
London EC4Y 0DZ
An Hachette UK Company

10 9 8 7 6 5 4 3 2 1

A CIP catalogue record for this book is
available from the British Library.

Hardback ISBN: 978 1 4091 5979 7
Trade Paperback ISBN: 978 1 4901 4106 8

Typeset by Input Data Services Ltd, Bridgwater, Somerset

Printed and bound by CPI Group (UK) Ltd, Croydon, CR0 4YY

The Orion Publishing Group's policy is to use papers that are natural,
renewable and recyclable and made from wood grown in sustainable
forests. The logging and manufacturing processes are expected to
conform to the environmental regulations of the country of origin.

Every effort has been made to fulfil requirements with regard to
reproducing copyright material. The author and publisher will
be glad to rectify any omissions at the earliest opportunity.

www.orionbooks.co.uk

For Nick McGregor

Contents

Acknowledgements

I never would have made it across the river of shit to find the gold on the other side, only to lose it again, if it hadn't been for the depthless kindness and generosity over the years in question of the following incredible people, some of whom don't speak to me anymore but all of whom I will carry in my heart until the grave. They are, in no order: Ross Halfin, Peter Makowski, Steve 'Krusher' Joule, Sandy Robertson, Geoff Barton, Malcolm Dome, Lynne Seeger, Julian 'Auntie' Isaacs, Danny Heatley, Mick Bevan, Alison Warr, Jo Cohen, Bareen Shah, Joe O'Neil, Sandra Casali, Kelly Pike, and . . . others that will now hate me even more for not remembering to list them here.

I also wish to extend my thanks to the following people, without whom this book would not exist: Anna Valentine, Robert Kirby, Malcolm Edwards, Linda Wall, Vanessa Lampert, Emma Smith, Amy Elliot, Mark Foster, Ian Preece, Susan Howe, Margot Weale, Jessica Purdue, Rebecca Gray, Gail Paten, Richard King, Krystyna Kujawinska, Isadora Attab, Marianne Ihlen, Anna Hayward; not forgetting Ian Clark, Steve Morant, and all at the SNC, especially Stefan and Olivier; Harry Paterson, Philip Maynell, Neil Cross and Gavin 'Young' Fowkes.

1. Rock and Roll Fantasy

It must have been around the third day when I decided I'd had enough. It wasn't that we'd run out of coke. We had enough of that to keep going for ever. It was that I came to on the floor of my hotel room, looked around and realised there were no women left in the place. Not a single one.

'What happened?' I croaked. 'Where did all the girls go?'

'What girls?' asked some biker-looking dude, all bad teeth and worse tattoos. 'I didn't see no fuckin' girls.'

Wait. Was I even in the right room? I tried to think, reconnect, get it together. Was I still asleep, still out for the count, maybe? *Dreaming this?*

I stood up and began moving around, tiptoeing over the dead bodies. Yep, there was the typewriter on the desk, borrowed from reception. Next to it the big wodge of paper, bottles of Tipp-Ex, ashtrays and bottles. And on the coffee table the little Dictaphone I'd started using for interviews. Wait, was that still going? I picked it up and looked at it. What a scene if that had recorded everything . . .

Nope. That was dead too.

I put it down and went looking for the mirror. Chopped out a couple of fat ones, did them. The biker dude looked at me expectantly but I ignored him. Who the fuck was he anyway? Found a warm can of Sapporo, pinged it. Lit a cigarette and gagged.

Let's see . . .

I had been sitting with Warren DeMartini from Ratt, listening to their new album, liking some of it, disliking the rest, not really caring much either way. Warren was a nice guy and it was a cover story for the mag, so what was I gonna do, blow him and his new CD out of the water?

It was also important to remember that it was Ratt's record company who were picking up the tab for all of this. Business-class flights to and from LA; poolside suite at the Sunset Marquis. And that chick with the thunder thighs who knocked on the door that first morning carrying the breakfast tray of Margaritas – and who then settled down by the pool to help me drink them – I didn't know if that was directly to do with Ratt too, but it must have meant something to somebody. It certainly felt like it when she asked if I wanted to take a bath. 'On the house, baby.' And I'd said, 'All right, then . . .'

I hadn't come about the new Ratt album anyway. I'd come because I loved LA. The album was just my ticket to ride. I'd happily give it five stars in return for this.

I loved waking up to smoggy sunshine, eating a late breakfast by the pool, sitting in my shorts and shades, taking it all in. Watching Michael Bolton sitting over there eating breakfast with the phone permanently glued to his ear, same as he did every day. Loved it that at the adjoining table was Bruce Springsteen in deep conversation with Steve Van Zandt, even though Steve hadn't played with Bruce for years. You noticed it, wondered for a moment what was afoot, then forgot about it as your own breakfast arrived and the sun took over your mind.

I loved taking a stroll up Alta Loma to Sunset Boulevard and Tower Records, just to load up on vibe, then across the street to Book Soup, where the ditzy chick behind the counter always had a gossip about who'd been in lately: 'Oh, Mick Fleetwood was here Monday. I mean, he was *high* but he was *cool* about it also, you know?'

'Yeah?'

'But guess who came by the *same* afternoon? *Stevie Nicks!* Like, wow, *coincidence*, right?'

'I don't believe in coincidence.'

'Me either!'

'Was she high too?'

'Who?'

'Stevie.'

'I couldn't tell. She had her hat on.'

Unlike London or New York, where you had to run around town for interviews, in LA in the eighties they just came to you. I imagined my room at the Sunset as like a salon for passing rock stars and their old ladies. But it wasn't like that. The hotel was simply one of those places those kinds of people were just born in.

You had to watch it, though. You could walk into the tiny corner bar by the entrance and not stagger out again until the next day. Time would run over you, leave you for dead in the road. If the party then moved on to your room it was over. Like with Warren. I had a bag of weed and some coke in my room and he had his shiny new CD, so we made straight for there. As Ozzy always said, 'You're never alone with a bag of coke.' Sure enough, as the afternoon collapsed into evening more and more people seemed to arrive out of nowhere. A couple of the guys from Cinderella and their roadies, Lars from Metallica, and a pet fan, Slash from Guns N' Roses, on his own as usual, at least at first. He walked in through the poolside doors, no hat or shades, though you still couldn't see his face behind all that hair, saw what was going on, had some, then tried walking out again but was cut off at the pass by two chicks in teeny-weeny bikinis and fuck-me kitten-heels.

'Hey, Slash, can we get autographs?' said the blonde one.

'Sure, baby. Where do you want me to sign?'

He stood there lighting a new cigarette with the butt of the old one as they ran around trying to find a waiter to borrow his pen.

The rest of us looked on, vaguely interested. Did they have any friends?

Then the girls were back. They both had pens but no paper.

'Here,' said the other blonde one, thrusting out her chest. The first did the same. They giggled again, that warm, Tinker Bell sound all blonde chicks made in LA when they wanted something. Were they twins?

Slash patiently applied his signature to their proffered breasts then added little drawings of a bad man in a top hat smoking a cigarette. They both shrieked with delight.

'We love you, Slash!' the blonde one cried.

'I love you too, baby,' he said back.

'Hey, what about me?' the other one pouted.

'I love you even more,' said Slash, grinning.

'Can we come in, Slash? *Pleeeeease?*'

'Sure, baby.'

And in they came. Then more girls in bikinis and whatnots began trickling in from the pool area, attracted by the music and the buzz.

Time passed. Everyone was doing coke and smoking weed and talking very fast. I ordered a tray of stuff from room service and what seemed like a second later it arrived. Bottles of beer, bottles of Jack, bottles of vodka, wine, cola, cranberry juice, buckets of ice . . .

The room-service guy sniffed and smiled. 'Hey, smells like somethin' good's cooking.'

Someone offered him the joint and he took it, had a few hungry puffs and passed it on.

Then a couple of the Iron Maiden guys were there. In town for what I didn't catch. Then a Dogs D'Amour guy, talking about how he'd met his dream chick and was gonna live here for ever. Then a guy and some girls from what sounded like somebody's record company. Then some other people that knew somebody or were to do with something. It was getting crowded. All the seats were taken, even the bed. People just sat on the floor or stood, or crowded in the bathroom. The party was spilling out through the sliding glass doors and fully into the pool area. Some other hotel guests began wandering over. As soon as the Ratt album finished Warren would put the CD back on.

'Hey, turn that shit off,' someone yelled. 'Put something good on.'

Warren left soon after. I felt for him: not long before, Ratt had been the hottest new band in America, now they were already on the way out. It wasn't Warren's fault. He was the talented one of the band. The rest, though, were now finding their true level. Guns N' Roses and Metallica had begun the job of demolishing them; Nirvana and Pearl Jam would soon finish it. Someone flipped on the set and MTV filled the room with Guns N' Roses and Def Leppard videos. Then Steve Clark from Def Leppard walked in and everyone started laughing while Steve just hung there in the doorway like a ghost. A most nervous cat. I got up, handed him a bottle of vodka. He'd brought his own coke but didn't want anybody to know, so we went into a closet and closed the door behind us. I snipped on my lighter while he fumbled with the gear.

After he'd had a few tokes he felt better and we left the closet. Steve was always hiding himself. I hadn't figured out why yet. Then the most welcome sight of all: Skinny Pete, a 250-pound former Vietnam vet from Texas who dealt the best blow you would ever have but had this thing about never selling any to rock stars or their people, only giving it to them for free. This made Skinny Pete the most popular man at any gig on any night of the week in America, always backstage in the singer's dressing room or riding in the back of the limo with the lead guitarist. Skinny Pete didn't have a home, just travelled the road, staying in the same five-star hotels as the bands, buckled up next to them on the leather couches of their private planes, or simply crashing on the back bunk of the tour bus.

He wasn't choosy; he just went where the action was. Half the time, Pete *was* the action. And he had a thing about always 'taking care' of anyone that crossed his path. He'd leave out gigantic lines of coke by the side of his hotel bed every morning just so the chambermaids would have a nice day. No one really knew how he made his money and no one cared. Just as long as he was there when you needed him. Which meant just as long as he was there. Word was, more rock songs had been written about Skinny Pete between 1981 and 1988 than any other person, real or unreal, on planet rock. Or maybe that was bullshit. Who cared? As long as it sounded true.

All that mattered was that when Skinny Pete showed up you knew the party had started. It was like that now, as he pulled what looked like a sack of white powder from his leather satchel.

'This will sort out the men from the boys,' he said, instantly commanding the best seat in the house. It also sorted out the serious party people from the simple joy bangers. The lightweights began abandoning ship almost immediately. That must have been when the girls started drifting away. When fuckers like biker dude and some other weird-beards nobody knew showed up.

Night came and things started to smooth out. Lars left. So did Slash. Pete said something about the Rainbow, next thing we were all down there, taking up the half-moon seats at the back that used to belong to Led Zeppelin, back when the world was wrong but still better than now.

The usual suspects were there, like Jimmy Bain, bassist in Dio, smack buddy to Phil Lynott, until Phil checked out; a short, skinny devil with a face like baby Jesus who could out-snort, out-drink, out-shoot any fucker you put in front of him, including Skinny Pete. Go figure that one out.

The Rainbow toilets were upstairs, but nobody used them because they had no doors on the crappers. The management had taken them off to discourage people like us from using the stalls to take drugs in. Boohoo! It was just something they did to keep the cops happy, though. Instead they let the people like us – that is, rock stars and their great many dear friends – walk through the kitchens to the staff bogs at the back, where you could spend all night if you wanted to, which sometimes you did.

It was Jimmy Bain who had introduced me to that little dodge. I'd worked with Jimmy in London as a PR in the late seventies when he was partners in Wild Horses with ex-Thin Lizzy guitarist Brian Robertson. Back when everybody seemed to be on smack. But I'd dug myself out of that grimy little corner and by the time I hooked up with Jimmy again in LA I was a gym-going, Filofax-wanking, eighties rocker. That is, I would do anything you wanted to do but I wouldn't do smack. I'd assumed Jimmy was the same. How else was the fucker still alive?

But no. 'Not even just a wee bit?' he smiled, as we stood in the kitchen bogs at the Rainbow that night.

'No, man. Thank you. *No . . .*'

He seemed pissed off.

'Don't let me stop you, though . . .'

'Naw, fuck it, I'm cool.'

We were all cool, baby. Just some were cooler than others.

On the way back I noticed Ozzy's drummer Randy Castillo hiding out at a side table. Randy was half-Red Indian, half-Harley Davidson, one of the friendliest road companions I'd ever shared a groupie with, but a very cold, unfunny fucker when he didn't want you around. You had to read the signs. Tonight they said: stay the fuck away from me. It took me a moment to notice, though. As I slid into the booth next to him, one of his weird friends, who looked like a tramp, grabbed me by the throat: 'Who the fuck are *you*?'

'It's OK,' drawled Randy. 'He's just saying hello.'

Trampus let me go but didn't take his glassy eyes off me. Randy looked away. I said my hellos then got the hell out of there.

The last time I'd seen Randy he had been on the road with Ozzy in Germany. Ozzy had freaked out and refused to come out of his hotel room for three days. So the whole tour had come grinding to a halt until Sharon could fly in and fix the fucker. We were somewhere hopeless like Mannheim, where the action was minimal – just one rock club full of autograph hunters, so the band decided to simply sit it out at the hotel until Ozzy came back off of whatever black cloud he had floated away on.

The chicks had found them, though, like the chicks always did, and Randy had ended the night taking one up to his room. A real looker, too, maybe six feet tall, blonder than blonde with that special light surrounding her that some chicks have. The one that says, 'I will fuck you but it will be you who feels bad about it afterwards.' Not Randy, though.

Around 3 a.m. there was a knock on my door. 'Here,' said Randy, 'birthday present.' And in walked blondie with her special light now not so special. I had barely got the words, 'It's not my birthday,' out of my mouth when she was on her knees yanking at my sleepy knob.

'What a nice guy,' I thought. When I went to thank him the next day he'd merely shrugged. 'Hey, man, I'd had my fuck. Bitch wanted to sleep in my bed! I said, "Fuck that. Sleep on the floor." She didn't like that, so I said, "Wait, I know whose bed you can have . . ."'

Back at the table, Vince Neil of Mötley Crüe had joined the party. I didn't really know Vince, but he'd spotted Skinny Pete so that was that. We would be good friends for the rest of the evening, maybe for ever.

Vince was still on probation for his part in the death of Hanoi Rocks drummer Razzle after he'd crashed his sports car while driving it out of his fucking mind. As a singer, Vince was less than zero, but as a frontman he had it all: an arena-sized ego, hepatitis-yellow hair and silvery Spandex pants so tight they could make a dead girl come. One of those LA dudes the Rainbow was made for. And like Randy you didn't mess with him. A fierce little Mexican kid from the barrio, Vince was street-level tough. I had interviewed him several times, had hung out with him and had a gas. So I would always say hi to him whenever I saw him, and he would always very enthusiastically say hi back. But I was always sure he had no fucking idea who I was.

There were others – over there, W.A.S.P. singer Blackie Lawless, still living off the fumes of their anthem 'Animal (Fuck Like A Beast)'; over here C. C. DeVille from Poison, who Slash said he was gonna kill for wearing a top hat in their videos. All over everywhere the dawn chorus of would-bes and wanna-fucks, all dressed like they were in a Whitesnake video, chicks with dicks star-tripping on their old-fangled fantasies of what it would be like, honey, to be David Lee Roth just for one fuck-rocking day.

The Rainbow closed at 2 a.m., so after that we all went back to my place. I was the only one stupid enough to let people like that in at that time of night. The only one who Skinny Pete was hanging out with anyway.

We got back and I got on the phone to room service again. There were only about eight or nine of us left, including some hotties from the 'Bow, but that just made it more fun. You could actually have a conversation now and again.

It must have been a few hours later, because the sun was up, when I got a phone call from my favourite record company girl, English Rose, so called because she was an English chick working in LA. Her real name was Maggie. Maggie was a little bit in love with me and I was a little bit in love with Maggie. That is, we both liked to fuck and suck and pull and drool and do anything and everything we could think of to each other whenever we got together. Maggie was simply the dirtiest girl I'd ever known, even dirtier than me, and I was fucking filthy.

The only reason we didn't end up together was that I already had a live-in girlfriend back in London. But whenever I was in LA . . .

'Check it out, honey,' she purred down the phone. 'I've got a limo to myself for the next twenty-four hours. I was supposed to be taking that dick from MTV out to Long Beach for something he's doing on Whitesnake. But they cancelled so I've got the limo to myself for the day. Wanna go for a ride?'

I looked around the room. Vince had taken off with two of the girls, hours ago. Even Skinny Pete looked like he was starting to fade. It was just that time of the night. Day. Whatever.

'Great,' I said. 'How long will it take you to get here?'

'I'm right outside, honey . . .'

I picked up my cigarettes and jacket and left them to it.

The limo was laid right outside the front door of the Sunset, engines gloating. The uniformed driver jumped out when he saw me coming and opened the door. I fell in.

'Hey, baby!'

I kissed her, a good one, tongues and everything. As usual she had painted her lips bright cherry red. I broke off and looked at her face. She was dark-haired, pretty, with plenty of meat on the bone. So different from the plastic fantastic look you got used to in LA.

'So great to see you,' I said.

'You too, honey. What have you been up to? You look like shit.'

'I feel like shit. Where we going?'

'Fancy some breakfast?'

'No!'

'Sure?' she said. She pushed a button and the grey shield between the driver and us slid up. As it did so she unbuttoned her top. Another cool thing about Maggie, she had great tits. Everyone agreed. Again, not the pointy, bulgy fake cakes you got in LA. These were real *woman's* breasts. Not some pouty little chick from the Rainbow but a real king-size babe. You could get lost in a woman like that.

I fell on her like sack of shit. Gorged myself on those magnificent tits. She laughed and pulled at my jeans until they slid down my arse just far enough for her to grab my hopeful cock and guide it into her. I reached down and pulled her pants to one side. She wasn't even wet yet. I was barely hard. But in it went, like it just belonged there. My spirit gusted out of my body, clouding up the windows. She yelled and bit me on the shoulder. Hard! I banged into her six, seven, eight times and came. Now it was my turn to yell. 'Jesus fucking Christ, that nearly killed me . . .' I rolled off and lay on the floor of the limo, panting. I felt my heart trying to jump out of my throat.

'I think I'm having a fucking heart attack,' I gasped. Sweat poured down my face. I looked up at her. She just sat there staring at me, smiling, legs spread. I knew she hadn't come but she knew it was only the start.

'Play with yourself,' I said. 'I want to watch.'

'No. Later. *You* play with me first.'

I did as I was told. I put my head between her legs and got into it. My throat was chokingly dry and my tongue blistered and swollen from all the coke and cigarettes, but that only made it feel more intense. She began to whimper and moan and grind her pussy into my face.

I stopped and looked up. 'I know who you wish this was,' I said.

'No, don't!'

'You wish this was David Coverdale, don't you?'

'No!' she heaved.

'Yes you do, you filthy cow. You wish this was David Coverdale sticking his big white snake into you. *Don't you?*'

'Yes! Yes! Now shut up and get on with it . . .'

Afterwards we snuggled up together in the back of the limo. Maggie had her eyes closed and her breathing was deep, like she was asleep. I wanted to join her but felt like I'd never sleep again.

More time passed. I didn't know where I was, what was supposed to be happening. Then the intercom light came on.

I picked up the car phone. 'Yes?' I said.

'Sorry to disturb you, sir. Just checking if there is someplace you folks want to go. We've been on the kerb at the hotel now for a while. They're going to get mighty pissed off if we don't move off soon.'

'Sure,' I said. 'Actually, I'm getting out now. Please take the lady home, OK?'

'Yes, sir!'

He jumped out and ran around to open the door.

I kissed Maggie, smoothed her skirt down over her thighs and got out.

She opened her eyes. 'Is that it? You're not even going to invite me in?'

'I'm really sorry. I've been up all night. I've really got to sleep. Call you later?'

She ignored me. The driver shut the door. I tiptoed back inside the hotel, properly tired now. I still didn't know if I could sleep but knew I needed rest. A bath maybe and a cup of tea and then bed, with the TV on and maybe one last joint . . .

But when I got to my room there was a guy standing guard outside. I vaguely recognised him, I thought. Though I couldn't be sure. There were guys that looked like this guarding dressing rooms doors at every gig you'd ever been to. I reached into my pocket for my room key. He caught the movement and put out a hand.

'I'm sorry, sir, but you can't come in here.'

'What? But this is my room . . .'

'I'm sorry, sir, but you still can't come in here. It's *occupied.*'

I stood there waiting for the words to come.

'What do you mean "occupied"? This is *my* room. These are *my* guests! Who are you?'

'I work for Mr James, sir. And I have instructions not to let anyone in under *any* circumstances.'

'"Mr James"? Who is Mr James?'

'Mr James, the musician, sir.'

I racked my brains. There was Brian James once of The Dammed now of the Lords Of The New Church. But it couldn't be him, he wouldn't have a bodyguard, no fucker knew who he was any more. Mind you, this was LA, where even the nobodies had bodyguards.

James, James . . .

'Look, this is ridiculous,' I said. 'This is my room. If you don't let me in I'm gonna call the hotel security.'

'I *am* hotel security, sir.'

I thundered back to reception. Unloaded on them. It was morning; the breakfast crowd was starting to drift in, all smiley gorgeous cleanly soberness. People were looking then turning away. There was a dead person in reception, *shouting* . . .

My guy finally came out from the back office. Knew me of old. Dr Cool.

'Mr Wall,' he beamed, 'I hear we have a little problem. And that it's to do with Mr James?'

'Yes. Who is Mr James? And why is he in my room?'

'Mr James is the famous musician, Mr Wall, and I think you'll agree there have been quite a lot of people like that in your room these past couple of days.'

He smiled some more. Was he taking the piss?

'Tell you what we can do for you, Mr Wall. How about we put you up in another room for today until we can get you back in your room tomorrow? After Mr James leaves.'

'But what about my stuff?'

'Oh, I can promise you Mr James won't be interested in that. He just doesn't want to be disturbed right now. Andre will show you to your *new* room.'

I followed Andre back down the hall to my new room, about three doors down from my old room. As we passed it I could hear loud music, funk, soul, stuff like that, but really loud. That and the hum of a crowd. What the fuck was going on in there?

'What's going on in there?' I asked.

'I don't know,' he said, 'But it's been going on for a couple of days now. Some kind of party.'

'Yeah, I know. But who is Mr James?'

'Oh you know, the "Super Freak" guy? He's always taking over people's rooms. I think he thinks he owns this place.' He chuckled good-naturedly.

I took it in, floated it around in what was left of my heavy metal brain and still came back with nothing. Fuck this, I decided. I waited till Andre had gone then slid open the glass doors to the pool. Crept back along the patio to the sliding doors to my old room. They were closed now but you could just see through the drapes. It looked kind of like how I'd left it, only now there was a major party going on. I tapped on the glass. Pressed my room key to the glass and waited.

One of them, this huge spade in full spade's clothing – fur collar, killer shades, gold everything – came over and slid open the door.

'I get it,' he said. 'You're the dude who's *having* the party, right?'

'That's right,' I said.

'Well, come on in, brother!'

I walked in and it was the same room I'd left but with added glitter. Skinny Pete had vamoosed, as had most of the other people I knew, except for a couple of the biker-looking dudes. Only now there were all these black guys and white chicks about the place too, dancing, laughing, smoking, toking, chugging and a-lugging.

I looked over and the typewriter was where I had left it. That was a relief. The tape-recorder lying next to it. Big relief.

'Hey, man, say hello to Rick,' the guy said.

I looked and there was Mr Rick James, stretched out on the bed with a couple of babes next to him and a big mirror with a hill of white snow on it. I recognised the mirror. It was from the bathroom wall. Someone had unscrewed it and placed it on the bed. I'd try to remember that one.

'Hey, man,' said Rick, looking up. 'Make yourself at mother-fucking home . . .'

So I did.

The next day, week, year, whenever, I wondered: did that *really* happen? *Could* that have really happened? Or was I just *imagining* it? I would find myself asking that question a lot in times to come.

2. **Born Too Late**

I was eighteen and dealing speed when I met somebody that actually had a better job. His name was Pete Makowski and at first I was only vaguely interested when told he was a music journalist. I'd read *NME* in its heyday, back when Charlie Murray and Nick Kent ruled the roost, but I'd lost the habit since leaving home and renting my own room at the big house on Ealing Common. It was the cold, grey winter of 1976 and the house was full of hippies. They were all older, came from a different time, before Bowie had cha-cha-cha-changed things. So now I was into J. D. Souther, Sun Ra, Dan Hicks and His Hot Licks ... stuff you didn't find in the music papers. Also, I was told Pete worked for *Sounds*, and I'd never really bought that. And anyway, writing about music – how dull that must be. I imagined Pete going to concerts, then coming home and sitting up all night writing about them. It sounded like homework. That's why he needed the speed, I supposed.

We were sitting cross-legged on the floor in my room, me on the thin, fag-burned mattress, him by the electric fire. Summer was over and the ratting wind swept in under the door and through the single-pane window in cold waves. Some mornings you could hardly breathe for the cold. I would lay on the mattress, bundled in my sleeping bag, with the fire, both bars blazing, up near my head. I would reach across with a cigarette and light it off one of the orange bars, then sit up on one elbow and tip some sulphate into a cup of water, stir it with my finger then drink it down, trying not to gag. The days of taking a couple of dabs with a wet finger were long gone. When you're swallowing down half a gram of foul-tasting white powder at a time, you need something to take away the awful sting.

Pete didn't look like one of those. He liked his speed, didn't mind hanging out in my shithole, playing records and talking, talking, talking till the room fell finally to zipped-up silence, the way it always does when you mix your speed with your dope and alcohol and melancholy no-woman blues ... you know the fucking scene. But Pete didn't *live* there like I did. He lived somewhere else, in my imagination somewhere nice and clean that smelled warm. Pete was just dropping by to score, not hanging on for wherever the next deal might take him. Or not.

Consequently I looked down on him a little. He was an amateur. I was a pro. It was OK for what it was, being a part-timer, but what it was wasn't much. Not really. Then one night my ears pricked up. He was saying something about America. Going to America. With a band ... for a band ... what did he say?

I was used to people talking about going on the hippy trail to Morocco, India or Greece – six months at a time; two years – you and your old lady. Sri Lanka was the latest. The beaches were *amazing*, man. I couldn't remember anyone talking of America, though. The States. We'd had a chick staying at the house in the summer who came from Canada via Goa, but never anybody who had been to America.

It was a couple of days later, I was thinking about what he'd said, but I couldn't remember if I'd heard right. He was going to America to be on tour with Lynyrd Skynyrd? That didn't sound right. Were they even still going? Did people go to America to be on tour with Lynyrd Skynyrd?

I asked his sister, Yvonne, about it. Yvonne lived in the house too, and I had a thing for her. She was twenty-four, gorgeous, but screwed up. Anorexia. She'd had it as a kid and never gotten over it. Not properly. She still couldn't eat without making a big deal of it, so just drank little glasses of sickly sweet white wine and smoked Silk Cuts, the long, light kind no one else could even taste. Some guy had already done for her; whoever came along next had to listen to her going on about it, over and over, until finally you gave up.

She tutted and rolled her eyes. She'd been asked about her brother before. 'He's always going somewhere like that to write about a band,' she told me grudgingly. 'I don't know about this one, though. He never tells me anything . . .'

And he got paid for that? Or did he have to pay for himself? She looked at me, as if reconsidering. 'It's his job. God . . .'

The subject was simply too irritating, too old news for her to pursue any further, so that was the sum total of all my knowledge. Pete went to America to tour with bands then wrote about them and, yes, he got paid for it. 'Cos it was his job. Stupid.

A few weeks later he was back and full of stories. How he'd been down in the Deep South with the band. How he'd ridden on the back of their motorcycles. How he'd been to some club with them where someone pulled a gun. Then how they rode off into the night with some crazy bikers who had this atomic fucking speed, man – meth, crystals, ice-on-fire, then something, something . . . I couldn't keep up. How they all nearly died but then this chick got up and slapped Johnny's face and everybody laughed and fell about the place . . .

I noticed how the older hippy guys in the house hung on his words, how deeply impressed they were by his stories, while trying not to show it. Not really knowing much about Lynyrd Skynyrd or where the Deep South might be, exactly, I locked on to them locking on to him. Everyone was buzzing. Then after he'd gone it all died down. I was alone in my room again – just the speed and me. That had always suited me, only now it didn't. It had been getting that way more and more lately.

Pete and me became chummier after that. He had two tickets to see Thin Lizzy at the Hammersmith Odeon and asked if I'd like to go with him. I thought he'd bought them because he was a fan. It wasn't until we got there and I asked how much they'd cost that he explained they hadn't cost anything. He'd been given them.

'By who?'

'The band.'

'The *band*?'

'Yeah. Well, the band's record company. 'Cos of all the stuff I've done with them.'

I had no idea what 'stuff' he might have done with the band or their record company, but sensed it would not be cool to ask, acted like it was no big thing. I'd never seen Thin Lizzy before, either, but I had their *Jailbreak* album and Pete had played me some tracks from their new LP, *Johnny the Fox*. We took our seats at the front of the balcony and when the band came on to the sound of a deafening police siren my lid just fucking flapped open. They were amazing! Brilliant! Amazing!

'Tonight there's gonna be a jailbreak,' the singer, Phil Lynott, sang, *'. . . somewhere in this town . . .'*

He was right and it was happening right here, in this room, for all of us. I stood up like everybody else did and began weaving around, singing along. A minute or two in, lost in my own speed-crazed movie, I glanced to my side, ready to commune better with Pete. But he wasn't there. He was sitting down! Just staring, his head vaguely nodding a bit.

I leaned over. 'AREN'T THEY GREAT!'

He barely looked up, just nodded slightly, not even smiling. Then went back to just sitting, as though lost in some deep, more interesting thought.

Things stayed that way for the rest of the show. Every now and again I would glance over, see him sitting there while everyone else around us stood, not unhappy, but hardly delirious in the way my fellow escapees and I were.

'FUCKING AMAZING!' I would scream.

But it was as if I wasn't even there with him. Or rather, he wasn't there with me. There was something separating us – whole worlds, as it turned out. But I didn't know that then. I just saw the band and the music, felt the crowd and the collective joy; getting off on the absolute thrill of being there as it all happened around us, in the middle of something unbelievable.

When it was over, so was I. Finished off good and proper. Exhausted from yelling and stamping my feet, clapping as hard as I could in order to persuade the band back for an encore, until – far out! – they came back on!

'YEAH! YEAH!'

What an ending. I could not imagine a better one. Not for Pete, though. As we made our way back down to the lobby, people kept coming up and shaking his hand, hugging him, saying how great it was to see him; how great it was he'd made it. Women too. Lookers. Coming up and pressing their bodies against him, genuinely excited to see him.

'Who was *she*?' I asked, as one broke away, her face still in my eyes.

'No one,' he said. 'A friend.'

I followed him outside where another friend offered to drive him – us – to the party.

'Cool,' said Pete, still distant, still apparently thinking of something else.

'Where we going?' I asked, as we walked through the cold November night to the car park.

'The band are having a do,' he said.

The band? A do? What sort of a do? Would they be there too? Bloody hell . . .

It was at a posh hotel somewhere in Kensington, a few floors up. A big room full of people I didn't know or knew existed. Everyone knew Pete, though. All were pleased to see him. I tagged along, walking a couple of paces behind, grinning to cover my embarrassment, my lack of basic knowledge as to where I was, who these people were or how any of this worked. I had never felt so lost, not even when surrounded by strangers, all older than me, at the house whenever they had a gathering. At least there you could make friends easily just by letting them know you had speed. Here was different. The speed alone wouldn't make it work for this crowd. You needed some other in. One I didn't have. Not like Pete.

Suddenly he was talking to Phil Lynott. I didn't know where to look, what to do, how to stand, where to put my face. I just stood there behind Pete and waited.

They hugged each other and Phil said something in Pete's ear. Some secret only they could share. Pete grinned back and for the first time all night he looked fully turned on. I was stunned at how well they appeared to get on, to know each other.

'This is my mate, Mick,' said Pete, waving an arm in my general direction. Lynott just nodded and kept on grinning. Then went back to talking to Pete.

As a little kid my dad – forced to look after the boy for a few hours while my mother went God knows where – would take me with him to the pub on Chiswick High Road, then make me stand outside while he went in 'for five minutes'. It was horrible, having to hang around waiting for whatever was going on inside this place I wasn't allowed into. So I would stand outside, rigid like a statue, imagining that if people thought I was a statue they would simply pass by without a thought for my predicament. I did the same now with Pete and Phil, willing myself invisible while they did whatever it was they were doing in this place I didn't belong, while I waited for Pete to finish and come back for me, a bit like my dad, who would eventually remember to come back out for me.

Then this other guy came over. A truly ugly looking thing with weird orange hair, spiky, his face all pink and raw, his shoulders hunched, his eyes black and beady like a rat's. He didn't look like he belonged there either, yet here he was anyway.

'I thought the gig was farking great, Phil,' he said, the voice all cockney wind-up. 'Up the farking IRA, you knoworrimean?'

Phil just grinned at him.

'But I can't stand these parties. So farking *boring* . . .'

I was shocked. The party was boring?

'Ah, go on wit cha, Johnny,' said Phil in his low Dublin brogue. 'Have anudder fookin' drink and grab a burd. Enjoy yersel . . .'

Rat boy laughed. But even that came out vaguely insulting, like the sandpaper cough of an old tramp that had stopped finding things funny lifetimes before. 'Ark, ark, ark. Ark, ark, ark . . .'

Then he wandered off. Pete said see you later to Phil, and I finally got to say something: 'I didn't know you knew Phil Lynott!'

'What?' he said looking sideways at me. 'Yeah . . .'

'And who was that guy?'

'What guy?'

'The horrible-looking cunt in the hair, who said how bored he was?'

'Oh, that's Johnny . . . Johnny Rotten.'

I snorted with laughter. 'That's not his name!'

'Yeah. You know, from the Sex Pistols?'

'The sex what?'

'Doesn't matter. He's all right, actually. Just a bit weird.'

We pushed through to the bar where they were serving free drinks. I couldn't quite believe it was real. Free drinks! I ordered two beers and two whiskies. Pete ordered a wine.

'They're free!' I told him, in case he'd missed it. '*Free*. You can order whatever you like!'

'I'm all right,' he said. 'You go on, though.' Then he wandered off to say hello to someone else I didn't know.

Truly this was an odd night. It occurred to me there was a whole side to Pete I didn't know at all.

I waited around at the free bar while Pete did a circle of the room. I waited and watched. There were chicks everywhere. Really dolled up, like on telly, page-three quality. Even the guys were dolled up. I felt like a fraud standing in that crowd, people talking over me in the crush for the free bar. I wasn't moving, though.

Wait – was that George Best over there? GEORGE BEST!! No, it couldn't be. Could it? Yes!

'Let's go.' It was Pete. I downed the rest of the beer but couldn't manage both whiskies too. 'Come on,' he said. 'You can crash at mine. Got any more whizz?'

I pestered him about it all night, but he really didn't have much to say on the subject. Lynott was 'all right'. A 'good bloke'. Lizzy were 'a good band'. More 'good blokes'. But there were none of the stories to back up these glib observations the way there had been when he'd got back from Lynyrd Skynyrd in America. I sensed that was because it would have been too much effort for him. That, in truth, there really wasn't much special to tell about Thin Lizzy. That getting free tickets for the gig, getting a lift to a party for the band afterwards, getting to speak to Phil Lynott and drink free drinks was just somehow . . . normal. It felt like the wrong word to me, but it seemed like the only way to describe whatever it was Pete felt about it.

Weeks went by and I kept thinking about it. Then one night another speed freak named Pete (Lewis), who was an artist, said out of the blue, 'Did you see *Sounds* are looking for writers? You should go for it.'

I looked at him. How did he know I was a writer?

'Well, you are, aren't you?' He forced a laugh. Like he'd just come in and caught me wanking. 'You've always been a writer, haven't you? With your poems and stuff?'

It was true about the poems, but I'd never have used the word 'writer' about myself. That was reserved for people who had actually had something published – not somebody who sat up all night speeding out of their brains, making up would-be lyrics.

But Lewis talking out loud about it like that, it drew my attention to myself in a somewhat different manner. Like maybe I had a secret superpower that I could use for the good of mankind. Sitting there, hiding behind my secret identity as a respectable speed dealer. It didn't matter that I'd never thought of writing for a music paper. It was just the sound of it. *Sounds* needed writers . . .

I began to bother him for details, but he was already losing interest talking about me when we could be talking about him. Fire signs are the worst like that, and Lewis was a born Leo, right down to the great mane of curly dark hair.

'There's an ad in the paper. I don't know how I know. Perhaps Yvonne told me. I don't know. Anyway, it says they're looking for writers.'

Wow. All right, then. Thanks.

The next day I made it down to the newsagent's and bought a copy of *Sounds*. There was a band on the cover I'd never heard of. I opened it up and began turning pages, looking for this ad. There it was:

SOUNDS IS LOOKING FOR NEW WRITERS.
NO EXPERIENCE NECESSARY.

Those were the magic words: 'no experience necessary'. I'd seen ads for filing clerks that asked for more than that. No experience necessary . . . 'That's me,' I thought. All it asked for was that you write something – anything – about a musical artist you knew something about it, then send it in. The lucky entries would be interviewed at the magazine's London offices. All entries in by—

That night, I made myself an extra-specially strong cup of water. There was so much sulphate in it I had a job getting it all to dissolve. I choked it down. It tasted fucking awful. Jesus God! I thought I was gonna chuck-up. My poor, sleep-starved eyes began to water and my hair frizzed right up behind my ears. I could feel it. I smoked a couple of cigarettes, gave the gear time to kick in, then picked up my biro and began writing.

It was about David Bowie, a subject I felt I knew more about than practically anyone else in the world, including Charles Shaar Murray, who'd been good during the Ziggy period but had got *Diamond Dogs* and *David Live* all wrong, from start to finish. I had never really forgiven him for that, and I felt Bowie hadn't either. I would set the record straight. In the form of a review of *Low*, which had just come out and which I alone knew to be a masterpiece of desolation and icy peeks into the future, our future, the one waiting for us now we'd broken all the rules and there was no going back. This was David allowing us into his room, blue, blue electric blue: us and all that broken glass. When he sang about always crashing in the same car, I knew *exactly* what he was talking about, almost as if I'd been in the passenger seat next to him. And when, on side two, on 'Weeping Wall', the synthesiser sliced open 'Scarborough Fair' so cleanly the two halves spun all the way round in a circle back together again, I knew he had to have been up speeding too for a very, very long time. That neither of us might ever sleep again. Experiencing first hand that terror. I knew that when, on the final, blissfully psychotic track, 'Subterranean', when in his wordless vocals he sang *'Kay line, kay line, kay line, kay line, briding . . . lee shelly shelly, shelly omm . . .'* I would join in, howling like a brother wolf separated from the filthy pack, looking down with hungered yellow eyes from that thin, crumbling ledge high above the abyss. Me and Bowie; Bowie and me. Let me tell you about it, properly this time.

I wrote and I wrote, the pen dug into my speed-frozen fingers like a knife, and when the sick grey winter sun came crawling up the walls I carried on writing until I really had run out of ways to express it. But my mind wouldn't switch off, and so I kept on. Knowing to keep on would be to destroy it, trying to say too much of what was really all too little. Wordless lyrics. Inside-out melodies. Upside-down rock that despised having to roll. I knew I would ruin it, and I did, but still I couldn't stop.

Finally the buzz and burn blew itself out and I dragged myself over to the mattress, pulled the electric fire nearer, and lay there, my eyes staring open as I slept, the room full of cigarettes smoked and unsmoked. The way I supposed I liked it. Or said I did.

Later that day – or the next, it was hard to tell – I propped myself up again and read through the pages. Some of it was illegible, even to me. Some of it started well and went nowhere.

Some of it just disgusted me. It said nothing whatsoever. Not even close to what it was I'd been thinking at the time, what I'd meant to say.

But at least you could see I could write. There were enough words, surely. Long and short. Writer's words.

I carried it to the post office, bought a big envelope. Wrote down the address copied from the ad, torn from the magazine, and bought a first-class stamp and posted it. I cringed as I did so, imagining someone coming across it and holding it aloft from its furthest corner, by the tips of their fingers, regarding it as one might a soiled tissue found on a toilet seat.

Then I shuffled back to the house again, where I slurped more speed and this time imagined them reading it aloud to each other, amazed at the discovery of a new genius. Then I went back to seeing them crumpling it into a ball and hurling it on to the fire. Where it belonged. See that a mile off. Still, you never knew, maybe the right guy would get it and he would like it, see the potential, persuade the others to give this newcomer a chance.

Jesus God Christ . . . I knew the comedown would be horrendous and tried to postpone it for as long as possible. Knowing it wouldn't work.

3. Lurking

The delay was long enough for the letter to be a surprise, but not so long I'd completely forgotten about it. I already knew what it would say, anyway. Sure enough: *Dear Hopeless Sap, you didn't get the gig. We gave it to some people who knew what they were doing.* I sloped back to my room and dropped down on the mattress, flattened. I felt under the mattress for the polythene bag with the three grams in it and sifted out enough for a few dabs off the wet finger. Flattened and freaked out and failed and fucked. What was I thinking? Maybe I could write lyrics, but you really had to know how to write in a certain way to write for something real like *Sounds*. How had Pete done it? Where did he go to learn? Or was he just born with it? Could that happen? That some were born with it and some – most – like me, weren't?

I thought about trying to review something else, but I knew I'd never get around to it. I did still buy *Sounds* occasionally, just to see how Pete was getting on. There was another writer they had, too, Giovanni Dadomo, whose name I could not guess how to pronounce but whose writing really turned me on. The clincher had been a three-part story on the Velvet Underground. This was higher-ground stuff – the kind I knew I'd never be able to reach but didn't feel at all bad about. It was just so good to read, to witness a real master at work. The reader in me would always trump the writer, I realised. But maybe that was OK, after all.

By the summer of '77 I'd crashed big time. In the end, no amount of speed worked any more. It just sent me down Doolally Street, round the Mulberry Bush and up Shit Creek. I couldn't sleep but I couldn't stay awake. I was down to seven stone, always hungry but unable to eat. Bread and a small tin of spaghetti hoops was a banquet for me. Breakfast was a Mars Bar and a can of Coke.

Finally, I fell out with the older hippies when I couldn't afford the rent one month and they ransacked my room, stole what was left of my speed and took some pictures I'd taken on an instamatic camera of an old girlfriend, posing nude. I came home one night and found them sellotaped to the walls of the toilet. If I'd had a gun I'd have done a Travis Bickle on them. But all I had was my mattress and electric fire. The next morning I got a friend to come round in his car and take me back to my parents' house. My old room had been taken over by my youngest brother, so I slept on a camp bed. I really had no idea what was what, just that I'd never be a writer. Not for *Sounds* anyway.

It wasn't just my life that had changed. That summer saw the big switchover to punk. Suddenly everything that came before was out the window. The weird, arse-faced guy I'd seen moaning at Phil Lynott had ascended to messiah-hood. His band, the Sex Pistols, had singlehandedly changed the game for everybody.

I liked it and I didn't like it. Pete Makowski had been the first person to play me 'Anarchy In The UK' and I had become addicted – instantly. I still hadn't really heard the word 'punk' being used to describe it, and the music, as such, didn't sound very different to what else was going on. More like the culmination of years of listening to Bowie, Mott The Hoople and Hawkwind. In fact, it reminded me of 'Urban Guerrilla', the Hawkwind single from a few years before, that had been banned by the BBC then withdrawn by the band's record company. When the same thing happened to the Sex Pistols' single, it seemed impossible, ridiculous. Surely we'd moved on from the antique values of 1973?

I also really liked The Damned. They were the first of the new generation of bands that actually sounded like they were from the future. Fast, fast, fast, yet brilliantly witty. They didn't have the same brutal lyrical imagery of Rotten and the Pistols, but they had the speed and punch and weird, Luis Buñuel quality I was a sucker for. Like early Alice Cooper but much more real.

Far more interesting were American artists like Patti Smith and Television. I'd bought *Horses* on the strength of the *NME* review and I had no recollection of anyone describing it as punk, though maybe they did. But the word had no *frisson* when *Horses* was released in 1975.

Compared to *Horses*, albums that followed, like ones from The Clash and The Jam, sounded like playground spittle. Patti had so much to say she couldn't even sing Them's 'Gloria' without packing it with reams of symbolist poetry. Compared to 'Land', everything the British punk bands, including the Sex Pistols, were attempting was just angry mulch – worm food for mental cases dancing on one leg. This, surely, was the real future of rock 'n' roll. Music that referenced the past, renovated it with present-time lyrics and poetry and ground-floor, free-flowing jams, then sent it whoosh into the sky like indoor fireworks. *'One who sees his possibilities . . . One who seizes possibilities . . . standing there with my legs spread . . . his hand on my knee . . . the boy looked at Johnny . . .'*

'Land' was like 'Stairway To Heaven' for a generation who didn't believe in heaven any more. Patti was by consequence a greater artist than Led Zeppelin and the Rolling Stones put together, neither of whom had said anything of interest for donkey's years. Only Lennon and Dylan had previously been there, done that, come back and grudgingly let us in on it. Or Bowie on *Low*. But that had been after *Horses*.

The other clincher that summer had been *Marquee Moon* by Television. Had there been no punk, no Johnny swearing on telly and the music papers fawning over him, no boring Joe Strummer going on about 'the kids', like anyone gave a fuck about that, had rock not digressed to its grotty adolescence and incoherent air-punching, Television would have been seen as the latest in a line of brilliantly realised rock bands, touched by Bowie, as everything now was, but stretching back far beyond Ziggy to the Velvet Underground and The Doors, to Creedence Clearwater Revival and The Byrds. Staring at the lyric sheet that first time, when Tom Verlaine sang, '*I remember how the darkness doubled, I recall, lightning struck itself*', I gasped out loud. How *the darkness doubled*? How *lightning struck itself*? This was a whole new way of saying the unsayable, and it spoke to me on a level far deeper, more shockingly painful yet more achingly zestful than anything Johnny or Joe or Paul or whoever might be on stage at the 100 Club that night could ever do.

I wouldn't have known how to write about it, though, not even to myself. Instead I took a job in an employment agency – offered after they gave up trying to find me a job somebody wanted me for. They needed somebody young and cheap who could answer a phone and make tea and generally just laugh at their jokes.

Then one day, on one of those days off I was beginning to have more and more of, I was rummaging in a drawer at my parents' place when I found the original letter from *Sounds*. I'd been drinking all day and everything was funny. Picking it up and reading it again, though, was like finding a map to the treasure. It was buried deep on an island far away that I'd already tried and failed to find my way to, and if I hadn't been drunk I'd never have given it another thought. Instead I decided to give the magic lamp another rub.

I rang the number and spoke to their reviews editor, Geoff Barton.

'Perhaps we should try a live review,' he said. 'What sort of music are you into?'

My eyes opened. I wasn't ready for that question. I tried to think of something but could only come up with the usual. 'Um . . . Bowie.'

'Yes,' he said, seeing his mistake, perhaps. 'I tell you what, there's a band called The Lurkers playing at the Red Cow in Hammersmith next week. Do you know them?'

The Lurkers? I had never heard of them. Had anybody? 'Yes, I think so.'

'Punk band,' he said. 'How are you with punk?'

'Yeah, I like punk,' I said back.

'All right. So, look, why don't you go along and write something. See how you get on. Have you got a pen? I'll give you the details . . .'

It was a rainy Tuesday night in September and I was worried. I'd been to punk gigs before – The Damned, who were brilliant, at some college in London; the big gig at the Rainbow with The Clash, The Jam, Subway Sect and all that stuff, that had also been good though not that great – but I'd never been to a scummy pub in Hammersmith to see bottom-rung punk lobsters like The Lurkers.

Fortunately, Pete Lewis had offered to come with me. Said he'd take some photos. He also had his dad's car, which meant we could get the hell out of dodge quickly when it finished. The band was already on stage when we arrived. I was surprised by how many people were there to see them. A big gang of them down the front pogoing and gobbing at them. All uniformly punk, short, spiked black hair, worn leathers, a few swastika armbands, all clearly way ahead of me in terms of Lurkers knowledge.

I'd brought a pen and pad, assuming the correct thing would be to take notes. But I was too self-conscious to pull them out in front of this mob. I was worried it would attract their attention, and that was the last thing I wanted. I already felt out of place in my flared green cords and long silver scarf. I'd heard about what that Sex Pistols fan did to Nick Kent. I was not impatient to give these hungry young sharks the smell of my blood so easily.

I couldn't tell if the band was really any good, but the crowd went bonkers for them. It was hard actually to tell the band from the crowd. Several times they all jumped on the stage together, all pogoing and falling over together while the band did same-sounding songs like the one called 'Shadow' that went '*sha-dow, sha-dow, sha-dow, sha-dow, sha-dow, sha-dow, sha-dow . . .*' Seven times. I counted and made a mental note. There were other numbers. I had never heard any of them before but you got the idea pretty quickly. There was another one called 'Freak Show' that went '*I don't wanna go, be in a freak show, I don't wanna go, be in a freak show, freak show, oh no, freak show, oh no . . .*' Four times. I counted.

By the time it was over Lewis and I had drunk quite a few pints of beer. Towards the end of the set he had been inclined to join in by also throwing himself at the stage. Thankfully, I managed to persuade him not to. I may have had both feet still in the glam, art-rock past but Lewis still looked like an unreconstructed hippy, all long, uncombed hair and – most sinful of all in this context – a full Guy Fawkes beard. I felt sure he'd get beaten up if he allowed himself to converge in any meaningful way with this crowd.

I was already anxious about his girlfriend, Josie, a tall, stunning-looking beauty who looked like one of those pillow-fairies Leonard Cohen always had hanging round him, smoking cigarettes while fluttering their gossamer wings, and as at home here in this environment as Lewis was. I was frightened one of the butch-looking punk girls would take offence at just the sight of her. They were all so ugly looking and aggressive by comparison. Worse than the guys, even, who just romped around like little kids trying to act tough.

The next day I sat down and began writing. This time nothing of how I really felt about it came out – in fact nothing about anything at all, other than what I'd read in lots of other live reviews in *Sounds*. When it was finished I had no idea what it was worth. I just sent it in and sat back for the final countdown. The big kiss-off. Boy no good. At least, now it was over. Relief. There was no point even in phoning the guy. I already knew the reply.

A few days later, unable to stop myself, I switched the soft, feeling part of my brain off and rang Geoff Barton.

'Yes,' he said, 'very good. We're running it next week, I think.'

'*What?*'

'Yes,' he said again, 'it was good, I thought. Very fresh.'

Fresh? What the fuck did *fresh* mean? 'Wow,' I said, 'great.' Then thinking quick, quick, quick, 'Can I do another one, perhaps?'

'Yes, absolutely. Let's see. What have I got . . .'

Shit!

4. **All the Old Dudes**

God it was awful. What had I done?

I'd only thought as far as actually getting something published in *Sounds*. I hadn't imagined what might happen then. I just saw myself interviewing big rock stars, hanging out, having my name in the magazine next to theirs, the guys who really knew how to say it. Me and Pete Makowski and Giovanni Dadomo. *Sounds* had a lot of good writers by then: oldsters like Barbara Charone, but also a lot of new dicks on the block like Sandy Robertson, who seemed as fascinated by Patti Smith as I was, and Jon Savage who used to write in such a weird way I could never quite stand it but seemed to know a lot about art history and genres and all that stuff. And, best of all, Jane Suck, whose confrontational penname perfectly mirrored her barbed-wire style of writing. Everyone wrote with forward slashes in those punk days, so that everything became/had become/might never be something/anything you wanted it to/didn't want it to/whatever. But no one did it quite like Jane. There was something terrifying about her, as if you knew she despised you before she'd even met you.

I needn't have worried. I hardly fitted into this picture at all. What seemed like a breakthrough quickly revealed itself to be little more than the shit end of the stick. Every week I would ring Geoff Barton and he would kindly scramble to find me something totally unimportant to do. Like reviewing the New Hearts at the Nashville. Or The Crabs at the Marquee. Or No Dice at some pub in north London I had to take a train and two buses to get to.

I would always be alone. After the first couple of gigs I couldn't persuade any of my friends to come with me. The novelty of getting in for free with me quickly wore off as the direness of the situation began to dawn. None of these bands were memorable, whatever I might have written, and the whole strangeness of the situation – forced to sit through bands whose music you could barely stand and would otherwise have had nothing to do with – was simply too much to bear after a while. I could see the panic in their eyes whenever I mentioned I was going off to review something that Thursday or Tuesday or whenever, getting their excuses in quick or simply telling me to fuck off, not that again.

At least I was getting paid for it, they didn't say it but I knew they were thinking it. Yeah, on average about £10 a review, if it was big and came with a headline and picture; half that if less. Usually less. Yet I kept on going, kept on churning out those copycat-style reviews, and *Sounds* miraculously kept printing them. One, sometimes two a week.

Then one day, about three months in, the breakthrough.

It was Barton on the phone.

'Do you know anything about Ian Hunter?' he asked.

I was at work at the office, no personal calls allowed, and had to whisper into my hand.

'Ian Hunter from Mott The Hoople?'

'Yes,' said Geoff, 'only he's not with Mott any more, you know that?'

'Of course.'

After Bowie and Roxy and Lou Reed and Bob Dylan, Hunter and Mott had been one of those artists that I'd once put pictures of on my bedroom wall. 'All The Young Dudes' was up there with 'The Jean Genie' and 'Brown Sugar' as one of the greatest singles of all time, no arguments allowed. When the less-good but still great follow-up, 'Honaloochie Boogie', came out, I'd been so excited I'd stolen a ten-bob note from my mum's purse to buy it, then kept playing it until she banged on the ceiling for me to stop.

After that my interest had waned. I became irritated by Hunter's habit of putting the words 'rock 'n' roll' into every song he wrote, grew to dislike his self-absorbed, ponderously autobiographical lyrics and cosy relationship with music-press kingmakers like Charles Shaar Murray, who seemed to idolise Hunter at a time when he was writing off Bowie, who was making much better albums but who no longer favoured Chuck with his time the way Hunter still did.

Nevertheless, I'd bought his first solo album, *Ian Hunter*, featuring Bowie guitarist Mick Ronson and killer-heels rock classic 'Once Bitten, Twice Shy' (even if he did shoehorn-in the words 'rock 'n' roll' three more times). It was OK. But I liked his second solo album, *All American Alien Boy*, more. Even though it was an obvious attempt at emulating what his songwriting mentor David Bowie had done the year before with *Young Americans*, at least it was different – for Hunter, anyway, and he hadn't done anything as bold since, going back to the same old rock 'n' roll routine for his next album, even bringing in yet another former Bowie guitarist to help him do it, in Earl Slick. By which point I'd zeroed out. As had most people by 1977.

'He's in the country producing an album for Mr Big,' Barton explained. 'Do you know Mr Big?'

I did. Pop-rock dandies with one hit: 'Romeo'. I recalled they had a singer with a face that looked like it had been hit with a sledgehammer, and a preposterous name – Dicken. God love 'em, they were average. I already knew enough not to say that, though, until I found out what Barton was after.

'"Romeo",' I said.

'That's right,' he said. 'Good band. Now Hunter's producing the follow-up, and we're looking for someone to go and interview him. Would you be interested?'

He explained that Hunter didn't actually have much going on, personally, and that he'd probably only want to talk about the Mr Big album. But if I went along to the studio, heard what he had to say . . . then maybe they could turn it into something.

It sounded tricky. Not really the straightforward thing I would have preferred as a first interview. I wondered if I had what it took to do something like that – go and see what I could 'get'. The only thing I knew for sure was that saying no would not work, either.

'Sounds great,' I lied. 'When is it?'

I wrote down the details on my hand. A lady named Jill from the record company would phone me to arrange things. The studio was in Oxfordshire, wherever that was, but Jill would get me there and back no problem. How many words would they need, though, and by when?

'See what happens,' he said, and rung off.

Then Jill from the record company rang. She sounded nice. Asked for my address. Explained the limo would pick me up on Friday around six. Added that there would be another journalist coming too, from *Melody Maker*, Roxy Red. 'So it should be fun.' Then rung off.

Shitting God! The *limo*? Picking me up at my parents' place at 'around six'? And with Roxy Red coming with us, whoever she was. 'Another journalist.' Like I was a journalist too. Christ almighty!

I spent the rest of the afternoon at work blown to bits. I had wanted something like this. Now it was here I didn't want it at all. Or rather I did, just not all in one big dollop of anxiety-inducing detail. I thought about ringing Pete Makowski for advice but I'd only spoken to him once since becoming a reviewer on the paper and he hadn't seemed that impressed. He'd just left a salaried job there on the editorial staff and seemed to be so far over the other side of the *Sounds* rainbow as to be nowhere near at all. 'I read your review of Clover,' he'd said at one point. 'I liked that line: "elemental funk",' he smirked. 'That made me chuckle.'

Why? What was so funny about that? I'd thought it was rather a good line. He seemed to suggest it was just fakery. Which it was, to a degree, in that I didn't actually know what it meant, just that it sounded right. Or was I just too late for my own funeral?

I decided I would never ask Pete about anything to do with *Sounds* again; that I would stand or fall on the basis of my own efforts. Bloody well good for me.

Friday evening came and with it – miracles of miracles – a long black limo pulling up outside my parents' house as every net curtain in the street shook. We lived in a cul-de-sac, in Ealing, once known as the Queen of the London suburbs, now just another rundown working-class neighbourhood, the bit where we lived anyway. My mother had told all the neighbours about the big car coming to pick her son up. Secretly I was pleased. What was the point in being picked up by a limo if no one gets to see it?

I was less pleased when my mum came to the front door to wave me off.

'Ooh, who's that older lady?' asked Jill from the record company. 'My name's Jill.'

'Oh . . . no one,' I said. 'I'm Mick.'

'Is that your mum?' asked the other woman in the back of the car, who I assumed must be Roxy Red.

'What? Um . . .'

I sat there struggling how to answer that and retain a soupçon of cool, but they had both already moved on. Back to whatever they'd been talking about before the limo got to my gaff.

'. . . he's such an arsehole,' Roxy was saying. 'He absolutely promised me the interview then gave it to Jim Stott. Fucking cheek! I told his PR, that awful cow from RCA, "I'll never write about him again. . . "'

'Good for you,' said Jill. 'Awful cow . . .'

'It's not her fault, though, it's *him*,' said Roxy.

'I *know*,' said Jill. 'Fucking arsehole!'

The limo had left my street behind and was nosing through the early evening traffic towards the M4. I sat back and drank it in, imagined myself as Bowie in *The Man Who Fell to Earth*, a stranger in a strange land.

'Would you like a drink, Mick?' asked Jill. She gestured to the bar set up on one side of the limo. There were decanters full of booze, fluted glasses, silver cocktail shakers, ice buckets, red cloth serviettes. It was incredibly glamorous, right out of a film.

'Great,' I said, trying to act as if this was the most natural thing in the world. Of course I'd like a drink from one of those panelled glass decanters with the dark gold liquid in it.

'Great,' she said. She lifted a heavy-looking glass and filled it nearly to the brim, with what turned out to be brandy. I took a swig, managed not to gag, then lit a cigarette to take away the foul burning taste.

'We should be there in about an hour,' she said, as though it mattered to me how long this all took.

'Great,' I said.

'How long have you been writing for *Sounds*?' asked Roxy.

'Not long. A few months.'

'Oh,' she said, losing interest. 'I haven't seen your name in there much. Have you done many features?'

'Not many,' I said. 'Mainly reviews.'

'Oh.'

She turned back to Jill and they launched into another long rant about some other complete arsehole that'd fucked them around. They seemed to know a lot of these arseholes that fucked them around.

My glass was quickly empty. Jill noticed and filled it to the brim again. She seemed like she was good at her job. I lit another cigarette and went back to being Bowie staring out the window at my hallucinations. The drive took forever. It was made slower by the lack of any opportunity to join in with their conversation. They'd both obviously been doing this stuff for a while.

Jill was cute. About twenty-three, I guessed; long brown hair, short skirt, tights, nice cleavage. Definitely beyond my reach. Roxy was older, muttony, lots of make-up and hairspray to disguise the fact that she wasn't a young chick any more. She looked like she'd been around the block and pissed on every corner. Now there was a sour taste in her mouth. I had no idea how to handle her at all.

The more lost and out of reach of the conversation I became, the quicker my glass kept emptying and Jill kept refilling it. I had never drunk brandy before. But there was no beer in the car, only spirits. Jill was drinking too, but not Roxy. 'I'd better not,' she said. 'I want to keep a clear head for Ian.'

'Have you ever met him before?' I asked.

She looked at me the way a teacher would the class idiot, before reaching for the cane. 'Of course I have,' she said, pursing her thin red lips. 'We're very old friends.'

That made me flinch. I sat back and tried to let that one seep through, the idea of being very old friends with someone like Ian Hunter. How old *was* she?

The car left the motorway and was now making its way through grey-green country lanes. There were fields with black-and-white moocows in them. I pointed to them.

'"Moocows!"' laughed Jill. 'You're funny . . .'

I played along, like I knew what the hell.

It was dark by the time the limo pulled into the courtyard of the studio. The brandy decanter was now almost empty but I didn't feel drunk. I was too nervous to feel drunk. Until I stepped out of the car and the fresh air hit me. I wobbled, staggered then righted myself as I saw a tall, familiar-looking figure walking towards us. It was Hunter. *Shit!* Looking just like he did on *Top of the Pops*, all shaggy curly hair and big sunglasses.

'Hi, Ian,' chirped Jill. 'You remember Roxy . . .'

'Course I bloody do!' he beamed, 'Come 'ere, darling . . .'

They embraced and kissed and Roxy suddenly looked ten years younger, became giggly and girly and smiley and almost nice. I was strangely jealous, awaiting my turn.

'And this is Mick from *Sounds*,' said Jill, nudging Hunter in my direction.

I stood there with my hand outstretched. 'Hello,' I said, 'pleased to meet you.'

He stopped and looked me up and down. Ignored the hand. No welcoming smile. Just waves of suspicion and hostility.

'How old are you?' he asked.

'Nineteen.'

'I've got a son about your age,' he said, then turned around and walked back towards the women, who pretended not to notice his rudeness and carried on fussing him and hanging on his every word. I dragged behind, feeling like I'd just been shot in the head. Like I was walking through flames before the fire had even started.

I followed them inside to the studio. I had never been inside a recording studio before, but it was pretty much as I'd imagined it: two rooms separated by a big pane of glass. On one side a large room with all the instruments and wires and microphones in it; on the other side a smaller room with a control desk with lots of buttons and faders and twinkling lights. Most of the people were in the smaller control room.

Jill introduced us around. They all made a small fuss of Roxy, knowing her name, I imagined. Nobody knew what to do with me, never having heard of me. I waited for something to happen. Nothing did.

Jill went to get more drinks. I lit more cigarettes. Occasionally someone would say something to Roxy, who always seemed to know exactly what they were talking about and what to say back. I sat there decapitated by silence. It went on like this for a very long time. Two hours. More. I couldn't understand what I was doing here. Why no one seemed interested. If they hated me being here so much, why didn't they just get on with the inter-view and let me go home?

At one point they played an unfinished track for us. Loudly. I had no idea what to make of it. It was fast then slow then fast again. Nothing really stopped me in my tracks, though. When it was over, Roxy gushed at them: 'Wow! Fantastic! If the rest of it is as good as that it should be great!' They all looked at her and nodded and smiled and murmured their collywobbled consent.

I spotted my cue. 'It's really good,' I said. They glanced at me, as though seeing me in the room for the first time, then, deciding I wasn't worth it, went back to doing whatever they were doing.

I gave up and concentrated fully on the drink and the smokes. The brandy was all gone but Jill – good old Jill – kept refilling my glass. I didn't know what I was drinking. It didn't matter. I began to not care what any of this meant. When, finally, Hunter gave Jill some sort of signal – a nod, a grimace, some telepathic message – that he was ready for his interview, I was put out. I'd gotten used to sitting around drinking, just watching and listening as Hunter and the band went through their boring paces making their boring album. Now I had to get up and follow them into another room.

We went into a small lounge area and arranged ourselves around a table.

'I don't have time for two interviews so you'll have to take turns asking me questions,' said Hunter.

Shit. I began taking out my little Phillips cassette recorder and microphone.

'No tape recorders,' Hunter said, looking straight at me.
What?

'I don't do interviews with tape recorders any more.'

'But how will I remember what you say?' I said, sending hailing signals with my eyes to Jill.

'Shorthand?' she said breezily.

'Fine by me,' said Roxy, pulling a pad and pen out of her bag.

'Shorthand? I don't do shorthand,' I whimpered.

Hunter ignored me. Like he gave a fuck.

'You'll just have to write fast, then,' said Jill, still trying to make it all sound eminently normal and doable.

Fucking shorthand? I didn't even have a pen or a piece of paper with me.

'I'll get you some,' said Jill.

By the time she came back with a biro and some sheets of A4 the interview had already started. Roxy just fired off question after question. By the time I'd written down what she'd asked and what Hunter had said – or approximations of that – she'd already moved on two or three more questions and answers. I didn't know what to do. The long drive with two people

I had nothing in common with, the long wait in a room full of hostile strangers . . . I had hung on in there well enough with that, even though it had nearly killed me. This, though, was a disaster.

Fifteen minutes in I gave up for good. I'd filled two or three sheets of paper with scribbles but I could hardly read what they said. Now I'd lost the gist of the conversation as they drifted into small talk, about the good old days of New York and champagne and Bowie and Bad Company and so on and so forth.

'What's he like? Bowie?' I blurted, at one point.

Hunter turned his sunglasses on me, with more of his death rays. 'Depends on who's asking.'

'Me,' I said, trying for engaging, settling for silly little prick.

'I don't know about *you*,' he said. 'To *you* he'd probably be like some big hero.'

It was the final arrow through the head. I put down the pen, picked up the glass, went to light another cigarette but found the packet was empty. I sat, waiting for the nightmare to please God finally end, as Hunter and Roxy continued their little trip down memory lane together. The thing was, you could tell he didn't really like her, either. But, you sensed, he was prepared to make allowances for her. She was at least real. I was just some daft kid pretending to be a writer from a pretend music paper. His years of being on the cover of the *NME*, in major pieces written by genuine rock-writer giants like Charles Shaar Murray, had given him that special second sight that only old rock stars have. The one that tells them the pricks from the kicks . . .

When at last, mercifully, painfully, horribly, it did end, I was now so far out of the inter-dimensional loop that I felt like the astronaut at the end of *2001*, parallel universes and multi-realities zipping by me at such speed I felt my eyeballs turning inside out, my head bent back by unstoppable galaxy storms. Back at the limo I wouldn't have been surprised if they'd asked me to ride on the roof for the drive back. Instead, I simply sat there in shame as Jill and Roxy resumed their conversation about music-business arseholes and how they would not be fucked by them a minute longer.

It took a while for us to come down. Roxy, job done, and done well, began to nod off. Jill, still wide-awake on the buzz of her own good gig being over, began talking to me. Really talking. Not about music-business stuff I didn't know anything about, but things I could actually join in on. Records we both liked. Concerts we'd seen. Funny stories. She told me about her life. How she was shacked up in a pad in Hampstead with the singer of a famous punk band. A band I'd actually bought a single by not so long before. I was impressed, though tried not to show it, obviously.

We were both still drinking, but I was into some other realm now, beyond drunk. My head may not have had plenty of space in it for new things but my nineteen-year-old body could keep going for days. On speed or off. Now, as the limo scudded through the black night, and Roxy began to snore, we were moving slowly more into my world. The big surprise was that Jill seemed happy enough to go there.

Suddenly we were getting on like a house on fire. I sensed she was being kind, letting me off the hook, that she realised I was a novice, badly burned, but not entirely beyond help perhaps. She began to move nearer. Suddenly her long brown hair was in my face, her body close, I could smell her perfumed skin.

Then we were kissing. French kissing. Then groping. Squeezing, holding, pulling and pushing. She unzipped my jeans, pulled out my terrified cock and put her head down there and went to work on it. I looked over at Roxy, wondering if she was really asleep or just clearing the way for Jill to do her thing. Had they discussed it, perhaps? By the sounds of it, they had been on lots of these sorts of trips together before. Was this just their way?

The more Jill licked and sucked the less I cared. Suddenly everything that had gone on, in the long hours before, hardly mattered. My badly bruised spirit wafted up from my body, clung to the ceiling of the limo and looked down on the situation. Now this surely was rock 'n' roll. The limo speeding through the night, the record company chick giving me a blowjob. If we had only been on our way back to New York instead of London the fantasy would have been complete. As it was, this would do.

'Do you want to come back to my place?' she asked when she came up for air.

'What about your boyfriend?'

'He's away on tour. You can spend the night, if you like.'

'What about . . .?' I nodded towards the snoring Roxy.

'She's fine,' she said, some laughter in her voice. 'We live round the corner from each other. I'll drop her off first.'

She did.

5. Jam No Bread

I fretted over that Ian Hunter non-story for days, weeks. I didn't know what to do with it. I rang Barton for advice but he didn't seem bothered either way.

'Just send in what you've got and we'll take a look,' he said.

But I didn't have anything. Or rather I did, I just didn't know it. Instead I tried to put some notes together based on the indecipherable scribbling I'd managed at the so-called interview and what I could remember of what else Hunter had said to Roxy. But I'd been toast by then. Burned and buttered both sides, face-down on the floor. I couldn't remember him saying much of interest at all.

I sent a couple of pages in to Barton and waited. And waited. Nothing. It was never mentioned again, not even in passing, not even when we spoke about what my next review might be.

Instead I fell into a down groove of reviewing low-rank punk bands and trying to make my way through the clutter of mid-week night-time London. In an effort to try to push the boat an inch further forward through the swamp, I'd given up my job at the employment agency and become a full-time writer. My parents were perplexed, but then everything perplexed them.

The only real problem was money. None of us had any. My dad had once been a working musician, playing accordion in

Scottish and Irish pubs and clubs. A born Paddy, who claimed he'd run away from home when he was fourteen after 'breaking a chair over my father's back', he made all our lives hell with his drinking and his violence. Most especially my mother's, who had been educated in an Irish convent and had only married him when she became pregnant with me. He would still talk of his time playing with Jimmy Shand. But that had been before I was born, before my mother had even known him, and the only ones who still cared were the gang of down-and-outs he thought of as friends: Packi Rice, Northern Ireland Jimmy, Johnny Lynch and the crew.

The lack of cash meant I was always hanging around in clubs like the Marquee and the Vortex, the Rock Garden and the Nashville, all those places that put on second-rate bands for fourth-rate pay. On a good night, I would take a pound note with me: 50p for my tube fare there and back, 50p for one beer. On a bad night, I would take nothing, bunk the tube and stand around hoping some record-company drone would spot me and buy the important *Sounds* journalist a drink.

It was through this that I got to know some of the regulars on the scene, older men and women who would sidle over, buy me a drink then not let me out of their sight until I'd done whatever it was they had in mind. Usually, this meant telling them how great their rotten band was. Sometimes, it meant more. Not knowing the protocols, I tried to keep them all happy – if I could. This was not a good strategy and I rarely succeeded in pleasing anybody, least of all myself.

One evening, the phone rang just as I was putting my one good jacket on. It was a guy I'd met a couple of times at the corner of the bar in the Marquee, next to the dressing-room door.

'Hello, Mick,' he said, all friendly. 'It's Roger. I hear you're coming to see my little superstars tonight, is that right?'

'Yes, looking forward to it,' I said, panicked.

'That's lovely. Why don't you come to my office first and we can have a drink, then go to the gig together?'

'Great.' I wrote down the address and went to hunt for some change for the tube fare from my dad's trouser pockets. He was asleep on the couch after an afternoon bender. As always, he'd taken off his trousers as soon as he'd lurched through the door. I could hear the change in his pockets jingling as his trousers hit the linoleum floor.

Luck! Both pockets were full of coins. I took a 50p and some five- and ten-pence pieces. Stuff he'd wouldn't be able to remember he'd had when he woke up.

I was pleased but worried. Roger was one of those guys I'd been warned had 'shit on his breath' – meaning, he liked to eat pretty young boys' arseholes. I wasn't a pretty boy but I knew I'd have to watch my arse anyway. Roger was also a former pop star from back in the sixties, who'd had a couple of hits. 'A poor man's Frankie Vaughan' someone called him, and you could see it. That same oily smile, those same oily dark curls. And the suits: pure would-be mobster, always a carnation in the buttonhole. Now he was some big wheel in the music business, managing punk bands and doing whatever it was guys like him did. He had a flash office in Carnaby Street, gold records on the walls, secretaries, assistants, and a well-stocked bar. I knew I'd be all right for a drink at least.

When I got there Roger was smoking a thin needlepoint joint. It was like a magic straw hanging from his gob.

'Here,' he said, 'have a bit of this.' He held it out. 'Oops,' he said, 'I've bum-sucked it a bit, but you won't worry about that, will you?'

I took it and put it in my mouth. The end was soggy and sweet. I inhaled as deeply as I could, held it, then inhaled some more, held it – until the smoke came gushing out again like an overexcited chimney.

'Good boy,' he said. 'Drink?'

I nodded what was left of my head. Had another hit. The smoke exploded out of me.

'Good boy,' he said, handing me a beer. Then stood behind me rubbing my shoulders.

I tensed up, freaking about where this was going. He felt it and let me be, grinning as he came back behind his desk.

'Tell you what,' he said, 'we'll get down to the Marquee now, nice and early, say hello to the boys, catch the gig, then go out and grab a bite to eat afterwards, with the band. What do you say?'

'Great,' I said. What else would I say? No, I'd rather go home to my dreary life on the cot bed in my brothers' room, thanks. I hadn't gotten into this writing for *Sounds* game to say no to invitations like that, however dodgy they sounded. I stayed out late for a lot worse reasons than putting up with some old music-biz predator. I thought I could handle it.

The gig was dreadful. One of the worst I'd seen lately. I knew, though, I'd give it a decent review. I depended on guys like Roger just to survive most nights at places like the Marquee, regardless of what band was on or whether they were any good. I knew what was expected of me, if I was to stay in their good books. It wasn't like this was the real world where anything actually mattered. For all I knew, I'd be back where I started soon enough. I'd hang on for the ride, see where it took me, then jump off when it became too much.

It was gone 11 when we left the Marquee. The tube would be finishing in half an hour and I began to fret about how I would get home.

'Don't worry,' said Roger. 'I'll get you a taxi. On the company account.'

That sounded good. Where was the band, though?

'It's OK. They're still fighting over something in the dressing room. They'll follow us down when they're ready.'

He led the way down Wardour Street towards Leicester Square. 'I know a place . . .' We came to a nondescript-looking door in a side street and he rang the doorbell. It buzzed open and we walked into the darkest darkness, down some stairs and into the basement. I had thought we were going to a restaurant but there were no tables down there, no waiters, only a long chintzy bar at which stood a few very still figures, mostly men. Just one woman, well dressed, old school like Roger, who she looked at without smiling as he said hello.

Roger introduced us. 'This is Mick. He writes for *Sounds*.'

'Oh yes,' she said, regarding me without interest. I got the feeling Roger introduced her to a lot of guys called Mick who wrote for *Sounds*.

They stood talking while I stood smiling along, pretending to know what it was they were talking about. But I didn't know anything. Just that I'd changed my mind about being here.

'Actually, Roger,' I interrupted. 'I've just remembered, I've got to go.'

'But why?' he said, alarmed. 'The boys will be here in a minute, we'll have a party.'

'Wow. Sounds great. But I just remembered – I have to get going.'

He shifted his body so that he stood squarely between me and the stairs to the front door. It was now or never. I pushed past him.

'Wait!' he said. 'You can't go yet!'

I ran up the stairs, my eyes now adjusted to the darkness, found the door and yanked it open. Ran into the street, Roger close behind.

'WAIT!' he roared.

I kept running. There was a taxi. Not on account, but a taxi all the same. I waved. It stopped. I jumped in.

'Where to mate?'

'Oxford Street! Fast as you can!'

Roger was now gaining on me, almost to the taxi door. The driver must have cottoned on to what was happening. He put his foot down and the taxi moved off just as Roger caught up with it.

'Sorry!' I yelled through the open window.

He kept running, trying to catch us but the taxi was ahead of him now. I looked out the rear window and I saw him finally stop, his arms still in the air, his once-handsome sixties' pop star face ugly with thwarted rage.

Others I got to know of a similar vintage weren't so predatory but they all still wanted something. There was one, Kit, a Canadian, who worked as a PR for an independent company that represented lots of big stars, The Who, the Stones, Status Quo, and the better-off new punk bands, the ones that had hits like The Jam and the Stranglers.

He also took a shine to me, but in a way that was far more unfathomable. He wanted to offer me a job.

I'd reviewed a couple of Kit's bands. He rang to thank me. Then asked if I'd care to meet him for a drink one evening, tomorrow maybe?

He suggested we meet at the Speakeasy, the basement club in Margaret Street where bands and the people who knew them liked to go after the pubs in Soho closed. You were supposed to be a member but if they knew your face they would just wave you in. The first time I'd been taken there, Sid Vicious and Nancy Spungen were lying in a heap at the foot of the stairs. Nancy looked completely out of it, one torn fishnet leg dangling through the bottom banister. Sid was also flat on his back, but with one eye open.

'I say, old chap,' he announced loudly as I stepped over him, 'would you be so kind as to send over some champagne?' He lay there cackling at his own joke. A cackle that almost instantly turned into a nasty cough. He ran a thin white hand over his face and came back with blood. Like his nose was bleeding. Or his mouth. I hurried on by.

I liked the Speak. The punks hadn't overtaken it as they had the other London clubs I was now a regular of, you actually saw musicians you'd bought records by, with long hair and very good-looking chicks. Cats like Brian Robertson of Thin Lizzy, Lemmy who used to be in Hawkwind, Frankie Miller, Jeff Beck, the singer from the Stranglers – bad cats who had no place better to go on a rainy Tuesday night in hell. You would see them sitting in large gaggles at their tables, surrounded by girls and hangers-on, drivers and drug dealers, guys who'd made it further than most punk bands ever would but who hadn't quite reached the tax-exiled heights of the Stones or Zeppelin. You would see them hanging out, then later, around 1 a.m. you'd see some of them get up with whoever the house band was that night and jam. Very cool.

The night I met Kit the band booked to play was the Snivelling Shits. This added an extra edge to the evening as the Shits was the band recently formed 'for fun' by Pete Makowski and Giovanni Dadomo: Pete on guitar, Gio on vocals, and whoever fancied turning up on bass and drums. It didn't sound much on paper but on record – a double A-side single, 'Terminal Stupid' and 'I Can't Come' – it was the most revelatory thing I'd heard since the Sex Pistols and the Modern Lovers. Better than, even. But because they were still high-profile music journalists they felt impelled to act like the whole thing was some big put on. It was, but not like that. Once they started playing they were as serious – more so, actually – than all the other new bands on the scene.

Gio sounded like you imagined Johnny Rotten would if he ever let his guard down long enough to say something *really* clever. Pete sounded more garage than Lou Reed in his early Velvets plume. The rest of the band didn't really matter, they just chugged along. In true punk spirit, it wasn't about musical accomplishment, more a certain unhinged but highly informed *joie de vivre*. The only reason they weren't bigger than biscuits was because they were all ex-music journalists, and not even *Sounds* would ever forgive them for that.

I tried to say hello to Pete while I waited at the bar for Kit, but Pete was into some new trip, something much deeper than being the new kid in town at *Sounds*. He had left my kind far behind, said the big black circles around his eyes. Now he was out there somewhere where he did not wish for us to follow. I dug that and left him to it. Gio I was too intimidated to speak to. He'd been such a great rock writer, now he too had taken off on some wholly unforeseen trip, and he was even better at that than being the main man on *Sounds*. I hid at the bar, sneaking glances as they set up their gear, sipping my half of lager and lime.

When Kit arrived he jumped when he saw me, as though it was some big surprise. I reminded him he'd asked me to be there, but he still looked as though I'd ambushed him.

'Yeah, right, OK, cool, yeah . . .'

He spoke to the barmaid, whose name he knew, ordered a beer. Didn't order one for me. He drank it half down, then finished the rest, ordered himself another. This time he looked at me out of the corner of his eye.

'You OK or do you want another?'

'I'll have a pint, please, cheers.'

I was still the newcomer, on all levels, but I'd learned how to ask for a drink a long time before.

Kit led the way to one of the booths. We sat down. He gulped his drink down again, waved at the barmaid to bring another. Looked at me sideways. Didn't offer.

'So, yeah, anyway, what I wanted to say . . . We're looking for someone to come into the office?'

'Yeah?'

'Someone new . . . young . . . someone to learn the ropes but someone who gets the new bands. These fucking punks . . . ha! 'Cos I sure as shit don't! Ha!'

I pictured the scene, getting up in the morning and going to work again, being on the phone all day, having to deal with rude stuck-up music journalists whose boots would need regular licking. Then out every night, holding everybody's hands while they pretended to get on, when they could be bothered. Footing the bill. Begging for mercy. Eating shit. There didn't seem much to tempt you. Except for the money. That was the one thing I would get from it that I wasn't getting now. It might be enough . . .

'Hey,' he said, getting into his stride. 'You want another?' He waved at the barmaid – Elsie, who I was also getting to know now – for two more beers. 'And a menu!' he called after her.

Ooh, we were going to eat. I was hungry. I was always hungry, had been for years. I became more interested.

'So when you say you're looking for someone . . .'

'That's right. You! What do you say? We're a big agency, getting bigger all the time. But we need fresh blood. Someone who . . .'

'. . . gets the punk bands?'

'Right! You're about the right age, right? What are you, twenty-two? Twenty-three?'

'Nineteen.'

'What? No way! You look older! Are you sure?'

'Everybody says that . . .'

'So you're really nineteen? Far out . . .'

Elsie dropped off the new beers and two grubby plastic menus. I lit a ciggy and stared at the prices. I already knew what to have: scampi and chips – with peas and a twist of lemon. But I took my time, thinking it over. Panicking about how I was going to say no before we'd even ordered the food.

He read the silence.

'I know what you're thinking. That's it's shit having to deal with fucking music journalists all the time. And it is, it is! *Fucking shit!* Like that bitch Vivian on *Sounds*. She calls up, says, "But Kit, I didn't get my Rasta Pastor LP!" I'm like, I *know* I sent her two already, but watcha gonna do? Get into an *argument* with her over it? She's the features editor, Christ's sake! So I get into it with her and the next time I need a favour for something she's gonna shit all over me, right? So you have to play your cards right, absolutely. But it's worth it in the end. You get to work with all the bands and get paid for it, right?'

'Right.'

We ordered the food, plus a couple more beers. I was relaxing and getting into it. Kit had also loosened up. He was smiling.

Then suddenly his face changed. 'Ah, shit . . .'

I looked over and it was Paul Weller from The Jam with some girl. He looked just as miserable as he did on stage and in all his photographs. Dressed in the same suit and tie, his hair all kiss-curled at the sides. 'It must take him ages to fix it that way in the mirror,' I thought idly.

'Hey, Paul!' cried Kit. 'How ya doin'? Looking good, my man! Looking good!'

Weller looked over at him as though regarding a turd. Said nothing, just plonked himself down in the booth next to us.

'Buy us something to eat then, Kit,' he scowled.

'Hey, buddy, you know we don't do you guys any more. I don't have expenses for that.'

'Fuck off, Kit. Buy us a meal. You're good for it and I'm skint.'

Kit's face tightened, his smile thinned out, then he seemed to change his mind about something. Like it wouldn't pay to make a scene, not while he's trying to sell me on how fun it was working with the 'new' punk bands.

'OK, man, but this is positively the last time,' he said, affecting an avuncular chuckle that came out sounding like the cackle of a dying man. 'And only because I like you, man.'

Weller turned away and motioned Elsie over, ordered, then jerked a thumb in our direction. 'He's paying,' he said, then went back to his girl.

Again I pictured some future scene where it was me being chivvied for a meal on expenses from some wanker in a group. I knew I would never be able to handle it. Not like Kit.

The night wore on, me and Kit getting drunker and drunker. I used the booze to blot out any more talk of taking a job at Kit's office, knew I was leaving him with the impression that it was practically a done deal, but knew I could get out of it by phoning him whenever and giving him some excuse. Something, anything, I didn't want to think about it.

The Shits came on and they lived up to their name. They were terrible. All the songs were too fast, like Pete couldn't be bothered to play them properly. Gio had swapped the leather jacket he'd arrived in for a deliberately naff – I assumed – brown suit, and didn't seem to give a shit whether anyone got the joke or not. I got that they were making a statement of sorts, subverting the usual context of a gig and all that sort of guff. That they were saying they were above such post-punk conceptions. But all it did was make them appear as though they didn't know what they were doing. I was embarrassed for them. People didn't even boo. Not the crowd at the Speak, too knowing for that. They simply tuned out, wandered off, left the band to fizzle out in its own self-absorbed fumes. It was a drag.

'Wow, these guys are fucking terrible!' declared Kit, yelling into my ear. 'Just goes to show it's true what they say – all music journalists are really frustrated musicians. Really *bad* frustrated musicians.' He laughed, and that's when I knew for sure I would never work for him.

Not all nights went so well. Often there was nobody there to buy the drinks, to front the cabs or make you feel like any of this was going somewhere good one day, maybe. Mostly, I was on my own. The trouble was, you couldn't make it on your own. So you made friends where you could. Two o'clock in the morning on a cold wet Thursday in Nowheresville you took whatever ride you could that got you closer to home. Except I never wanted to go home.

What made it doubly hard was the whole punk death trip. They were anti-life. Punks didn't seem to have sex, not that I could pick up on. Not like the hippies, who oozed sweet love, baby, share the one you're with, no hang-ups, dig it? The punks were my age, or older, but they all acted like they still went to school. They dressed in costumes, assumed poses, didn't know what to do when confronted by a beautiful girl. And they all took speed. I'd left the costumes behind, couldn't handle speed any more, and really was looking for love. But the only girls you ever talked to at punk gigs were the fucked-up ones, the ones with short black hair, too much make-up, spots and torn stockings, torn minds, pimply black hearts you sensed were there for the taking if only you could get past the shtick and spit, which you knew you never would.

Even when you did there was always something wrong about it. Some book you found with half the pages torn out. One night, short on cab fare, nothing left to lose, I wound up with one at some council block in Ladbroke Grove. Said she was in a band that was better than The Slits, said she'd met Iggy Pop, sung with Siouxsie Sioux, knew the guy on the door of the Marquee. She was on all fours as I prodded away diligently from behind. I looked down at the badly drawn, inky tattoo scrawled in a wavy line across her back. At first it didn't make sense. Then I got it: B-O-R-N-T-O-L-O-S-E.

Her dark, once-blonde hair was dreadlocked and now thick and stale as old rope. Neither of us was enjoying it but somehow the situation demanded it. The speed and whiskey and beer and wine and endless joints demanded it. The copy of Lou Reed's *Transformer* that played over and over in the background demanded it. Side two. I must have heard 'Goodnight Ladies' three times. But still I couldn't quite come.

Eventually, I gave up and flopped over on my back. She didn't move, just looked at me.

'What's the matter? Don't you like girls?'

What? I looked up at her, now standing angrily by the bed, hitching her black bra back into place. God, how had it come to this? Once I'd had a nice girlfriend. She would come to my parents' house and we would disappear upstairs to my room together. The first time it had been a cold day in April, so we'd put the little paraffin heater on. After that, it became like a ritual. Even on a warm day we'd light the little paraffin heater and turn the dial down to Low, then take off all our clothes and snuggle into bed together. It felt magical, warm, right.

This, I decided, reaching over for my cigarettes, did not feel right.

She walked around picking up the rest of her clothes, putting them on, her angry back to me.

'I want you to go now,' she said over her shoulder.

I looked at my watch: 2.14 a.m.

'I can't go now,' I said. 'The trains are all finished and I haven't got the dough for a cab.'

'GET OUT!' she screamed, turning to face me. 'GET OUT OR I'LL CALL THE FUCKING COPS! YOU TRIED TO FUCKING RAPE ME!! GET OUT!'

It was like something out of a horror movie. I jumped from the bed straight into my jeans, got the rest of my stuff and flew out the door. She stood there like a vampire denied its blood, eyes full of hate, pointing at me with one long, heavily ringed finger, her witch's mouth quivering. 'GET OUT!' she screamed. 'DON'T EVER FUCKING COME BACK!'

She slammed the door behind me and a dog began to bark somewhere on the estate. It was a high-rise in Ladbroke Grove, who knew which one, they all looked the same and, as usual, the lift was broken. I tiptoed down the five flights of stairs.

6. **Doing it for the Kids**

His name was Nick and he was not my friend. He just said he was.

We'd met one middle-of-nowhere night when I was out there reviewing one of his little punk bands – Chelsea, loathed by everyone, for being 'fake', quite liked by me because they had a frontman with cave-deep cheekbones and an interesting name, Gene October, and a guitarist, named Dave Martin, who looked like Mick Ronson's little brother, right down to the low-slung Les and dyed-blonde feather cut.

Chelsea had earned their place in London punk mythology for starting out with Billy Idol on guitar and Tony James on bass, who both went on to form Generation X, another barely tolerated punk-lite group, but one that at least had hits. The highpoint for Chelsea had been their first single, 'Right To Work', which tapped into the same the-kids-are-all-right dole-queue mentality that The Clash had made their calling card. By the summer of 1978, however, it was over for them. Gene couldn't really sing – not a huge handicap for a punk frontman, but that wasn't what the music press held against him. He was just horrible to be around. A male model who'd lost his way in the netherworld of dreadfully exploitative old music-biz benders, Gene was so insecure about his talents he rubbed everybody up the wrong way. He saw himself as the consummate blagger; everybody else saw him as a mouthy thicko who hovered around you like a tsetse fly waiting to bite his poison into you.

As the last music journalist left standing who had anything goodish to say about Chelsea, Nick had zeroed in on me for special treatment. Somebody up there had put a good word in for Gene and it was Nick's job to do whatever he could to get something – anything – positive about the band into the music press. He'd worked his way through all the scene-makers with the by-lines that everybody recognised. No chance. Now he'd worked his way down to me.

I didn't mind. A dog will take a slap round the ear rather than no attention at all. I knew Nick was desperate. So was I. If he wanted to buy me drinks he knew I couldn't afford to buy him back, that was fine. The little independent label he worked for, Step Forward Records, was quite cool too. It wasn't all dross like Chelsea, they also had Alternative TV, the band formed by Mark P – now going by his full name of Mark Perry – who'd started *Sniffin' Glue*, other something-happening new bands like The Fall and Clock DVA, and weird outsider shit by old timers like Spirit, Kim Fowley and Wayne County. Different artists were given nominally different labels: so The Police were on Illegal Records – geddit? Squeeze, who were from Deptford, were on – wait for it – Deptford Fun City Records. And so on. But they all came from Step Forward, were all run by the same small, punk-crazed team.

The label was actually owned by a guy named Miles Copeland, who looked like Andy Warhol's little brother, all fly-by-night white hair and weird Aunt Mable glasses. Miles had made his money managing Renaissance and Curved Air. But they didn't talk about that as any whiff of such old-wave connections were likely to make the label seem somehow fake, the most unforgiveable sin of the new wave where nobody was fake. The other don't-mention-the-war thing about Miles was that his father had been a bigwig in the CIA. But no one really believed that anyway. Even though it turned out to be true.

When out of the blue one day Nick asked if I'd like to 'come and join the crazy gang', I couldn't see why not. I'd been out of full-time employment trying to make it as a *Sounds* writer and getting nowhere for nearly nine months and the prospect of £40 a week – what the gig paid – sounded a fortune right then. I was to replace Nick as the label's 'press guy'. That is, the sap whose job it is to try to get the records and bands reviewed in the *NME* and places like that. It sounded straightforward enough. My only concern was that I'd have to stop writing for *Sounds*. Nick said not to worry, that it was only a temporary job, filling in while he was away with Mark Perry's band Alternative TV, and that I could carry on with the *Sounds* stuff, as long as I did the job for him too. Unlike the full-time job in PR that Kit had offered me just a few months before, this was different, it seemed to me. For a start, by now I really needed the bread. What I had hoped to parlay, over time, into a better-paid writing gig on *Sounds* had simply not panned out. I was starting to doubt it ever would. Suddenly £40 a week cash looked mighty good. That, plus the little bits of extra dough the occasional *Sounds* job would bring, would lift me back out of Shit Street. At least for a while, I hoped.

We met for lunch at a greasy spoon round the corner from the crumbling Step Forward office in Blenheim Crescent, near Portobello Road. Mark was also there when I arrived. They were talking about the forthcoming American tour and Nick's role in it. I thought I was hearing things when it turned out Nick was going to be the drummer in the group.

Mark was still only twenty-one, he didn't sport the usual punk regalia – his hair was combed flat and footballer-styled, his clothes working-class bookworm – but he walked with a lot of punk-cred wherever he went. I didn't know how old Nick was but he looked like an older leftover from the hippy house in Ealing I'd lived in two years before: thirty-something, Lennon glasses, beard, like one of those ban-the-bomb types who always knew more than you. He looked like he was into jazz or classical. Politics.

But Mark had left punk behind, was busy finding out all about the big wide world beyond the *NME*, and he sat there talking about this dream he'd had about Delius. How it had inspired him to write a new piece called . . . 'Delius'.

I felt surprised and encouraged. Maybe these were punk people I could actually talk to. But they wouldn't let me in. It was all about how great Mark was and how cool Nick was, despite his old-fart appearance. It was all about how great the American tour would be and how great the world was, once you got to know it – from inside the safety of a cool 'new wave' band.

'And Mick here is going to feed the cat while I'm gone,' Nick quipped.

Mark ignored that. We both did.

Three weeks later I started work at Step Forward – only Nick was still there. The American tour had been cancelled. I forgot the reason even as they were telling it. But there was only ever one reason any British band cancelled a tour of America – lack of ticket sales. No money. No use. Rain, rain, go away, come again another day. Maybe.

Nick was determined, though, not to let this latest setback hurt him. I would still be employed, not as a temp but as a full-time employee, while he got on doing bigger and better things. Again, he tried listing what some of those things would be but it was way too blurry and I stopped listening after a couple of days. Instead I went to work doing . . . nothing.

I had started writing a couple of press releases – one for Chelsea, who had a new single coming out that August called 'Urban Kids', with lyrics by Mark Perry, that the label hoped might finally be the one to make them seem less of a joke, and one for this American biker chick named Vermilion, who frankly scared me, called 'I Can't Stop Fucking Around', with a picture of Vermilion on the cover with her tits peeping out of a leather jacket.

Nick sat there reading through what I'd written with a constipated expression on his face, his little round granny glasses twinkling evilly. Then he took both pieces of paper, scrunched them up and threw them at me.

'You don't get it, do you?' he said, looking ready to explode. 'You're not writing for *Sounds* now, this stuff is meant to be *real*.'

He was right. I didn't get it. I genuinely liked both records. I tried to show that in my press releases. What had I done wrong?

'Everything! The whole tone is just wrong! It reads like something out of the *Melody Maker* from 1968!'

He pulled a couple of older press releases that he had written from a drawer and shoved them across the desk to me.

'Take a look at those then try again.'

I took them and looked at them, then read what I'd written again. I couldn't spot the difference, except maybe mine were a bit better written.

I tried again. Cut out the superlatives and gave it to them straight. Showed them to him.

'What's this?' he said. 'Any monkey can type out the release date and the track titles. Where's the *personality* behind them? Where's the *energy*?'

They were press releases. Whenever I had been given a record to review and it came with a press release, I would check it for the title and the release date and any other background info then throw the damn thing away. It had never occurred to me they might have personality or energy or what the fuck.

'Tell you what, make us a cup of tea and I'll write them, then show you what I mean,' he said, exasperated.

And that pretty much defined the job thereafter. I would make the tea and Nick would huff and puff about press releases with personality and energy. Sometimes I would put a record on but even that I got wrong. The Cortinas were the first band the label had ever released a single by. When I found an old box of their albums one day I took one out and put it on the office record player. Not cool.

'Take that off,' said Nick. 'The very thought of it offends me.'

'Why?'

'They blew it the day they signed to CBS.'

One or two knowing nods around the office. I was baffled. I took the record off and looked at the label: CBS. Punk sacrilege, apparently. Never mind that The Clash had released *all* their records on CBS. I took it home with me that night and played it in my room. Well, well. Pretty damn good. Not punk, not thick enough, but reaching towards something like Television or a British version of the Modern Lovers. I was genuinely baffled as to why no one at the office seemed to care.

The next day, in front of Nick, I took my life in my hands and put the record back on, starting with one of the best tracks, a rave-up version of an old Motown hit for The Contours called 'First I Look At The Purse'.

I watched as his face contorted into a sneer.

'Do me a favour.'

'You don't like this?' I asked as innocently as I could manage.

'It's all right. But what a *waste*. You know what their first single for us was?'

'No.'

'Well, go downstairs and ask Dexter then. You want to know about The Cortinas, he'll tell you all about them.'

Dexter was this kid who worked in the small basement room where we kept all the records, ready to be sent out to shops in the battered old transit van. As well as signing shitty little punk bands, Step Forward also distributed reggae singles and other stuff by other tiny independent labels: Tapper Zukie, Burning Spear, all kinds of one-off stuff. It was like a proper little hole-in-the-ground record shop down there.

I would wander down sometimes to help bag up the singles when something new came in they had a big order for. They always had good sounds going, and the air would be thick with dope smoke.

I liked Dexter because he didn't dress like a punk. Most of the other kids we had working there looked like Sid Vicious. Dexter looked more like me, more normal. Which made us both look abnormal in those surrounds.

I went downstairs and found him and told him what Nick had said.

He laughed. 'Don't worry about Nick,' he said, 'he's just a bitter old cunt who wishes he'd been a rock star.'

He explained that the first record The Cortinas had released was called 'Fascist Dictator'. But that it had just been 'silly'. Just something they'd done in the heat of the punk moment to get noticed. That the album was much more how they really felt.

Wow. OK. But how did he know all this? Was he a fan?

'No, you twat. I was *in* them.'

Turned out Dexter was Dexter Dalwood, the bassist in The Cortinas. Oh. Sorry. But what was he doing working here in the basement if he was in the band?

'Oh, we broke up months ago,' he said. 'As soon as we finished the album we were dropped. It had all gotten a bit crap by then anyway so we just sort of stopped.'

Oh.

And now?

'I'm just doing this until something else comes along.'

What, like another band?

'Maybe. It's all bollocks, though, really, isn't it? Here, do you want a hit on this . . . ?'

He pulled out a Rasta-sized joint, already half-smoked but still longer than your mind, and lit it, took a few hungry puffs and passed it to me. The smoke plumed out of it like a fucking chimney, I gave it a few good tugs. Felt my lungs catch fire.

'Careful!' he sniggered. 'That's not your run-of-the mill shit. One of the reggae guys sold us this weed. I swear to God it blows your fucking head off.'

How many times had I heard that before? Everybody always had the best dope. 'Yeah?' I said. 'Give me another go, then . . .'

This time though it was true. By the time I went back up to the office where Nick was talking to some band, I felt like I was carrying the pieces of what was left of my head in my pocket. The rest of the day slipped by nice and easy and I began going down to the basement to see Dexter more and more often. So much groovier than hanging around upstairs pretending to be busy in the office.

I never really knew who was what or what was where at Step Forward. Some of the artists were fun. Vermilion took to coming by most days while we were trying to get press for her single. She was the real deal. A genuine American biker chick who made the most ardent of the punk boys – jittery Joe Strummer, big softy Johnny Rotten – look like what they were: pretend rockers.

The day her single was released she brought with her a drunk and speeding bunch of biker friends and family. The girls, tattooed in the days when tattoos meant you were criminally insane, were far scarier than the guys, who seemed to be running on their own interior highs that meant as long as you didn't pull their beards or look at them funny they were content to let you live.

One of the girls – a big, full-bodied redhead with earrings all over her face called Mental Maureen or Sick Sister Sue, something like that – climbed right on to my desk and pulled my astonished face into her cleavage. It was warm in there and surprisingly soft. Then pulled me out again, licked her finger like a lollipop until it was dripping wet, then stuck it in my ear.

I sat there, too scared to move, just staring at her tattooed tits.

'Wassamatter, pretty boy? Are you too love-struck to speak?'

I found a shaky smile. She leaned over and stuck her face into mine, used her mouth to force open mine and stuck her long thick tongue in there and had a damn good feel around. I nearly gagged.

She broke off and looked at me, laughing.

'Ooh, that was *nice!* You better be careful though, pretty boy. If my old feller finds out you've been snogging me he'll have your guts for garters!'

'But, you kissed me!' I squealed like a tiny girl.

'What?' she said, turning fierce, 'Are you saying I'm a *liar?*'

'What? No, no, no . . .'

'Good,' she broke into a big smile again. 'So you *do* fancy me? Naughty boy. Wait till my old feller hears about *you* . . .'

One morning when I turned up for work and found – oh God, please no! – Gene October waiting for me at my desk, my boiling blood simply took over. I felt for Gene. His band was a joke in the music press and he was a joke around the office. The only one who seemed to care was Miles, which meant we all had to pay Gene a certain amount of lip service – but not much. Mainly it was left to me to placate him. Which was doubly difficult, as I could never get anyone in the music press interested in Chelsea, unless it was to take the piss, and even that they had now grown bored with.

Gene would come in with a copy of the *NME* rolled up in his hand and immediately start on me. Why was such and such a band on the cover when they had been supporting Chelsea less than three months ago? Why wasn't I able to get someone along to at least review their next show at the Marquee, or whatever hellhole they were playing. Why wasn't I *doing my job?*

This particular morning it was worse than usual. Not helped by the speed hangover I was suffering. I hated speed by then but it was what everyone else there was into and sometimes it just felt like I had no choice but to join in. But all it did now was prevent me from sleeping or even having a wank, and I would turn up at the office the next day with knives for eyes.

Gene was merciless. Their new single 'Urban Kids' had been out three weeks and so far there had only been a shitty review in *Sounds*. What was I doing about it? *Well?*

He followed me into the slender kitchenette where I was making tea. I couldn't hear what he was saying any more, he'd been saying it for so long. Sensing this, he turned up the volume, his mouth almost touching my ear. Well? *Well?*

Something snapped. Something bad. I swung round and threw the tea in his face. It was hot and very painful. But all it did was enrage him. He launched himself at me. I launched myself back. We stood there toe-to-toe fighting each other in the kitchenette. I was going to kill him. That was all. I began punching him in the head and he began retreating. He got me a couple of good digs to my face but I didn't even feel them.

Then Miles appeared from somewhere – Gene's saviour once again – and pulled us apart. He didn't swear, he just shouted at me to get back to my desk. Took Gene off to his office to calm him down and find out what had happened. I sank into my seat out of breath, out of everything.

Nick looked at me. 'You shouldn't have done that.'

'Fuck off, Nick.'

He laughed. Nick didn't care what happened to Gene or me. He looked down on us both the same.

I waited for something else to happen – the sack, the demand of an apology – but nothing did. The next day Gene was back at my desk and we carried on as if nothing had happened. *Well?*

The only group on the label Miles really cared about was The Police. Which, as it happened, was the group most of the rest of us *least* cared about. At least Chelsea had some genuine punk credentials, the 'Right To Work' single and the blessing early on of the sainted Mark P.

The only reason I could see why The Police got a deal was because their drummer, Stewart Copeland, was Miles' younger brother. Before The Police, Stewart had been in Curved Air. Good band, but definitely not punk. Before The Police, the guitarist Andy Summers, who we all joked was old enough to be Miles' dad, had been in definitely-not-punk groups like Zoot Money and Soft Machine, and had played with the likes of Kevin Coyne, Neil Sedaka and Mike Oldfield. Which meant he could really play; a cardinal sin in the 'new reality' being sectioned by punk.

Even the singer, named *Sting* (the kind of vanilla-punk name that forced fingers down throats) was really an old jazzer from Geordieland just going through the motions. If it had been five years earlier they would have all worn make-up and glitter suits.

As it was they had all dyed their hair blond, donned parachute suits and pogoed on stage like older dads dancing at the works' Xmas party. But they were Miles' favourites and we all had to play along.

So clearly was The Police not the type of band we'd normally have had on Step Forward that Miles gave them their own label, Illegal Records. Sure enough, their first single, 'Fall Out', was two-minutes two-seconds of punk-by-numbers bollocks. Now they were working in a rehearsal room with a black guy named Joe who would come by the office every day to play us cassette copies of the latest demos, all of which sounded the same.

But Joe had a reggae background and would groove around the room going on about 'the feel' and how he was teaching the band how to really capture it. Joe was a tremendously friendly guy, but we would all inch out of the room every time he started up about 'the feel' and the latest news on what new tricks he'd showed Stewart or Sting the night before. We would do impersonations of him going on about 'the feel' behind his back, while playing the latest bones-into-dust contraption from The Fall or whoever.

'You see, mon,' said Dexter-as-Joe, 'the thing I taught The Fall is how to get *the feel*. Now that crazy Marky Smith guy, him wanna rename the group *The Feel* too . . .'

Joe stopped being a joke the day he came in with his latest Police demo with *the feel* called 'Roxanne'. It was an instant hit, like heroin. You just had to do it again and again. And by God, yes! It had *the feel*! It had so much feel The Police at once abandoned their plans to become the punk band your mother actually would like and transformed themselves into a white rock-reggae band. A week later, Joe came in with another song called 'Can't Stand Losing You', which was a rewrite of 'Roxanne' with the same rock-reggae feel, and it seemed like they had really hit on something. There was no way, though, that they could parlay that sound into a whole career, surely?

I wouldn't survive long enough at Step Forward to find out. I grew so bored and tormented by Nick not allowing me to do anything that I began skipping days. Began to come down with a lot of colds. Began to not even bother to come up with excuses, and would just show up on a Friday to collect my £40 cash.

Then one dull November afternoon Miles and Stewart entered our shabby office just off the Portobello Road and issued an invitation. Wishbone Ash were playing that night at the Ipswich Gaumont. Miles and Stewart were going and so could anyone else who fancied it. Being as this was 1978 and Wishbone Ash was about as fashionable as the plague, nobody fancied it except Doreen, the middle-aged office receptionist – and me. What the hell, I was twenty, no money, nothing doing, and this was Friday night. I knew it probably meant free drinks, maybe even free drugs. And, besides, I didn't just like punk, I liked rock music too. And I'd never seen the mighty Ash before, though I still owned a couple of their early albums. I still recalled how, some years earlier, *Sounds* had voted *Argus* their rock album of the year. I wondered vaguely if they still did 'Blowin' Free'. And that really bloody long one about the phoenix rising from the ashes. What was it called again? Oh, yeah – 'Phoenix'.

We all piled into a car and sped off. Sure enough, there was beer and Scotch in the car, and a little speed and dope in my pocket. It was a long, tedious drive up the motorway from London, though, and I kept plugging away at the booze and the drugs until I was almost comatose. By the time we got to the gig, I had just enough brain cells left to find a seat and collapse into it. At which point, I promptly blacked-out.

When I awoke, the show was over and everybody was going backstage to greet the band. I tagged along behind them, not really knowing what the fuck. I still didn't know whether they'd done 'Blowin' Free', or the one about the phoenix.

Backstage the band was partying like it was 1969, all long hair and warm white wine and ladies in flowery dresses showing plenty of freckly cleavage. I staggered into a room where their bassist Martin Turner was entertaining some of the ladies. He was explaining something deeply interesting. They all listened intently, their flowery cleavages heaving with enthusiasm.

I tried to join in the conversation, which was a mistake for two reasons: a) I didn't actually know what the hell they were talking about, and b) I was still semi-comatose, half-speeding, half-dozing, half-drunk, half-insane ... way too many halves bouncing around my skull to put them into any order, let alone allow them out of my mouth.

Instead, I found myself ranting at them about who knows what. Something about blowing up a phoenix, I dare say. Then someone, possibly Martin, possibly some sort of tour minder, politely suggested I shut the fuck up. Cue an even bigger rant, this time sprinkled liberally, as they say, with expletives ... how dare they try to shove their fucking phoenix up my arse, the fucking fuckers!

Nobody seemed to know what to do. Suddenly it was all too much for me and I vomited, not just a little but a lot – a long, gushing fountain of vomit that managed to spray all the ladies and a fair bit of Martin too.

The ladies screamed. Martin swore. The minder stepped in. And I vomited again. With my recently dyed-and-spiked black hair and borrowed leather jacket they must have thought me a punk, possibly making some kind of 'statement'. But of course I wasn't. I was just a drunk kid, a stupid rock fan, drugged-up and bored and unable to hold any of it in any longer.

Suddenly I was alone in the room, covered in puke and no glory. I looked around, squinting into the shadows, realising I'd put a foot wrong somewhere but not quite able to discern where or why.

Later that night, on the drive back to London, Miles and Stewart ignored me, for which I was grateful. I was starting to come down now and couldn't bear to think of what I'd been doing for the past few hours. Doreen, the middle-aged receptionist, offered to put me up in the spare room at her house.

'There's just one thing,' she advised me sternly as she tucked me up in bed that night. 'You must promise to leave your underpants on. I don't want any pubic hairs in the bed in the morning.'

I looked at her. Was she kidding? She was not. I left my underpants on and in the morning swept the sheets with my hand for stray pubic hairs. Well, you can't be too careful. You don't want to upset anybody.

Then Nick sacked me. With great relish, he took me into a side-room after I'd returned from one of my colds, handed me £40 and told me not to bother coming back. He did it with a most serious expression on his face. Nick still believed punk was a promise, not a pose. And, as he'd long suspected, I didn't believe in anything. So off I fucked.

7. **Co-caine**

So there's this chick. Well, older lady. Maybe twenty-nine. Maybe even thirty. Old, you know? She's in PR and she's driving me home from one of her gigs. I was still bottom rung on the *Sounds* ladder, but I'd been plugging away for about a year and occasionally I'd be given something big to do that the punk-blinded, uptight rabble on the staff now deemed beneath them. This had been one of those, and I was grateful. No bunking the tube to get there, no worrying about paying for a drink. The older lady had taken care of everything.

So she's driving me home and it turns out her house is not far from where I live with my ma and pa. And she says, look, it's too early for home, fancy coming in for coffee?

I jump at it, anything that meant I didn't have to go home always sounded good to me. And when we get there it's the full rock-star shtick, six-inch-deep white carpets, gold records on the wall, decanters of brandy and such. Even by 1978 standards it was dated. I'm sitting there digging all this, trying to act like no big deal but then she pulls out the coke and, ah, OK . . . I've never done coke before. Not that I let on. She feeds me line after line, talking about New York and LA and all these scenes she's been in, and I don't know what's going on, I'm just hanging on to be polite and not seem like a complete amateur.

Then she says, 'Now, am I going to drive you home to mummy, or are you going to take me upstairs and fuck the arse off me?'

And that's how I got my first proper job in PR, after being sacked from Step Forward. Casting couch? Not by then. This was the debauched end of the most uninhibited decade of the twentieth century. Everybody fucked everybody. Can't stand the heat? Put your clothes back on and let someone else have a go, then.

This was more of a kindness. The job offer didn't follow the fuck. It was more like the lunch we had a few weeks later. More specifically, the phone call I made some days after that begging for some work, any work. Well, they had a temporary gig, she said, paid £50 a week. Would that tidy me over?

I started work the next day. The company specialised in rock bands – Black Sabbath, Hawkwind, Journey – and a couple of new wave bands like The Damned and, later, Ultravox. After the strictly enforced punk rules and regulations of Step Forward, none of which I was ever able to get to grips with, this was like escaping Alcatraz and finding yourself in the best little whorehouse in Texas. Only we were in London. Well, you get me.

Cocaine was everywhere, every day and every night, and so was the money. It felt big league rock 'n' roll, and in some ways it was. You'd go off on tour and wouldn't come back for days, weeks. Or until you'd run out of coke. We would bill the bands back for all the coke, itemised as 'champagne and flowers for the band'.

I was enjoying it so much I gave up trying to write for *Sounds* at the same time, and gave myself over to becoming the most popular rock PR in London. The journalists may not have liked all my bands, but they sure as shit liked hanging out with me. I seemed to spend most of my time standing in the toilet stalls of whatever hellhole gig we were at, shoveling coke up the noses of music journalists.

It was strange. Some of them, you had this big idea of what they were about from reading them in the *NME* or *Time Out*, *The Times* or the *Daily Mirror*. But they dropped all the pretense once I beckoned them to join me. The women were as bad as the men, often worse. They had no qualms about following me into the gents for a quick snort or two. Occasionally, while in-situ, they would offer me a different kind of a snort and, very occasionally, I would take them up on their kind offer. But if you've ever tried to have a shag in a toilet stall at a concert venue you'll know how unwelcoming that prospect can quickly become – especially when some inconsiderate bastard decides to lock himself in the stall next to you and actually have a shit.

The benefits of being even an average rock PR far outstripped those of being a good rock journalist, on every level. Rock PRs made more money than rock journalists, had more real involvement with the artists, and weren't treated with suspicion (at best) or sheer contempt (at worst) by every other branch of the music business.

This then, I decided, was definitely the life for me. So much so that after the lady that had 'talent spotted' me left, I became a partner in the firm myself. Not that I had to fuck anyone else to get that far, though I did have to pop my cherry in other, more metaphorical ways. For example, becoming skilled in the Art of Lunch. No internet or email, not even any fax in those days, all you had to persuade journalists to write about your bands were your phone manner and your ability to 'connect' in person.

Hence the importance of a 'good lunch'. The revolving restaurant at the top of the Post Office Tower was a regular haunt. Writers seemed to love it there. Especially after I'd slipped them a few white lines on a shiny side-plate while the friendly (read: well-tipped) staff turned the other way. Other times, there was a basement place in Soho. Dark as death, you could stay there all day and night, snorting whiskey, drinking cocaine, as the old Pat Travers song (another client) used to go, and no one would be any the wiser. The amount of bands I talked on to the front cover of magazines from that vantage point . . . well, you'd have to have been there to believe.

Other useful PR devices included sellotaping grams of cocaine to the white inside paper sleeve of albums, before biking them over to certain favoured writers on the music weeklies. Not merely to ensure good reviews, you understand, but as much to keep the flow of goodwill going. Other times we used more imagination. On a whim, I once stuck a writer on the back of a motorbike, with me following on my own bike behind, as we raced to Heathrow in time to catch a flight to Edinburgh where one of our least popular bands was playing that night. The writer had a girlfriend up there and was so delighted to be unexpectedly whisked to her side that giving some nothing band a good review was the least he could do for me, stout fellow.

The only time I was momentarily flummoxed was when a writer named Malcolm Dome from *Record Mirror* turned up at the office one day to interview Hawkwind. Not at all sure how the teeny mag would treat space-ritualists like the Wind, we laid on a buffet of dope, coke, speed and shots, only to be rebuffed by Malcolm, who announced he was a booze and drug teetotaler, a species we had never before encountered on our planet. In which case, what would he like instead? 'A cup of tea,' he said. We were thunderstruck. 'And a doughnut, perhaps?' Was he taking the piss? Had our bluff been thoroughly called? Naw. We just sent the office dolly-bird out for a tray with a dozen different glazed pastries on it, churned him up a bucket of leafy stuff, into which we couldn't resist adding a couple of grains of this and that, and served it to him hot. The following week – hey presto! – Hawkwind revealed in *Record Mirror* as shock-horror good guys definitely worth taking home to mother! Slapped backs and fat cheques all round. Oh, and yeah, a couple more lines to celebrate.

It couldn't last, and it didn't. My life became a series of flashbacks, or flash-forwards. Disjointed scenes from a movie no one wanted to see. Like the time . . .

. . . I was lying on the floor as it all went off around me. I couldn't remember if it was my room. I thought maybe we'd started there then moved on to Phil's room. It's all the same in Holiday Inns. Anyway, now it was all going off again.

From where I lay, I could see at least six pairs of cowboy boots stumbling around, making a lot of noise. They were all laughing and talking and drinking and smoking and taking turns to bend their heads over the large mirror that someone had thoughtfully taken from the wall and placed on the bed.

'What about yer man on the floor?' I heard some voice I recognised ask. One of Lizzy's roadies. A good guy, couldn't remember his name right this second, just the beard. And that big knife he carried. 'I wouldn't bother,' I heard someone else say. 'He's out for the count.'

I wanted to join in with them, of course, but not as much as I just wanted to lie there. No, I was fine, thanks. It was just those downers I'd taken earlier that had gone weird on me, that's all – probably in reaction to the speed, or maybe the dope. There had been a lot of that since we'd hit the road two weeks before. I'd be fine, though. I just needed to be still for a minute . . .

Phil never batted an eye. He knew. The rest of them, as always, took their cue from him and did the same, stepping over me carefully as they bustled around the room, telling a dirty joke or two, as the song went. I began humming it: The boys are back in town/The boys are back in town . . . *then those big crunching guitar chords . . . Dern! Da-dern!*

Suddenly Phil was standing over me, staring down hard, his long black face filling the indoor sky. 'Are you taking da piss?' he said in that hoarse Irish brogue.

What? Oh . . . no. Never, mate. I stopped humming. I hadn't realised I was doing it out loud. I tried to tell him but my mouth wouldn't move. Then his face vanished again and I heard someone say, 'I want whatever he's on!' Then more laughing.

I felt like laughing too. 'This,' I thought idly, 'is the pinnacle; about as inside the inside story as you can get without actually being in the band.' And that felt good to me. Fucking good. I had promised myself as a teenager that my life would be a rock 'n' roll one and now here I was, just turned twenty-one, and actually out there doing it. All of it.

I would never have gotten this close to them if I had remained a journalist. As a PR, though, I became someone they relied on, someone they liked having around, a great kid, a cool customer. An it's-all-right-he's-with-the-band kind of guy. Much better than just being a music journalist, who the bands always felt very uncomfortable around, no matter how well they disguised it. Not with me, though. With me they could be themselves and that made me proud. I lay there on the floor, basking in my new-found glory . . .

Some time passed. I must have drifted off again. The next time I counted there were only two pairs of legs in the room. I could hear them talking.

'I don't know,' one of them was saying. 'Why don't we just take him out into the corridor and leave him there? Throw a blanket over him, he'll be all right . . .'

'Naw,' said the other voice, which I recognised as Phil's. 'You can't do that, he doesn't know what fookin' time o'day it is. Look at him . . .'

Momentary silence. Then the first voice again. 'Which room is he in? Has he got a key on him?'

I felt their hands on me, checking my pockets. Nothing. I wanted to help but didn't know how. I tried to get their attention by humming again but Phil looked at me aghast.

'Jayzus Christ!' he said. 'His fookin' brain's gone! Come on, let's get him into da corridor . . .'

Phil got me by the arms, the other one, my roadie mate, got me by the feet.

'Christ, he's light as a feather,' said Phil.

'More like a girl,' said the other.

They got me through the door and carried me about twenty feet down the corridor, where they laid me out again. I wanted to help, to join in, but I was gone, gone, gone . . .

Phil stayed with me while the other one went to get a blanket and pillow from the room. He looked down at me and spoke. 'Look at it dis way, son. Either you've lost da use of yer fookin' legs permanently – in which case yer focked anyway – or dis is all a bad dream you're gonna wake up from in a few hours. Either way, I'm off down to da bar now, so I'll see yer later . . .'

'Yeah, sweet dreams,' smirked the other one, a good guy for getting me that pillow.

I watched their legs disappear down the corridor towards the elevators and I thought, 'I wish I was going with them. I'd love to go down to the bar with Phil and the lads right now. That would be great.'

I began humming again. The boys are back, the boys are back . . . It was, after all, one of the all-time classic rock songs I had always felt . . .

*

I was used to waking up in strange places. We all were, those of us who were young in the seventies. Like sex and getting drunk, doing drugs was just another rock 'n' roll rite of passage. Certainly nothing to get worked up about. Getting wasted was just where it was at. Elegantly wasted, like Keef.

I was good at getting wasted but I hadn't perfected the 'elegant' part yet. That would take years of inelegant practice and many times on that journey I found myself laying face-down in the gutter – the real kind and the worse kind. A crumpled black sack of rubbish left out in the street for the bin men to collect.

Sometimes you could laugh it off. Once with Hawkwind, I was leaving the tour in Scotland and was booked on to a 7 a.m. flight from Edinburgh to London. This was in the days when the Edinburgh-to-London shuttle was like getting on a bus: you could pre-book your tickets but it wasn't necessary to actually pay for them until you were on-board the plane. As soon as it had taken off a conductor would come round with a ticket-machine and collect the fares. If you only had hand luggage you didn't need to turn up drastically early to get a seat, either. You could arrive literally five minutes before flight time and they would simply open the doors and shove you on.

That's what happened this time. Fresh from a party for the band at the hotel that was still going strong when I'd crawled, stinking of sweat and booze and funny cigarettes, into the back of the taxi taking me to the airport, I'd arrived just in time to feel the whoosh of the giant mechanical door closing behind me as I hobbled to my seat in the smoking section. I was still drunk and fucked-up from the party but getting on aeroplanes still drunk and fucked-up from the party was all part of the deal, right?

I got to my seat and lowered my undercarriage as best I could into position. Then I did my seatbelt up and stared at the No Smoking sign blinking ominously overhead, waiting for it to switch off after the plane took off. The stewardess stood in the aisle and started to say something. She was young and good-looking and I imagined her strapped into the seat next to me, ready for take-off. Then I blacked out. Gone again, for ever . . .

When I awoke, it was from the not so gentle prodding of the same stewardess; her young, much too made-up face close enough to mine for me to smell it; her voice a mixture of concern and impatience.

'Wake up, please, sir,' she was saying. 'The plane has landed and we're disembarking.' She glanced around the cabin. I followed her eyes. The plane was virtually empty. Then all at once I got it. I had slept through the entire flight. Take-off, landing, the in-flight meal, free drinks, everything. In one way it was kind of thrilling – like I had literally travelled hundreds of miles in a second – in another way it felt strangely humiliating: I could have done with that in-flight meal. I got to my feet, feeling worse than ever.

It was only as I walked through the exit of the departure lounge at Heathrow that I realised I hadn't even bought a ticket. I realised with a cringe that I must have been totally out for the count when the conductor came round; that he would have tried to wake me, probably more than once during the flight, and that in the end he must have just given up. I'd seen these guys virtually slap people awake on other flights. I wondered if he'd tried doing that to me. I put my hand to the side of my face and imagined it – like trying to prise open a coffin lid with a spoon.

Generally, though, I spent most of my time at the company with both eyes glued open. So much of how I came to view both the music and media business would be informed by my experiences there. Did it make me cynical? Yes, of course. We would pull so many tricks to get our clients in the papers, literally making stuff up the music press and tabloids would reprint sometimes word for word. I have never been able to read a newspaper story since – whether it be on 'serious' issues such as politics and finance, or the usual bollocks about music and TV celebs – without keeping at least one jaundiced eye half-closed.

But it also helped me understand fully, for the first time, just how the game worked and why it was played that way. It was all about dreams and how to manipulate them, and it worked both ways. The fans fed off the stars and the illusions they peddled, unable to comprehend that people whose private lives are sad, neurotic, arid holes often create the most beautiful music. The stars fed off the record companies and managers, the agents and promoters, even the PRs like me, who only existed if the stars were making money, real money. As my partner in the company, Big Joe, used to say, 'Art for art's sake, hit singles for fuck's sake!' It was the complete opposite of the Step Forward credo, the one where a band like The Cortinas signing to a major money-making label like CBS was derided (as it would be when The Police did the same with A&M) but, like it or not, it was the one that had built the music business and allowed places like Step Forward to exist, the one that actually kept the entire music business going. And the one I was now thrilled to be a proper part of. I fed off the high-stakes corruption. It made me feel more real. Like at least I wasn't lying to myself like the one-inch intellect punks.

A year before I had written my first short feature for *Sounds*, travelling up to Bradford with The Lurkers in the back of a broken-down Transit van, squeezed in with all the gear, before watching them play to a half-empty pub on a Sunday night. In their heads they were The Ramones. In my head I was Nick Kent. In reality we were all consumed by the smell of our own farts. Trundling back down the motorway the next day in the same dirty old van it felt like all we'd done was go round in one big meaningless circle. No money, no honey, no dope, no hope.

Now I was travelling in a limo with Thin Lizzy, full of groupies and coke dealers, and I was getting paid big bucks for it – more in a week than my dad earned in a month; or The Lurkers would earn in a year. There was no way back for me now. I would make sure of it.

Everyone you met seemed to have the same understanding. Out with Brian Robertson one night we somehow ended up at this flat in Mayfair. It was full of scene-makers and the women they attracted. Not your average rock chicks, but a cut above: film babes, models; wives and girlfriends of distant millionaires from far-off scenes in other time zones. Brian was introduced as 'Robbo from Thin Lizzy'. He didn't bother to explain he'd left the band. That would only have made too much of it. I was introduced as his manager. Again, so what? Nobody was really listening anyway. They just needed to feel you were somehow already part of their deal.

Next thing Freddie Mercury was standing there. I had to look twice, though, because he was so short. I'd never met Freddie before, only seen him on stage or on TV, where he'd looked as tall and as lithe as a ballet dancer. In person, though, it was a case of big head, small body – huge teeth. And cloying in his shadow, two or three young and overeager male faces.

'Hello, darling,' he said to Robbo. 'Where's Philip?'

'He's not here tonight, Fred,' said Robbo. 'He's away with his boyfriend.'

Freddie gurgled with pleasure. 'If *only*, my dear! Have you said hello to Kenny?'

He waved his hand vaguely. We looked and there was Kenny Everett, on a couch, attended to on either side by a couple of leather-clad musclemen with preposterously large moustaches. He looked over when he heard his name, spotted Robbo and blew him a kiss.

'What's this?' growled Robbo. 'Are we in the wrong fucking place?'

Freddie smiled but his eyes remained cold.

'You don't know what you're missing, dear . . .'

We moved on further into the flat. It was like the Tardis, much bigger on the inside than you imagined from the outside. The chicks started to thin out. Then, just as we were about to give up, we found what we hadn't realised we were looking for. There was Keith Richards, stretched out in an armchair, a foot-long doobie dangling from his mush.

Someone whispered into Keith's ear, and he looked over. 'Hey, man,' he said, 'come join us.'

It wasn't clear if he knew who Robbo was, but it soon became clear he knew all about Thin Lizzy.

'I really like that one, "Dancing In The Moonlight",' he drawled, beckoning Robbo over to the seat next to him. Then, 'Hey, man,' – extending me his heavily ringed hand.

We settled down and acted cool. Like Freddie, I was surprised how short Keith was: not as short as Freddie, but not the larger-than-life rock zombie I'd gotten used to in pictures and on stage either. He also spoke with quite a posh accent, or so it seemed: articulate, switched on, despite the tumbler of bourbon that never seemed to empty, and the endless stream of smoke-ums.

Keith and Robbo talked guitars. Yawn. I sat and stared at the most beautiful woman I had ever seen, an Arabian princess with swimming-pool eyes and the whole cosmos swirling beneath her silk shift, her coal-size diamonds and her opium-enflamed perfume.

'Hi,' I said, cool as fuck.

'Allo, mate,' she said. 'Oo are you, then?'

It turned out the closest to the exotic Orient my Arabian princess had ever been was East Ham. Not that that made it any easier for me to talk to her. I was still just as lost in her staggering beauty, unable to make sense of it and remain calm at the same time.

'Yes,' I began. 'I am . . . I am . . .' I looked at over at Robbo, '. . . with him.'

I fumbled for a cigarette. 'And you?'

'I'm Keith's mate, Julie. Pleased to meet ya.'

Finally Keith broke the tension by asking Robbo, 'Fancy a Catherine Wheel?'

'Aye, that would be great,' said Robbo.

I had no idea what they were talking about, so just sat and waited, imagining an unexpected excursion to the garden maybe, for some fireworks. Then I watched in awe as Keith used a menacing-looking hunting knife to arrange an extremely chunky – not much chopping done with that knife – line of coke into one long concentric circle on the coffee table. Then he fished out a hundred dollar bill, already rolled, and nodded to Robbo to do the same, who pulled out a tenner and began rolling.

'Right,' said Keith, 'I'll start from the inside, you start from the outside. Last one home's a sissy!'

Robbo did as he was told, and for the next ten seconds we watched as their heads made sharp little circles as they snaffled up the coke, until their noses were virtually touching.

Keith laughed a horrible, water-disappearing-down-the-plughole laugh while Robbo sat there rubbing his nose, his eyes on sticks.

'My turn!' cried Julie.

'Me too!' I said, chancing it.

Once again, Keith obliged with the knife and butter. He passed Julie his hundred-dollar bill while I fished out a pound note. And we began, our heads banging at the end. Not that I noticed. By then my brain had left the building.

'Woo, woo!' yelped Julie.

'Yeah, baby!' shouted Keith.

Then Julie leaned over and kissed Keith full on the mouth for what seemed like a long time. Then, breaking off, she came and gave one to me. I nearly choked, terrified what Keith would do. I pictured that knife at my throat. But then she stopped and went over and gave Robbo a big smacker too. Keith just sat there grinning, taking it all in, slurping on his beaker of bourbon and his chimney smoke.

The next day, I had no idea where the evening had gone after that, other than recalling one passing conversation with Keith. We were talking about travelling the world, him going off on one about Morocco, Tangiers, Paris, New York, where all the best places to 'make a connection' were and where you had to watch yourself. 'You don't walk into one those gaffs in New York after dark without carrying a piece,' he advised, as I sat there nodding sagely.

One of his anecdotes ended with the words, '. . . but then you know what it's like when you're only twenty-one.'

'I'm only twenty-one,' I chirped.

He looked at me with suspicion. The first bad vibes of the night.

'What's that?'

'I said I'm only twenty-one now.'

'Fuck off, baby, you're thirty at least . . .'

'No. It's true, I'm still only twenty-one.'

Now he gave me the benefit of his complete attention. He studied my face carefully, dug deep into my aura, made his appraisal then sat back and pointed a bony, skull-ringed finger at me.

'What *happened* to you, man?'

I didn't know what to say. It didn't make sense, but everybody laughed anyway. It wasn't about making sense; it was about grooving on the riff. Though we didn't know it then these were the final days of the pre-AIDS era, and as long as nobody let the side down and ever stopped laughing one hell of a time would still be had by all. As long as nobody ever left the party early everything would be cool, baby.

Everyone seemed to be infected by the same idea, as though we all knew it had to end, and soon. There was the wife of the famous rock singer I worked for who came banging on my door in the middle of the night. We were on tour in Texas and she was gacked out and drunk and ready to try anything, she said. 'I know he fucks around, so why shouldn't I?' Yes, but he was asleep in the next room and this was too weird even for me.

Then there was the beautiful young fiancée of the famous record producer who grew tired of always being left behind while he went off to Jamaica or wherever to make another hit album for you know who. She used to take me to places in London I never knew existed and would never be able to find again. Then would fuck me on black silk sheets and talk about why oh why it couldn't have been a nice guy like me she'd fallen in love with instead of the famous millionaire who'd bought her the pad in Chelsea with the silk bed sheets.

Or the time Phil Lynott offered me a snort of smack in the dressing room at the Marquee and I'd recoiled in horror until he said, with that lucky black cat smile, 'I don't offer this to just anybody . . .'

That was the clincher. The choice of sticking with what I knew and being 'just anybody', or taking a leap of unfaith into full-blown rock-star hedonism, replete with its nastiest habit. I bowed my head in supplication and had a damn good snort. I felt my body give in, my mind concertina. I felt myself let go. Later that same night I bought my first £10 baggie of gear. I was on my way, never coming back, whoa yeah . . .

Other times it was just simple dirt. One of the crew would give over his hotel room for a bit of 'sport', a couple of groupies would set up shop, and for the rest of the night the room key would be passed around to anyone who fancied a blowjob or a fuck. There were always lots of takers. I recall one mother and daughter team from a certain northern English town who would show up at all the gigs. We even got to know their names.

The idea was you never stopped: why would you want to? You just kept going until the darkness descended; the candle having burnt itself out from both ends, now extinguishing itself with the same self-destructive haste of the snake that devours its own tail.

Or something like that. I just knew, eventually, that I had to get out. Then I arrived for work one morning and discovered the office had burned down. Big Joe, all innocent: 'Thank God, we've got the insurance . . .'

That was it for me. I saw it as a metaphor for my own burnt-out state. An omen. I was sick of waking up strange, tired of blacking out broken, astounded at my good luck and misfortune. Now I just wanted to go home.

If only I still had one.

8. Don't You Want Me, Baby?

The next couple of years were bleak. They shouldn't have been – I drifted back into writing for *Sounds* again and soon after took a job as press officer at Virgin Records, in Notting Hill Gate – but by then I had developed a taste for smack and, as any fool knows when it comes to smack, that taste will turn into a habit, that habit into a full-blown addiction. It meant any good fortune that blew my way during those dreadful years always took second place to the more pressing day-to-day need for a fix. And then another. And then another . . .

It's no way to live, who needs to be told that? It's also incredibly tedious, the ultimate groundhog day, except without the redemptive learning curve. It had started as a lark, like the cocaine. When Wild Horses had gone out on tour with Thin Lizzy I felt like I'd joined the circus and was never coming back. Robbo and Jimmy were already adepts, not shooting smack, but snorting it, like it was just a different coloured cocaine. So were Phil and Lizzy guitarist Scott Gorham, except they had both gone beyond snorting and were now playing with fire.

'Fleetwood Mac,' Phil would call it. The first time he mentioned it to me I started mumbling like an idiot about the Peter Green line-up over the later Stevie Nicks one and he just laughed, thought I was making fun.

'Here,' he said, offering me a hit off his plectrum.

I assumed it was coke but my antennae was still good and I stopped at the last minute and asked what it was.

'Fleetwood Mac,' he said, holding it out under my nose.

I looked at him, still puzzled.

'Fleetwood Mac,' he repeated. 'Smack!'

And then the clincher, 'I don't offer this to just anybody . . .'

Because back then I really did go home to my flat at night and put on the *Live and Dangerous* album. I really did stand there, drunk, making shapes as though I was Robbo about to launch into that eye-rolling solo from 'Still In Love With You'. I really did go home at night feeling like I'd jumped through the TV screen and landed on the other side. In colour, volume set to maximum. I really did think like that.

They even had a pet doctor in Harley Street they paid to cool them out when things got out of hand. 'Dr Jewel', they called him. Say you'd been on the gear for a couple of weeks and were now strung out – early cold turkey without the ectoplasmic nightmare of full-scale withdrawal enfolding you – you simply made an appointment to see the good doctor, who would load you up with pain pills and sleepers, and you'd taper off from there. Ten pills the first day, then nine the next, eight, seven, six . . . and so on until you got down to one then none. At which point you were 'cool' to start all over again. It was downhill from there.

By the time I'd found myself working at Virgin in the summer of 1981 I'd taken two cures – both successful – and was now on my third habit. This one, though, would not be so easy to kick. I'd made the big mistake of picking up the needle – the works. You got them, no questions asked, from a Chinese place on Shaftesbury Avenue. They knew what you wanted them for, but as long as you had the cash that was your look out.

I became lost in permanent midnight, my shadow taller than my soul. In my head, I was Keith Richards and Lou Reed and

William Burroughs all rolled into one. The Dirty Spike Kid with the magic medicine and the dead eyes and cigarettes that never went out. In reality I was the stinking, disgusting oaf who hadn't had a shower or even washed his clothes for nearly a year, who lived on Twix Bars and bottles of Lucozade, who stole records from his own office to sell on his way home each night so that he could run off like a rat to score.

Even after I got hepatitis I only quit for as long as it took for me to feel 'better' enough to go back on the needle. When I ran out of veins to hit in my arms I began shooting into my hands. Very fucking painful. When the needle scars got too bad I pretended to have fallen down the stairs and sprained my wrist. In fact, I'd bought a roll of bandage and – very badly – wrapped my own hand and wrist in it. I was fooling no one and when one day I came into the office and found one of my spikes sticking out of my desk I nearly had a heart attack. They were all now watching me. They all knew. I would have to do something drastic about it. To quit, even. I ran to the toilets, locked myself in, had another hit and tried not to think about it.

It was a shame because Virgin was then reaching a new dizzy peak, in creativity and commercial status. That was the year the Human League transformed themselves from electronic punk industrialists into full-on pop stars with 'Don't You Want Me Baby'. The one who came up with the riff, Jo Callis, was a little older than the rest and more my kind of guy. He'd been in The Rezillos and knew the 'hit singles for fuck's sake' rule by heart. He told me he'd bowdlerised the riff for 'Don't You Want Me' from 'Down, Down' by Status Quo. He also told me the secret ingredient behind most hit songs.

'It all goes back to the school playground,' he explained. 'When you're five years old and going nah-nah, nah-nah-naaah-hhh to your mates.'

I laughed my dry, junkie laugh, a short thin tree with no leaves. 'Think about it,' he said. 'It's true. Think of the greatest riffs ever – "All Right Now" by Free, "Whole Lotta Love" by Led Zeppelin or, going back, "She Loves You" by The Beatles. They all play off that nursery rhymey nah-nah, nah-nah-naaahhh. Same with "Don't You Want Me".'

He was right, and even today I can't listen to pop or rock music without hearing the connection.

Other than that, highlights, there were few. The only artists at Virgin I might have found time for didn't want to know anyway. Ice queens like David Sylvian from Japan. Their only big album, *Tin Drum*, was released during my time and I was intrigued enough to want to say hello on one of his rare visits to the office. But it was like talking to a ghost. But then Sylvian was always too precious for this earth. Like his music.

Mostly I ran and hid in the bogs whenever anyone showed up whom I might have to give a little too much face-time to. The upstairs toilet was my home from home. My little drug den. I began to spend more and more time in there . . .

When finally the axe fell, the irony was that I had cleaned up, and was determined to make up for my sins by becoming the best record company press officer in London. Too little, too late. My boss, a lovely man named Keith Bourton, had received too many complaints about my behaviour. No comeback for Johnny Junkie. Not this time. I wept all the way up Portobello Road to the tube station.

I didn't know who I was any more, who I was supposed to be, nor what mattered and what didn't. I had a feeling that if I hung on something might bob to the surface, but that was just what you told yourself when all else was lost. I knew that and would sometimes tap into the deeper underlying feeling, prodding at the truth like a bear prodding at the trap that has just cut his body in two.

I still managed the occasional bit of paid writing for some of the smaller pop magazines, found solace of a kind in interviewing artists I considered beneath even me, like Dollar and Bucks Fizz. Mainly, though, I drifted along with a quid in my pocket, sleeping on floors and couches, signing on and picking up a little extra from cash-in-hand jobs like furniture removing and dishwashing.

It wasn't long before I was back on the junk again. But even that didn't seem to work any more, you could never get back the highs of your first go round. Within days of starting on the gear again I would be back to simply maintaining. Not getting high, just not being junk sick, and eventually I quit it for the last time. By now the whole ritual of withdrawal was almost routine. It never got easier, but you at least knew how it would end – eventually. Still, there was no sense of triumph or validation. Just one less piece of shit to swim through each day. The only thing I knew for sure was that I was finished writing about or working with rock bands. It was time for something new. Only I didn't feel new any more; I felt old before my time. Gone home early . . .

I still didn't know who I was when I met her, just who I wasn't. It was 1983, springtime for Hitler, and I hadn't had a woman since the seventies. She was a friend's ex and at first I couldn't see it, didn't fancy her at all. Tits too small, hair too big, face too plain . . . I was blind with painkillers and alcohol. I hadn't slept right for years. What did I know?

Her name was Maria – Spanish, born in west London – and more beautiful than I realised, before it was too late. Like something you would draw on a beer mat in a figure 8, with kisses underneath and a big penis looking up in drippy wonder.

She liked to go to gigs, dreamed of fucking the guy in Dexys, had been told something that in her mind linked it all together, then for some reason fixed her sights on me. I read all that but didn't know what to do about it. She was from another time, when girls followed bands like they were the Monkees, all jolly japes and crazy fun. But she rolled joints of homegrown and always had a bit of dough on her, and I felt obliged to act half decent whenever she and her friend Beverly were around.

One long, nothing Sunday she rang. 'Hi,' she said, sounding alarmingly real, 'It's Maria. I'm with Bev and we were wondering what you're doing tonight?'

I glanced around as though checking my diary.

'Nothing,' I said. 'I'm skint.'

'That's OK. We'll buy you a pint.'

I thought about it. One pint and then what?

'Sorry,' I said. 'I'm really skint.'

'Come on! Me and Bev are going down the Barley Mow, in Chiswick, it's nice in the garden there. We'll buy you a pint.'

I thought of that one pint and what would happen afterwards, but she kept on and I was easily worn down in those days. Keep on long enough and I'd agree to anything.

When I got there it was an hour later. I'd walked all the way, made out like I'd had to wait a long time for the bus. They looked at me as I sat down and I could tell they were already regretting it. They thought I'd been exaggerating when I'd said I was skint. Now they could see for themselves. Bad shirt and shoes, wrong face and hair . . .

Good girls, they hid it all, tried not to spoil their own fun, and while Maria trotted off to buy me a Guinness, male tongues hanging out as they watched her go by in her short dress and bare brown arms, her huge red hair like an aura wafting around her, I pretended to be interested in what Bev had to say. Bev was Scottish, mouthy, always a fag on the go and always a half-bottle of voddy in her handbag, along with the too-red lipstick and the always at the ready condoms.

She always began talking the same way. 'It was really funny, right . . .' Then a long drone about something so unfunny you prayed for the Big One to drop.

Maria came back with the drinks and I sat there slurping at my pint like a thirsty dog. She offered me a cigarette, a Dunhill. I looked at it, impressed.

They both sat there for a while talking between themselves. A litany of 'really funny' things seemed to happen to them wherever they went, crazy chicks lapping up the sun.

Lightning another cigarette, Maria looked at me and asked, 'Do you have a girlfriend, Mick?'

'Not at the moment.' I tried on a smile. It didn't suit me.

She clocked it, let it go.

'Me too,' she said, though it sounded better coming from her. Then, from Beverly: 'Have you heard from Pete lately?'

Ah, so this was it? Maria was still broken up about my crazy artist friend Pete. Wanted to know if I had a connect, maybe? Some good word, anything.

'Haven't spoken to him for a few weeks,' I lied. 'What happened with you two?'

'Nothing,' she lied back. 'It was never really a serious thing.'

Now it was my turn to smile knowingly. She'd been crazy about him, would always be. Relieved, I settled back into listening to another long tedious duet of girly-gossip. My smile was getting harder to maintain. But my soul was only one inch tall, and that helped.

I didn't hear any more for a couple of weeks. I thought about Maria a bit for the first few days – that hair, that face, was she interested in me, maybe, could that be so? But it quickly wore off. Nobody from the opposite sex had been interested in me for years. I had gotten used to it, though I hoped the spell would wear off one day. Maybe I had to let Jesus enter my heart first. Or get a job. Shit . . .

Instead, I sat around, smoking dope, sitting on the bed in my room, in this squat in Acton, wondering, why me? It wasn't the smallest room in the flat but it was definitely the shittiest. The glass pane in the door had been shattered some time before and I hadn't been able to afford to replace it. People would walk up to the door and just peer in through the gap. Because it was next to the toilet there was an endless stream of faces going back and forth, day and night. I thought I'd get used to it but I never quite did. Even the passing faces got tired and stopped looking in, except when they thought I wasn't there.

I had a single bed, inherited from the previous occupant, a rail in an alcove for clothes, also inherited, and a very old semi-acoustic guitar bequeathed me by a kindly musicianly soul when I expressed a belated interest in finally learning to play. No longer a full-time junkie, lately I had actually tried it. I knew the chords E, A, D, G, C, F and F sharp. I also had E minor, D minor, A minor and a couple of alternate fingerings I'd been shown, some barre chords. I knew them but could only play them slowly, couldn't strum for shit. I would sit there, the guitar on my lap, half a joint saved from the night before in the ashtray beside me, waiting for the angels to descend, lend me a wish or two.

It never happened. 'You ever gonna be able to play that thing?' I was becoming a bore, even to myself. Actually I had been a bore for many years, but an overbearing, joke-cracking one. Now I was just a bore, almost invisible. I could see the world falling away and myself toppling over with it and had decided not to fight it very hard.

Then the phone rang again one day and it was her.

'What are you doing? Fancy coming out for a drink?'

'Are you with Bev?'

'No, she's spending the weekend at her parents' in Scotland and I've got no one to keep me company.' She laughed.

I felt for the fiver in my pocket. The day before had been dole day and I still had some left.

'All right,' I said, not at all convinced this was a good idea. 'Where do you want to meet – the pub?'

'Why don't you come to the flat? I'll give you the address. You can get an E3 from Acton to Chiswick. You'll be here in half an hour.'

I got off the phone and went and washed my face, wet my hair and pulled the brush through it, making it fluff up. I'd always had good hair, thick and wavy. I checked the mirror. Still there. I brushed my teeth then went and put my least dirty shirt on. One last look in the mirror. Who was I fucking kidding? I nearly didn't go.

I grabbed Colleen, one of my squat mates, asked her if she'd like to come along too. Colleen was always up for anything, I knew she'd say yes. We got there an hour later. The E3 had taken for ever to come and then when it did it went really, really slow.

When Maria came to the door she had that big smile on that she obviously knew worked, but there was something around the edges of it. Colleen didn't see – she never saw things like that – but I did. 'Come in!' she said, 'Great to see you both! What a nice surprise!'

I sensed my mistake but was still too raw, too long out of the game, to grasp the full extent of it.

Maria got the drinks and Colleen rolled a joint. I tried to look like I knew what the fuck. What was left of the afternoon passed OK and by evening it was like we had all planned it that way. Maria boiled the kettle and made some mash potato from a packet. Then added some things in vine leaves she said her mother had brought round. Poured olive oil over it all and added mayonnaise. It tasted good. We ate it all up.

We went down the pub for a bit. The Barley Mow again. Then we came back to her place. I was beginning to think about how to get home.

'Colleen,' she said, 'you find a record to put on. Mick, you come outside and hold the torch while I get some more leaves.'

She had all these dope plants in the garden. It was especially hot that summer and the plants were getting tall. 'You can just pick the leaves off,' she said, 'dry them under the grill and smoke them.'

'Yeah?' I held the torch while she got down on her knees in the dark and began pulling at the leaves. I couldn't help noticing how loose her T-shirt was, how it afforded you a good peek at her breasts. They weren't big but they weren't nearly as small as I'd thought. She was brown-skinned, Spanish, of course, so I imagined her nipples were brown too.

When she'd finished we went back inside and she laid some of the leaves on the grill over the oven. 'Just for a couple of minutes, helps dry them out. Then we can smoke them.'

She was standing very close to me, side on. I could still peek at her breasts but felt bad for doing so. Not so bad it stopped me looking though. Then Colleen came out and started jabbering away about this and that. All the it-was-so-funny stuff girls always did, me standing there looking the other way.

'How are we getting home tonight, by the way?' Colleen asked.

I wasn't ready to answer. 'Why don't you get a cab?' said Maria. 'I don't know if I've got the money for that,' said Colleen, looking at me.

'I can lend you some,' said Maria, quickly.

When the cab came, Colleen was in the bog having a piss. 'Are you going too?' Maria asked with that smile.

I looked at her. I was still unborn again, still growing my new skin. The years on the gear had robbed me of my memory, how any of it worked. I needed her to spell it out.

She took a step towards me, pressed herself against me and kissed me on the mouth. Using her tongue. Her hand squeezing my arse, what was left of it.

I lit up, like it was normal. Like I was normal. When Colleen came back Maria helped her get her things then took her arm and led her towards the door, to the waiting minicab. Some words were exchanged. Some laughs. It was all very pleasant.

'Bye, then!' called Colleen from the hallway. Then she was gone. And I was alone with Maria. Spanish Maria.

I didn't know what next. I waited for her to show me, give me a clue, something.

'Why did you bring her too?' she asked, the smile still there but no longer turned on full.

'I thought you'd like it.'

'Why? Were you afraid of what I might do to you?' She grinned.

Yes, I supposed I was a bit.

'No,' I said. 'I just thought you'd prefer it, so it didn't feel like anything weird.'

'Well, I didn't,' she said. Then looked at me, realised the worst but mistook it for the usual stupidity of men, of boys, walking dick sticks.

'Come here,' she said.

I did.

Now I thought about it, I'd had sex a couple of times over the past few years. Nothing though you could really count. A one-off bunk-up with some girl who thought she'd landed a prize but hadn't. I'd been semi-cold turkey and I came the moment I was inside her. She couldn't look me in the eye after that, though I hung around long enough to make a bad deal of it. The other time I could think of had been a hand-job, rolling around stoned on a mattress on the floor of the squat with some big old hippy gal. Felt like a pygmy on a pony. Again, I came quick and called it quits, though that one was harder to shake off, saw it as a preamble till I finally got the message across.

This was different. This was more like I remembered from before. There was kissing and holding and . . . love. Was that the right word? It probably wasn't, but I couldn't think of anything that described it better. I hadn't come so quick either. I imagined that came from being newly straight.

I savoured every moment. It hadn't been so long for her, obviously, but no man ever has as much access to sex as a beautiful young woman, it's just something you have to try to live with, especially in those too tender early days where everything that doesn't immediately melt your heart hurts to the touch. I let her undress me, giggling like a girl. Acting like it was nothing.

We lay on the couch while she gave me head. I lifted her up though. I hadn't finished kissing her, hadn't wanted to stop looking up-close at that face, so beautiful, so far out and unreal. All that hair, red and hellish and deep and dark and full of things I didn't know or ever would. Her nipples *were* brown and her bush was tight and curly. I buried my face in both, giving each its fair turn.

It went on and on. We moved on to the floor. I dug my cock into her, slowly, slowly.

'You don't know what you're doing to me,' she said through half-closed eyes.

'You're so beautiful,' I said. 'So beautiful . . .'

I kept going, gave it my all. Slow, fast, long, deep, short, tantalising, in out, in out. I could feel the sweat trickling down my arms and back, falling on to her naked brown body, grooving beneath me.

This was it, the real thing. I was back, maybe even better than before. I was back, I was back! No longer dead, fully in the moment.

'You don't what you're doing to me,' she said again. I didn't know it yet but it was one of those things she always said.

We got on to the bed. I pushed her head forward, doggy-style. Roughed it up a bit, gave it to her good. Used my right hand to find the clit and play with it. Grabbed her arse with my other hand and held on like in the rodeo.

It felt good, genuinely something. I wanted to come but was able to hold it back and back, waiting for her to go first. But she wouldn't. Couldn't? How much did she need to get there? I pulled out and went back to licking her. That had always been my failsafe. Not this time, though.

'It's OK,' she said, that gorgeous smile on that beautiful face. I could tell it was easy for her to do that, that it easily hid whatever might really be going on inside her head. I didn't mind. Not knowing what it was or if it might ever come again I just let it go.

I straightened up and put it back in, my face so close to hers our eyelashes were touching. She was still smiling, still telling me she didn't know what I was doing to her, though she obviously did. When I finally came I cried out, like a baby, completely unashamed. I felt insane for a moment, then lay there waiting for it to come back to me, who I was, what it was, before and after, all happening at once.

She pulled something out from under the bed and wiped herself with it. Stood up and lit a cigarette, stood there smoking it, naked, like a builder admiring his work.

'I'm going for a shower,' she said. 'Put a record on.'

I got up on one elbow and leaned over for the cigarettes. Lit one and lay there wondering. Opposite the bed on an easel sat a large canvas she'd been working on. She was a painter, an artist, and this was her latest thing. There were two bald figures in pink, one a man the other also a sort of man. One was holding the other. The one being held seemed to be ignoring the holder. In the background were swirls of blue and green and white. It didn't look very good to me, like something a first-year student might produce. But what did I know about art?

I got out of bed and pulled on my pants and jeans, yanked on my T-shirt, found some wine still in the bottle and poured it into my glass. I knelt by the record collection and skimmed through it. Bryan Ferry, Bowie, Dylan, the Stones . . . the usual stuff you might expect to find. Then . . . something different. Édith Piaf – a live album. *Zorba the Greek* – the soundtrack. Joe Cocker . . .

Joe Cocker? I put it on. It sounded good, actually. 'You Can Keep Your Hat On'. I lit another cigarette and sat there digging it, thinking: I just had sex. I just had sex. I didn't think she'd come, but that wasn't my fault, not this time.

Then she was back, that big smile blazing, that hair like a wedding train down her back. She was wearing a towel wrapped around her. 'I love this one!' she said excitedly, and began dancing. She moved around like it was a dance she'd learned or knew well. I got the feeling I wasn't the first guy to have sat on her bed looking at it.

I smiled back at her. I had no idea what else to do.

9. The Sound of a Guitar Being Struck Loudly

Getting off the gear is one thing. It was finding something else to do, to fill the yawning chasm inside that was the really hard part. But I was determined. I thought about college. Thought about jobs. But nothing jumped out. Nothing was easy. I decided to lay up. Take my time. See what came along.

I signed on and smoked dope cadged from my flatmates, or more and more lately Maria's garden. Nights were different, though. You needed money to get through the nights, so I signed on at this catering agency, gave them a false name, so that I could still draw the dole. It meant emergency tax, which meant less take-home pay, and blah, blah, blah, but I didn't care.

It nearly killed me having to get up early mornings to go and scrub dishes in some office restaurant kitchen. I was always late, sometimes I didn't make it at all and would have the girl from the agency on the phone giving me the spiel. Last chance, final warning, etc.

I never wondered where I was going, what was afoot. I liked Miles Davis, Bob Dylan and Mozart. I read William S. Burroughs, Hunter S. Thompson and Henry Miller. I knew I was in a tunnel and often I despaired. But not enough to make a change. That would require money too, and what I had I spent on beer and wine and dope and rent. On the wall in the corridor in the flat where I lived someone had spray-painted NOTHING IS TRUE. I agreed with that, but it didn't make any difference anyway. You might as well have spray-painted THE WORLD IS ROUND. So what?

I took to spending more and more time at Maria's pad. She was adamant she didn't want me to move in, and I would nod my head and totally agree. Then just hang around until it was time to go to bed. Once we were fucking I knew I wouldn't have to leave. Once I overheard her on the phone to Bev, talking about me.

'All he knows how to do is write and fuck. That's it. He's useless at everything else.'

I took it as a ringing endorsement. If I could write and fuck why would I need to be good at anything else? But it was clear Maria saw things differently. She'd known plenty of guys who were good at fucking. And the writing, well, what good was that if it didn't pay?

I was also starting to see things a little differently. I had lived in some shitty dumps in my time but Maria's room was on another level. There was all the usual I-am-an-artist squalor – the dried-up paints and stiff brushes, the broken, stubby charcoals and unfinished canvases and torn sketchpads, the empty wine bottles and the endless ashtrays spilling over, the dead cups of tea left to moulder, the wine-soaked, fag-holed carpet that made your socks damp and stinky. Then there were the little touches that only Maria would have thought of. The shit-stained panties on the floor. The heavy curtains hanging off the broken rails. The lampshades she had streaked with gold and silver paints. The phone numbers she had lipsticked on the wall. The photographs of old boyfriends lying naked on her bed she had blue-tacked to the mirror. All with enormous cocks out, hanging limp but still huge. The filthy bed with its grey sheets and thin pillows.

The second time we fucked there she had been on her period. No biggie, she said. She just pulled out the bloody tampon and threw it under the bed. The first time she did it I took it as a sign of total freedom, baby. Fuck the straight world! This chick lived by her own rules. Then when she did it other times I realised she was just a dirty bitch. Once, when I reached under the bed looking for a shoe, my hand settled on a cluster of them: old tampons now crusty and purple, dating back to before my time, I realised.

The problem was I hadn't had a woman in five years and had forgotten how these things were supposed to work. Maybe it was just me, and all girls behaved like this now. Could be.

Maria certainly didn't act like this was a thing. I was the weird one in her eyes. She knew I'd been a writer in the long ago and zeroed in on the hanging out with rock stars bit. She brought it up whenever her hip young friends from art college showed up at the flat. They were all younger than me, in years and everything else. They all did speed and drank miniature bottles of vodka. All chain-smoked and fucked each other's perfect young bodies.

I sensed they viewed me as an oddity, an unwelcome bafflement. That extra piece of the jigsaw you sometimes got that you didn't need. I'd start to talk about the dishwashing gigs I was doing and how I was resting up before getting back into writing, and she would shoot me that look that said, 'Shut up! You're making it worse.'

I was losing her. I knew it. So one day while she was at college I tried my luck on the phone. I knew *Sounds* would never have me back. Twice they'd hired me as a writer and twice I'd walked away just as things were getting good. I knew my career as a record company PR was over since Virgin had sacked me for doing gear in the bogs. Since then *NME* had passed on me and I'd passed on *Melody Maker*. The editor on the *NME* wrote and told me he thought I was too old. I was twenty-three. The editor of the *Melody Maker* asked me to come and be their heavy metal writer and I nearly died of embarrassment. You might as well have asked me if I wanted to move into an old people's home.

That didn't leave much. I'd done bits for *Time Out* but couldn't make it with that crowd. We spoke in different tongues. There was *The Face*, but that was even worse than *Time Out*. It was all fashion, and I'd once gone a year without even washing my clothes let alone buying shiny new ones.

Now, though, there was also *Kerrang!*, the self-styled heavy metal bible. Suddenly the days of me turning down the *Melody Maker* because I didn't want to write about uncool old farts like Queen and Led Zeppelin for a magazine that nobody bought any more seemed very far off indeed. *Kerrang!* was a colour monthly where the standard of writing was so low any half-wit could get in, surely? Compared to the *MM* it was barely a fanzine. But there were already a couple of old-school junkies I knew writing for them. I thought, 'If they can do it . . .'

I picked up the phone and dialled.

The first job I blagged my way into for *Kerrang!* was an interview with Trevor Rabin, the new guitarist in Yes. In the seventies, Yes had been progressive rock titans; in the eighties they had been bulldozed away by punk. There were still uneducated parts of America and Europe that lined up to see them do their consciousness-expanding thing, but the group had splintered so many times no one knew who was still in them let alone if they were still going. By 1983, however, a new line-up of Yes had congregated around the former South African star, Rabin, an over-achieving singer-guitarist-keyboardist-writer-arranger-producer-pretty-boy who had just gifted Yes the song that would bring it all back for them: 'Owner Of A Lonely Heart'.

Apart from the pixie-eared vocal from Yes regular Jon Anderson it didn't sound much like Yes, and that was the key to its success. It sounded more like what it actually was: a superior

Trevor Rabin solo track – with Jon singing lead – shot into orbit by a high-end, tricked-out eighties production.

I'd met Trevor before but knew he wouldn't remember. It had been one very late night at Konk studios in North London four years before, when he was producing an album for Wild Horses, the Thin Lizzy offshoot band I had been doing PR for. Rabin had sat at the desk in the control room like a sentinel, while all kinds of terrible shit went on around him.

At least, I hoped Rabin wouldn't be able to remember me. Just in case, I brought Maria with me. She'd borrowed a flash-looking camera from college and acted like she was the photographer. She didn't know what she was doing with the camera but she did know what she was doing to Rabin, who couldn't take his eyes off her.

He lay back on the bed posing while she crawled all over him in her leather miniskirt, boobs hanging out of her cut-down T-shirt, firing off flashbulb shots that exploded in his face like stage lights. Her blood-red hair hung down over him like a curtain as I sat there with a biro in my hand trying to think of the sorts of questions you asked in situations like this.

I had brought a cassette player but knew it didn't really record, so tried to write down his answers on paper. When I looked it over later I couldn't read my own handwriting. I would have to try to remember what he'd said.

Back at the flat that night, drinking vodka and water and smoking some homegrown Maria's speed dealer had given her 'as a friend', she showed me the bit of paper Rabin had slipped her when I'd gone for a piss. It had his phone number on it.

'He said he'd really like to look at the shots I took. That he might buy some off me,' she told me.

I laughed. Then realised she was serious.

'You're not going to call him?'

'Why not? If he said he might buy some of them off me . . .'

'Just remember to take your tampon out first.'

'Fuck off, you bastard! What do you take me for?'

I couldn't hack it. I walked out, taking my broken tape-recorder and my shitty scribbled notes with me. I would hole up at my mate Porno Paul's, so called because he worked in a porn shop in Soho. Paul had an old children's typewriter he'd told me I could write on.

Three weeks later when the piece ran I was secretly pleased that they didn't run any of Maria's shots – holding on inside to that small victory as she ranted and raved about what a piece of shit *Kerrang!* was. How she'd never want to see her stuff in there anyway.

I had no idea if she would ever see Trevor Rabin again. I had a feeling I might, though.

Meanwhile, I saw writing for *Kerrang!* as a temporary thing. I still signed on, still lived in shit, and more shit with Maria. But the *Kerrang!* gig was much easier money than the dishwashing. No more early mornings, staggering out the door still drunk from the night before. And I now knew what I really wanted to do. I was going to write novels – works of genius in the style of Henry Miller with extended streams of consciousness à la William Burroughs. I would carry on writing bullshit stories for *Kerrang!* about heavy metal bands I didn't care for while secretly preparing myself for a life of the mind.

It was Maria's idea. Like her, I would become a mature student. I would receive a grant while doing an English degree at one of the University of London colleges. It didn't matter that I didn't have the necessary A levels, I would simply blag it. This was 1984, long before computers ruled the world, and blagging was always an option. It would be the same with this university malarkey. I felt sure.

Meanwhile I would sit around smoking in the *Kerrang!* office in Covent Garden, waiting for them to go to the pub at lunchtime where someone would buy me a drink. I even had my own seat at a desk, with my back to the record player. This was how I first became properly acquainted with Iron Maiden.

At that time, Iron Maiden were the biggest heavy metal band in the world. When *Kerrang!* ran its annual readers' poll they would routinely win every category. And the better Maiden seemed to do, the better *Kerrang!* seemed to do. They had both been born of the New Wave of British Heavy Metal scene of the early eighties, and they were both now rulers of their respective corners of the heavy metal universe.

So when one day I was asked if I would like to review the new Maiden album, *Powerslave*, I knew what I was being offered. The clue was in the word count. Small insignificant reviews could be as few as 80 words; lead reviews usually came in at around 400 words, maybe 500 words if it was an actual stroke of genius. This Maiden review, I was solemnly informed by the deputy editor, a fully consecrated heavy metal priest named Dante Bonutto, would need to be 1000 words long. Forsooth, and so it would be written, upon this new Maiden album the very future of metal now rested. Was I up to the task? Was I hairy man enough for the job? Well?

The way I saw it, I had two choices: I could roll up my sleeves, baring my needle-scarred arms, and tell it like it fucking was, right, man. Or I could do what was unspoken but no less expected of me and give it a very, very good review, regardless of what it actually sounded like, or what I thought it actually sounded like. It didn't occur to me I might actually like the damn thing.

I was given the weekend to turn the review around. I knew I'd never get away with playing the record at Maria's place, so I

camped out at the flat of *Kerrang!*'s in-house designer in Rother-
hithe. His name was Steve but everyone called him 'Krusher'.
Another devout follower of the left-hand path, Krusher would
become my spiritual guide in all matters metal for the next few
years, beginning with this new Maiden album.

'You can't just give it a good review,' he said.

'What? Why not?'

'You have to give it a *fucking* good review.' He looked at me,
his raggedy Jesus-beard rippling.

I gave him the album to put on his record player. He lined it
up with the care of a matron handling a newborn baby. Before
we could begin, though, we had to prepare properly, he said. 'We
must first anoint ourselves,' he declared. I looked again. No sign
of mirth.

Krusher shuffled off to his bedroom. We were in his South-
wark Park council flat, on the seventeenth floor of a tower block
he told me the locals referred to as Terror Tower. He was joking,
though. Wasn't he?

He returned clutching several items. One was a jolly green
giant bong, another a plastic carrier bag full of weed. Weed was
harder to get back then than old-fashioned dope. I was suitably
impressed. He told me to 'load her up' while he went into the
kitchen for something else. He came back with two bottles, one
of Old Grand-dad bourbon, the other of Mescal tequila.

'First,' he said, 'we have to do some of this,' pointing to the
bong. 'Then some of that,' nodding towards the bottles. 'We'll
also need some of this . . .'

He pulled out a couple of tiny pills from his jeans pocket.
'Acid,' he said. 'Not the weak-as-shit kind. The good stuff.'

'Wait,' I said, nervous suddenly. 'I haven't done acid for
years.'

'Well, it's a good time to get back into it, then, isn't it?'

I looked at him again, wondering. Taking acid is not like taking heroin. A full-blown acid trip was impossible to escape from, you could be out there on the edge of the universe for hours at a time. While smack you could just doze off with if you wanted.

His glowing eyes looked back at me. 'What's the matter?' he said. 'Afraid to play with the big boys?'

Fuck it. I took one of the pills and washed it down with a glug from the whiskey bottle. He followed me. Then we settled down to smoke the bong.

For the first hour or so we simply sat there stoking up the green giant and pouring the Grand-dad down our necks. It went down like Lucozade. I had never tasted whiskey so sweet and thirst-quenching. Then it was gone and we were on to the Mescal. Krusher showed me the worm floating at the bottom of the bottle. The acid was now kicking in and the worm appeared to wink at me.

'We share the worm,' he explained patiently. 'But to get to it we'll have to drink the bottle first.'

Seemed reasonable. I ignored the giant worm that was now in the room, writhing on the floor – I wasn't that easily fooled – and urged him to put the fucking record on.

Finally, at what now felt like some distant point in space and time, he did so. The needle found the groove and the world suddenly tilted on its axis and began to fall away.

HOLY JESUS CHRIST!! SHIT!!!

I reached out to try to stop myself from sliding off the edge of the cliff but it was too late. I was already on my way. The abyss below opened its jaws and swallowed me whole. Me and Krusher both.

The next thing I knew he was standing on the couch holding a tennis racket in his hands, playing it like a guitar. He leaned over towards the lounge windows, the view of London below spectacular.

'LONDON!' he screamed. 'For one night only! We present you! THE NEW IRON MAIDEN ALBUM!' He began riffing with a vengeance on the tennis racket.

The music was so loud I wondered vaguely where the cops were, who would stop us, how it would end. Then I didn't care any more and jumped up on the coffee table. I stared down at the minions below, thousands of miles below, and I began to wave my arms and scream too.

'LONDON! LONDON!! FUCK!!! LONDON!!!!'

What happened after that would only come back to me, in flashes, the next day. We must have done the whole gig then done it again and possibly again. Each time to bigger and bigger crowds. Each time to greater and greater acclaim. Each time falling off a mountain only to land on the backs of giant eagles that whisked us straight back to the top of the mountain. Finally, after about four hours, we sat down and started thinking things through. We looked at the album cover, which was all Egyptian sphinxes and ancient symbols, all now dancing in 3D before our whirring eyes. After that . . . more and . . . nothing . . . and . . .

It was a turning point for me, in ways that went beyond any trip I'd ever been on. When, late on the Sunday evening, the smoke still trickling from my ears, I sat down to type the review, I made sure what I wrote wasn't just a good review but, as Krusher had wisely advised, a *fucking* good review.

It began, 'We are now *flying at 28,000 feet . . .'*

But it wasn't just the new Iron Maiden album I was reviewing, splendid though that was. It is clear to me now I was writing up my own make-believe future. I knew it even as my shaky hands tapped out the words. The only really good rock writers who had ever written seriously about Iron Maiden had been the snotty cunts on the *NME*. And all they'd done was take the piss. Obviously. Those were the rules. At the same time, the only writers who had ever given Maiden sincerely great reviews were the kind of well-meaning metal maniacs who wrote for *Sounds* and now *Kerrang!*. Genuine fans at heart, all about the music. But what good was that to me?

I would lavish something on Maiden they'd never had before, I decided. Praise from on high. Top-drawer material, not taking the piss, nor fawning at their feet, but something that flew as high as they did when they were tripping out in the studio on those blood-rushing rhythms and gurgling solos. Something that gave them a reason to hold their heads high and take themselves even more seriously.

That's what I told myself anyway as I sat there drained of blood and spunk, pecking away at the typewriter in Krusher's tiny council-flat kitchen as he slept on the floor, the album still spinning away in the background, more quietly now but no less haughtily.

I would write my review and they would read it and want to meet me, and that would be it: I would be in with the biggest heavy metal band in the world and so the adventure would begin.

I really did think like that. More ridiculous still, as I soon found out, they did too.

10. Heavy Shit

Writing for *Kerrang!* in the eighties was unlike writing for any other music magazine of the time. Until then niche music titles like *Folk Roots* or *Black Echoes* were regarded as marginal publications – small but dedicated circulation mags that, as a PR, you invited to the party because it was nice having them around, the artists liked it and, unlike their bigger, more important brothers on *NME* or *Sounds*, they could always be relied on for their full support. Nobody in the business took them *seriously* though. The markets they served simply didn't make enough money.

Kerrang!, however, was a different kettle of fish. The eighties was the decade when rock and metal sold more records worldwide than any other 'genre music'. It also sold more tickets, keeping the concert industry alive virtually singlehandedly. Because of the exaggerated theatricality of the music and live performances – before punk or even pop, rock and metal was virtually invented for the big stage, music where size and weight really did matter – metal also translated into any language. Hence its huge popularity in Japan, Germany, Eastern Europe and South America, places where the words mattered less than the enormity of the spectacle and ball-aching tightness of those monster footstep riffs.

And, of course, it was huge in America, very much the dominant music of the mid-eighties. MTV built its empire on Def Leppard and Mötley Crüe videos. Already choking on the massive pipeline of new money now pouring in from CD sales, major record labels like Warner Bros and CBS looked to the giant album-oriented white rock acts to keep the tsunami of cash flowing, and no more so than from the British and American rock and metal acts. As well as Leppard and the Crüe, the eighties saw the squillion-dollar emergence of Iron Maiden, Bon Jovi, Whitesnake, Van Halen, Poison, Metallica, and dozens of other platinum-backed copycat acts, all of them still in their musical sales-day prime. And, right at the top of the megabuck heap, Guns N' Roses. Oh, baby.

It was the same in Britain, but with one crucial difference. Maimed by punk, which ruled that 'old wave' rock like Zeppelin and Queen was now considered boring, irrelevant and even offensive, the British mainstream media – print, radio and TV – had effectively blackballed rock and metal from the club. Hence the unexpected success of niche outlets for the music like Radio 1's *Friday Rock Show* and, now, *Kerrang!*.

By the time I had my first piece published in *Kerrang!* in December 1983, the magazine had already established its reputation as being what was still then the world's only colour magazine devoted entirely to rock and metal. Over the next ten years, however, it inspired dozens of copycat titles around the world, including at least two more in Britain, its own industry-prestigious annual awards show and, not long after that, its own TV and radio channels.

The main thing the magazine had going for it when I lurched through the door in the mid-eighties was that it was pampered and fawned over by the record companies in London, New York and LA. That was because it was the only widespread outlet for rock and metal in the UK at a time when bands like Iron Maiden and AC/DC could have numerous hit singles and still not be invited on to *Top of the Pops*, still not receive any daytime radio play (or evening time play, outside the *Friday Rock Show*), and still be treated as a joke in the mainstream music press. *Kerrang!* then, whose circulation was growing so fast it eventually overtook *Sounds, Melody Maker* and even the *NME*, was the only game in town for these bands and their record companies. Consequently they lavished their huge, otherwise unspent budgets on making sure the magazine's writers and photographers got everything they needed and more.

At first, because I wasn't paying attention, seeing it as a stopgap between junk sickness and the dole, I didn't get it, what I'd stumbled upon. Writing for *Sounds*, I'd had my pick of whoever was then making the scene – I'd write about the Stray Cats one week, The Only Ones the next, with side-tracks into reggae, soul and rock of the Thin Lizzy variety. At first, writing for *Kerrang!* I felt like the cuckoo in the nest. I would cherry pick my features so that I wrote about people like Kate Bush, Genesis, Dire Straits, Pink Floyd . . . stuff I felt I actually knew something about.

But because I was penniless – I would arrive at the office with 50p in my pocket, some days not even that, then rely on some kind soul to buy me a sandwich (or not, as might happen too) – I would find myself out at gigs with the whole gang most nights, where I would always be treated to drinks. That was another thing: the staff at *Kerrang!* would go to concerts *en masse*, we would be given our own guest list, which also helped engender the idea that we were more than just mere commentators, we were actually integral to the whole rock scene.

This meant I got a crash course in eighties-style rock and metal, whether I liked it or not. Increasingly, I decided, I did like it. A lot. Not always the music, but the characters, the camaraderie, the humour, the devotedly non-PC aspect to the music and culture surrounding it. Finally, to my surprise, I had found what seemed to be my people. Or the closest I was likely ever to find in that world. People who profoundly did not give a fuck what the prevailing wisdom of the self-styled fashionistas was; people who still longed for their limos to be long and black, their drugs to be thin and white, and their music to be far too fucking loud.

As the weeks slipped by and some money of my own started coming in, I began taking more of a lead. I still rarely liked more than a track or two of the new Ted Nugent album, but by Christ I preferred it to *anything* by The Clash or The Jam or any of the other self-regarding strips of punk humanity. And you could have fun writing about guys like Ozzy and Lemmy. And they would let you in, because you were from *Kerrang!*, and they knew that you knew what we all should know. That it was about money, honey, and good times and not pretending it was anything else. Not fooling yourself by thinking what you did mattered. But living the life to the full. Smoke, drink? I thought you'd never ask. Line? Well, of course . . .

The real epiphany came, though, when I reviewed that Iron Maiden album at Krusher's flat. After that, it all made sense to me, and I embraced it like a long, lost brother. Or dog. Or misplaced dream. I gave up worrying about anything else and jumped aboard the crazy train, amused to see where it stopped next, no longer so afraid. Rocking.

There were occasional forays back into the so-called real world – a girlfriend who wanted to see The Smiths, so I blagged some tickets and took her to a show and they were good, very good, if you liked that sort of anal thing – but very quickly I left the whole bamboozle behind. Especially once I became an established cover-story writer and the foreign trips kicked in. On *Sounds* I had been used to being sent out to Germany or France – or Finland, maybe, somewhere dull and worthy like that – to write about the sorts of bands whose greatest ambition was to get played on the John Peel show. But you'd be parachuting in on someone's little scene and you were always considered an interloper, there to judge and be judged.

On *Kerrang!* you found yourself being flown out to Japan and America, Russia and Australia, where you would be welcomed as part of the team. Two months later you'd be back and begin to really feel like part of the scene. The giant rock bands toured the whole world and would take a year, sometimes two, to do it. On Def Leppard's 1987–88 world tour in support of their 20-million-selling *Hysteria* album, I showed up six different times to write about them: in Holland, England, Italy, and three times in America.

These weren't little day trips either. I would be on the road with these bands for weeks at a time. It got to the point where I would arrive in Boston to cover Def Leppard, fly down to New York to hop on to the David Lee Roth tour, then up to Boston to hop aboard the Whitesnake tour, then back down south to Miami where Ozzy would be headlining some huge outdoor festival. Finish that then fly down to LA for two weeks to interview half a dozen different bands, some of whom you'd never heard of. Today, I flick through the pages of old issues of *Kerrang!* from those days and I see stuff I did on bands like Malice, Femme Fatale and Prophet that I can't even remember writing. Stories written just to please some record executive who'd offered to pick up two or three nights at the hotel.

All travel and out-of-pocket expenses were always paid for by record companies with more money than sense, and no one in the UK to spend it on other than *Kerrang!*. I'd be lying by the pool at the Sunset Marquis in LA, squinting at an old *NME*, in which the writers regaled their loyal readership with on-the-road-in-Liverpool stories of The Pogues, or midnight feasts in the studio with The Cure – tales from the back of the van in which Shane McGowan would boast of walking on stage each night drunk, or Robert Smith would confess to staying up all night to work on his hair. And I'd think, 'Bollocks.' Then chop out another couple of fat white lines, roll myself a B52 bomber, and get ready to meet the limo for the two-mile trek up the street to the Rainbow, where groupies raised on Led Zeppelin and Alice Cooper would be waiting to wang dang doodle my ding dong doo.

On a more meaningful level, I suddenly found my stride as a writer. I may not have always adored the music the way rock writers were supposed to, but the stories the rock musicians told were so much more interesting and entertaining – at times funny, at other times disturbing – than the tedious fare offered up by the artists I'd covered on *Sounds*. In the punk years you had to sit through some horizon-limited band bending over backwards to give you their impersonation of Joe Strummer or Johnny Rotten, full of disdain for times and places they would never be talented or courageous enough to try to explore themselves; too busy posing in front of the mirror to see beyond the pages of the music press.

The superstar rock bands, however, had been around the world so many times, working their way from vans to station wagons to commercial flights to their own private jets, they were never short of great stories to tell. And they loved to tell them. Not in interviews, necessarily, but after the show, back at the hotel, the moon on the wane and the drinks and drugs flowing, out would come the truth – their truth. And you either understood it and revelled in being allowed into the club – the one most so-called music journalists didn't even know existed – or you could make your excuses and leave.

Of course, my background as a PR, working for acts like Black Sabbath and Journey, Rory Gallagher and Thin Lizzy, helped a lot. They provided my bona fides. The rest was up to me. Could I keep a secret? The only things in life worth knowing were the secrets – I wasn't about to give up my access to them to enlighten the readers of *Kerrang!*. At the same time, I wanted to give a real sense of what it was like to live in the same world as people like Jon Bon Jovi, W. Axl Rose, Joe Elliott.

Writing from home – which by the mid-eighties was a tiny loft apartment in west London – I would set up by a small table in the bedroom, where I would top myself up on dope, coke and cases of beer, and not type a single word until my buzz was fully on. It was the same out on the road: I'd unpack my old portable typewriter, set up at the vanity table where I'd drape a towel over the mirror so I didn't have to see myself as I typed, and drink and smoke then type.

Some of the bands did actually become friends, of a kind. Lars Ulrich would ask to sleep on my couch. Fish of Marillion did too, except that at 6ft 5ins he was much too long to fit on to my hash-burned couch. He just crashed on the floor. The Iron Maiden office would send me two laminated backstage passes before the start of every tour, which allowed me and a plus one into any gig they did anywhere in the world. I admired the logic: having access to any gig any time anywhere meant I went to a disproportionately high number of Maiden shows around the world, which in turn led to me writing a disproportionate number of whey-hey cover stories about them.

Some, like Lemmy, became almost like father figures to me. Lemmy was a dispenser of road wisdom to anybody ready to listen. But there were deeper levels to who Lemmy was that very few people, it seemed, including his own band, ever had access to. There was a poignancy to his élan that was both surprising and consoling. It was the same with Ozzy. Hanging out over a period of years with guys like that was like becoming a regular viewer of *The Simpsons*: you could enjoy one hell of a time in their company, but if you knew what to look out for, there were depths to them, hidden-in-plain-sight, that were much more intriguing, if sometimes shockingly unappealing, to investigate.

Then there were the kinds of bands like Guns N' Roses and Metallica. Too old to be a fan, more deeply immersed in the music business than they yet were, there wasn't much they could show me I hadn't already seen a thousand times before. But being offered a seat on their respective rock ships as they left the Earth's stratosphere for the first time was exhilarating in a new, sometimes better, way. You knew where they were heading, but they didn't. It was fun to see just how fast they would grow into their new skins. They were using the same road maps Zeppelin and Sabbath had plotted, but they were coming from a completely different place. It meant you could never quite predict the outcome, and that was great for a writer to be part of, especially one who found none of this strange, one who actively applauded and gave thanks that those places still existed somewhere far off in someone's imagination.

It was the eighties, the most buttoned-up decade since the fifties. So I would rarely refer directly to drugs – unless Ozzy or Lemmy or some senior rock wizard like that talked openly about them, which of course they did. But I would write a lot about drinking. Sex was another no-no: this was the decade of AIDS, and even rock stars were now supposed to be sensible. So, instead, I wrote a lot about 'partying'. But the message always came across loud and clear. 'In this world,' I recall beginning one story, 'there are three ways you can fly: first class, club class and cunt class.'

Writing about the rock stars of the eighties you only ever travelled first. And when you'd done it once, you never wanted to fly any other way. I didn't. I'd spent my life living with the shit end of the stick, now it had somehow turned into a giant lollipop I was determined to keep sucking until the teat ran dry, however long it took and wherever it finally led me.

11. 'Allo, Rockers

The other unforeseen benefit of writing for *Kerrang!* was that it led, in 1985, to my presenting a weekly rock show on the fledgling Sky channel. I fell into TV presenting and fell out again just as easily. I never felt I had any sort of career in it, until right near the end when people kept telling me how good I was at it. Just before the same people told me the show was cancelled.

It was the fledgling days of Sky in the mid-eighties, before most people in Britain had even heard of Sky, when cable and satellite TV was barely off the ground in America, let alone the Old Country. You could get it in Europe, across twenty-three countries, where the most popular show on the channel was *Mister Ed, the Talking Horse.*

They also did a weekly show they called *Monsters of Rock*, a bunch of heavy metal videos linked by a pretty blonde twenty-three-year-old named Amanda Redington. Amanda dressed in all the mid-eighties hair-metal gear but didn't know anything about the music. She was a professional presenter who would end up fronting GMTV breakfast a few years later. Good for her. So Sky decided to bring in someone with some rock 'cred'. They asked Geoff Barton to come on as a guest one week. But Geoff said no, he didn't fancy it, but why didn't they ask me? I was a pushy little show-off.

So on I went, acted like I knew something while trying not to stare at Amanda's tits, and went home again with £25 stuffed in my pocket. When the following week they asked me to come on again as a guest, I said, sure, thinking of those tits and that £25.

When after a few months Amanda left for bigger and almost better things, they asked if I'd like to take over presenting the show. I said it was one thing being the smart-arse guest, another to have to sit there and actually do a proper job. They said, oh go on, it will only be for a few weeks until we can find someone good, and we'll give you £100 a show for your trouble.

And so it began. At first I hated it. It was simply crushing to come away from the recording each week knowing you had been so utterly useless. Then one day, during what I had already decided would be my last recording, knowing I would never have to go through this again, I put on a show, wisecracking to camera, and drawing appreciative chuckles from the crew – always a good sign. By the end everyone was congratulating me on such a good show, and that was the turning point, the moment when I realised I quite fancied having my back slapped for acting the fool. I would start the show each week by yelling, ''Allo, rockers!' then lightning would strike a couple of times and dry ice would gust about the set – made up to look like a graveyard. It was purest crap, but as the weeks went by I began to invest it with my own sense of the absurd, and the catchphrase and cod lightning and cheesy coffins began to look like a rueful pun on the whole concept of rock and metal, I told myself. Soon the show was getting so much fan mail they had to employ a girl to work three days a week opening it all. Within a year it was the most popular original music show Sky had ever produced.

The money never changed, though – I was still being paid £100 a week, even as the show became the most viewed original programme on the channel – but everything else did. It was somewhat like when I'd worked in PR: the bands stopped seeing me as the bloke from the magazine, just as likely to bury them as praise them, and more as one of them. A performer, grinning through the shit, keeping the show on the road even as my trousers were falling down.

It was around then I cemented my friendship with Steve Harris of Iron Maiden. I'd been part of the Maiden scene since my review of *Powerslave* did what it was supposed to and opened the door for me there. I'd gotten to know them pretty well; we were all the same age, so that helped. The fact that they were then approaching their commercial zenith was another factor. They took me all over the world with them as I banged out cover story after cover story on Maiden. A band very close to my wallet, you might say. Except it was more than that. They really had something – something real – and the reason for that lay squarely at the feet of the band's creator and ruler, Steve Harris.

Usually it was the singer or guitarist you zeroed in on as a writer. But Maiden's singer was a pompous oaf named Bruce Dickinson. He never talked to you, but at you. It was not uncommon to signal for help whenever he had been babbling at you for too long. The man had talent, no doubt, but no one knew more than Bruce exactly how much talent. He wasn't just a singer, he would explain, his eyes bulging, he was an Olympic-level fencer. He was also soon to become a pilot, then a novelist, then ... who knew what? You were lucky to know him.

The guitarists, Dave Murray and Adrian Smith, were both super cool, but they had both learned long ago not to give too much away, on pain of death from Steve. Steve was bassist, main writer, lyricist, and overlord. He was also the most down to earth millionaire rock star geezer I had ever met. We had always gotten on well. But when I started doing the *Monsters of Rock* show we really got to know each other. Steve had a place out on the Algarve – private villa, pool, all that – and to go with it a whopping great satellite dish, with which he used to watch the show, or tape it if he was away.

We began hanging out, playing tennis together, drinking beer. Him and Maiden's manager, Rod Smallwood. One thing about Steve, he was straight as a die. No puff, no huff, no coke, no choke. He liked a beer and that was it. Not even any chaser. So while Rod and I would sit there snorting our way through grams of charlie and talking till our tongues fell out, Steve would match us crazy story for crazy story but with no chemical assistance whatsoever.

He was just one of those guys. Tattooed, principled, a hard as fuck Cockney Eastender who you didn't mess with, never, mate. When Adrian walked into the dressing room one night wearing a little eyeliner Steve 'fronted him' immediately.

'What's that on your 'ead?' he demanded.

Adrian touched his head, looking puzzled.

'On your 'ead!' Steve barked, pointing at his face, 'On your bleedin' 'ead?'

'Oh,' said Adrian finally, cottoning on. 'Just a bit of make-up . . .'

'Wash it off!' scowled Steve. 'Now!'

Adrian did as he was told.

It wasn't just the bands who you got to know better. It was other people in the business. The big-time agent who told me he kept a library of videotapes of my show. How he liked to watch them while he was stoned because they made him laugh so much. The even-bigger-time American manager who took to phoning me from New York or wherever, asking how I was doing? I *never* knew how to answer that one. I had no idea how I was doing. Feeling that the moment I stopped to actually think about it I'd never be able to do it again. What did these people *want* from me?

It was only much later, when it was all over, I was told that at least two of the American industry types that took such an interest back then had been thinking of offering to manage me, but had backed away when they realised I simply wasn't tuned into things the way they needed me to be. It wasn't just that I drank too much, got stoned too much or didn't care enough – where none of those things counted in my favour, the Americans were used to working with those sorts of guys, as long as they made plenty of money – it was mainly the sense that I still didn't see any of this as any sort of career. I was just cruising until the real thing came along, never fully realising it already had. I'd been faking it for so long I'd fucked things for myself. How could anyone like that believe in me when I didn't even believe in myself? I didn't blame them at all when they quietly changed their minds. It was the right thing to do.

It was a strange time, the 1980s. The seventies, where I came from, had been about sex and drugs and rock 'n' roll, in any order you fancied. Yes, there had been money too, for groovy pads and road trips to Kathmandu. Even occasional health fads: vegetarianism, TM, bathing more than once a week. But mostly there had been an overarching emphasis on simply doing your own thing. Taking it to the max, Jack. Especially if it involved a degree of what now they called self-medicating.

One of the perks of presenting a show called *Monsters of Rock* was that I was given special 'artist' passes each year for the Monsters of Rock festival held at Castle Donington. There is still a rock festival held there every year, only now it is called Download. This, though, was back when it was still a one-day event and men were men and women stayed well away.

My first visit had been in 1984, the year when Van Halen – with a JD-guzzling, ray-catching Diamond Dave – blew the place up only for AC/DC – with a cloth cap-wearing, possibly ferret-concealing Brian Johnson – to send the pieces spinning like shrapnel into orbit. I don't remember much about that end of the day, though. For me the festival was all but over before it had begun. I had driven up with Krusher in a car fortified with Krusher's usual rider: a bottle of Mescal, a bottle of Old Grand-dad, two cases of warm lager, three grams of sparkly pharmaceutical cocaine and a small plastic sack of jolly green giant weed. We were fuck-headed before we'd even hit the Watford Gap. How we got to the site without killing ourselves or anyone else, neither of us ever knew, but somehow we did. I remember falling out of the car in the VIP parking area before hobbling on my knees towards the backstage enclosure. The only bands I remembering reviewing were Y&T, who I enjoyed while lying face-down on the ground, and Gary Moore, who I managed to turn on to one side for. I was being sick at the time and it seemed like the right thing to do.

The following year, however, I was the TV guy. With no need to review anybody I'd spent most of the day holding court in the giant, luxury tent that EMI had put up. I had a hotel to stay in that year and I recall sitting in the bar the night before the show when an impossibly young and keen Jon Bon Jovi came bounding over to tell me how excited he was to be there. I remember smiling indulgently and waiting for him to go away so I could go back to my drinking. Later that same night, Venom singer Cronos, who was also there for some reason, passed out at the table and me and Lars Ulrich of Metallica had our pictures taken standing next to his prone, face-down figure. Our cocks out and pressed against his ears, big silly grins on our faces.

The following year wasn't much different, except the crowd was mean, throwing bottles of piss at the stage throughout the entire show – so much so that Radio 1 DJ Tommy Vance went on in an American football helmet. 'You'd think they'd be grateful,' said the presenter of the only national rock show in the UK in those days. 'But they don't give a fuck!' No one did. Hanging out with 'spoof' *Comic Strip* rockers Bad News, who were filming themselves pretending to be a real band, Ade Edmondson was so 'in character' he seemed genuinely upset when the crowd proceeded to bottle them off. Motörhead fared better, of course, as no one had the guts to try throwing anything at Lemmy. But only Ozzy, who was headlining, really got away with it, after picking up the first bottle of piss that hit him in the face and drinking it. 'More!' he screamed. 'I'm thirsty!' That halted the bottle-throwing – briefly.

The next year, 1987, when Bon Jovi headlined, was more to-gether but dull as ditchwater by comparison, enlivened only by a seriously pissed-off James Hetfield threatening to kill Jon Bon for daring to helicopter over the stage during Metallica's set, thus causing the for once female-oriented crowd to begin screaming at the clouds and forcing their boyfriends to take their eyes from the stage right in the middle of chanting 'Die! Die! Die!' during 'Creeping Death'.

Biggest and best of all, though, was 1988, the year it all went so spectacularly right with what we knew even on the day would be the best Donington bill ever – Iron Maiden backed by Kiss, David Lee Roth, Megadeth, Guns N' Roses and Helloween – and yet so tragically wrong when two young fans were trampled to death in the rain-swept swampland surrounding the stage during Guns N' Roses' set. 'Don't kill yourselves!' shouted Axl unwittingly as he exited. Oh, how we laughed. Not knowing yet how hard others would be left crying.

Earlier on the tour, when the festival reached Holland, where the TV show was big, I had been the onstage host. No helmet needed that day. The hash tents kept the crowd happy. Anthrax were on the bill and they dared me to jump on stage with my trousers round my ankles. Like I ever walked around any other way at festivals. I also recall standing with an intensely morose David Lee Roth as he perused the crowd before he went on. Within seconds of hitting the stage, though, he was the laughing, jiving, rock clown of all the videos. 'Wow!' he trilled. 'We've got a lot of people here tonight!' Paul Stanley, who was there with his new girlfriend, Samantha Fox, stood next to me watching Roth, mouthing the words. I looked at him, puzzled. 'Shit,' he smiled, 'Dave's been saying that every night for the past ten years.'

The one that really intrigued me during those years was Ozzy Osbourne. I'd met Ozzy during the PR years, when he turned up at Jimmy Bain's stag party, which was held at John Henry's rehearsal studio in north London over three hot and heavy nights in June 1979. There had been a few famous faces there – Phil Lynott, Bob Geldof, Midge Ure, others – but Ozzy outranked them all, not just in terms of global stardom but in sheer *otherness*.

'Who's the fucking rock star here?' he growled as he pushed his way to the front of the queue in the production office where one of the roadies was chopping out show-stopping lines of coke. Everybody made way. There was something about Ozzy in those days – a dark charisma – that people cannot grasp now, in these post-*Osbournes* days. Far from the loveable buffoon the TV world would come to know twenty-five years later, Ozzy was still the out of control freak that had fronted Black Sabbath. In an era when it was still possible to find the measure of a band's importance by how heavy they were, there were none weightier than Sabbath – or the self-styled madman who fronted them. There were also few more successful.

What added to Ozzy's edge, though, in the summer of '79, was that he had recently been kicked out of Sabbath. For being

'too out of it', according to Ozzy. Quite a statement consider-
ing just how out of it the other three Sabbath members were
at the same time. Or indeed most singers and bands were back
then. The difference was that most singers didn't pass out in
their own piss at rehearsals, or fall asleep in the wrong hotel
room thereby missing the gig when no one could find them to
wake them, or refuse to show up for recording sessions because
they thought the new material was 'shit', or keep referring to
Sabbath's darkly glowering guitarist and leader Tony Iommi
as Darth Vadar because, 'He scares the fucking shit out of me,
he does!'

It was Ozzy, though, who scared me the most. Everything
about him just screamed pain. Not in some rock-orthodoxy kind
of way, but in a much more personal and deeply out-of-sync-
with-the-rest-of-reality kind of way that defied comprehension.
What was *wrong* with him? Why did he always have the down-
trodden expression of a stray dog, its bones poking out of its
skin? What had happened to that fucker back there on the road
somewhere to make him like this?

I got the story slowly, over the years. The terrible impoverished
upbringing, the permanent outsider status of Black Sabbath –
'It wasn't just the critics, even the other bands hated us,' Ozzy
would tell me – the ridicule he suffered from Iommi and so
many others, not least the various managers who had treated
him like the broken-down circus clown he so quickly came to
resemble. Then the resurrection, under the tutelage of Sharon,
who had learned all the tricks (dirty and clean) of the trade from
her father Don Arden, the self-styled Al Capone of pop.

As we all now know – or think we know – from *The Osbournes*, Ozzy and Sharon made quite a double-act, with Sharon
as firebrand straight woman to Ozzy's melancholy funny man. I
always looked forward to hanging out with them, because you

really never quite knew what was going to happen next. Just listening to Ozzy reminisce was enough to make the occasion soar. The time he bit the head off a dove at a record company convention. 'The woman who was sitting next to me is still in therapy over that!' The time he left Sabbath to open a wine bar in Birmingham with his first wife, Thelma – then begged the band to take him back. 'Can you imagine *me* as the manager of your local wine bar? I'd be fucking dead in a month!' The groupies he used to sleep with. 'I was more interested in boozing and doing drugs so the only groupies left at the end of the night were all the ugly ones. I used to call them two-baggers. One for her head so you wouldn't have to look at her while you were slipping it in. And one for your head in case anyone walked in and saw you!'

We would sit in his hotel room doing an interview and you barely had to ask a question. He was just ready to let it all out. He'd talk about his newfound sobriety then phone me later to see if I could get him some dope. Once we were in a restaurant somewhere in London and Ozzy decided he wanted to order every item on the menu. 'Just to try it!' Fortunately, Sharon talked him down from that one. Then when the food did arrive he ignored it anyway, passing me a large, white wrap of coke under the table, which I took to the toilets and snorted straight from the packet, no straw nor rolled-up note, the same way I'd seen Ozzy do it. We spent the rest of the night going back and forth from the table to the gents, acting as though no one else could possibly figure out what was going on.

Sharon was unbelievably cool about the whole thing. Not because she approved of Ozzy's drug-taking. She just figured it was shrewder to keep the star writer of *Kerrang!* and *Monsters of Rock* presenter onside than make a scene. She'd seen my like come and go. And at a time when Ozzy needed all the friends he could get in the British media, he was always on a long leash when it came to his 'jollies' with me.

Consequently I wrote some of my funniest, best-known *Kerrang!* cover stories about the times I shared with Ozzy. We developed an almost symbiotic relationship, to the point that when Sharon was looking for someone to write Ozzy's official biography, *Diary of a Madman*, she approached me. But every time we scheduled an interview something always seemed to go wrong. First, Ozzy was out of town; then he was in town but 'busy'. One time, I turned up at his office and he just didn't show up. Another time, I turned up at the London mansion where he and Sharon were then living only to find them both in bed together with the flu. I sat on the end of the bed and we chatted, but we still didn't get our interview done.

Then there were the times I turned up somewhere on the road and he was either too drunk to talk or simply too stunned at being sober. Ozzy was always either on the wagon – or totally off it. There was never any middle ground with Ozzy. It was one of the big reasons why those of us who put up with the fucker loved him so. And why he drove us all so mad.

Finally, Ozzy offered to cook me Sunday lunch, after which he promised we would get down to the business of putting his precious recollections on tape. The thought of Ozzy actually standing in the kitchen with his apron on cooking was not half as surreal as the reality, though. I arrived at just after 1 p.m., and there he was, peeling potatoes, shelling peas and slicing carrots.

'Can I help?' I asked. 'No, no,' he shook his head, 'All under control.'

Right. I grabbed a seat at the table and waited to see what would happen next. Sharon and the nanny were busying themselves with the children, Aimee and Kelly – Jack hadn't been born yet – as they were going out to play in Hyde Park while

Daddy finished cooking lunch. As the front door closed behind them, Ozzy froze in his tracks – literally, turned into a statue.

I thought he was having a seizure or something. 'Everything all right, Ozzy?'

'Shut up . . .'

We both lapsed into silence as outside we could hear cardoors slamming and the sound of an ignition being turned over. We listened in absolute silence as the car drove off, Ozzy still not moving a muscle, his whole being tuned to the sounds of Sharon's retreat. As the car drove off, he exhaled hugely. 'Thank fuck for that,' he sighed. 'Do you wanna drink?'

I didn't know what to say. Ozzy was then supposed to be 'on' the wagon and I didn't want to get the blame from Sharon for being the one that had caused him to fall off – again. Before I could say anything, though, he shoved a pint-glass in my hand, two-thirds full of white wine. 'Cheers!' he yelled, downing his own pint-glass of wine in one long, ungraceful haul, the wine spilling down his chin on to his shirt.

'Fucking hell, I needed that!' he gasped as he set down the empty glass with a thud. 'Do you fancy another?' I had hardly started on my own pint of wine but Ozzy yanked another bottle from the refrigerator, corkscrewed it impatiently and poured most of the contents into his glass and a little top-up into mine. Down in one again. I began to fret. What would Sharon say when she got back and found him – us – like this? I began downing my own wine more eagerly.

The meal itself was a memorable affair. Ozzy had laden the table with roast beef, Yorkshire pudding, gravy, cabbage, carrots, peas and sprouts, and a large bowl of mashed potato smothered with melted cheese and garnished with parsley and thin slices of tomato. We filled our plates – Sharon, the nanny, the kids and myself. Sharon filled Ozzy's plate for him as he didn't look like he was going to manage it. I didn't know how many pint-glasses of wine he had put down by the time Sharon and the kids arrived home but I was on to my second which meant he was probably on to his fifth or sixth.

Typically, Sharon didn't bat an eye, just clocked what was going on and acted like it wasn't happening. Then, five minutes into the meal, Ozzy's head very gently lowered itself on to his plate until it came to rest in the peas and potatoes. Ozzy began to snore, the gravy bubbling noisily around his nose.

'Um, is he all right?' I asked, for what must have been the tenth time that day.

'Fuck him!' barked Sharon. Then, smiling sweetly, 'Pass the carrots, please, sweetheart . . .'

We sat and ate our lunch, passing dishes over his head while Ozzy lay with his head in his plate, snoring. When the meal was over, Sharon and the nanny had just begun clearing away the plates when Ozzy finally came to. Raising his head from his plate just as slowly as he'd lowered it half an hour before, he looked around and gave out the call now familiar to millions of TV viewers the world over: '*Shaaaaaaron!!!*'

'What?' she snapped.

'I'm all fucked up . . .'

'And whose fault is that?'

'Please, Shaaaaaaaron!'

Ozzy tried to stand but couldn't make it and found himself collapsing back on to the table. Sharon shook her head. 'Fuck's sake,' she sighed. Then she grabbed him by the arm, yanked it around her shoulders and helped him stagger out the door and up the stairs to bed.

When she came down a little while later she looked at me and smiled. 'Would you like a proper glass for that?' she asked, nodding towards my nearly empty pint glass.

'That would be great,' I slurred. 'Cheers!'

Sharon fetched me a proper wine glass and poured me a fresh drink. 'Right,' she said, 'get out your tape-recorder. Whatever you want to know, you can ask me. We'll be waiting for ever for that fucker to tell you.'

And that's what we did. When it was published in 1986 it became a bestseller. Not that I saw any real money for it. That was another important lesson Sharon had learned from her father. Laugh, smile, show everyone a good time, but always keep all of the money for yourself.

This would become more of an issue in the years to come, but for now I was simply happy to be 'part of the family', as Sharon always charmingly referred to me. Until one day many years later I joined the long list of black sheep that found themselves suddenly expunged from the Christmas card list.

But that was for the future, and as Ozzy was fond of saying: 'Fuck the fucking future!'

12. The Magus

I was sitting at my desk in the *Kerrang!* office when the phone rang. It was mid-afternoon, spring of 1988, right in the middle of the extended rock wars – you could really like Guns N' Roses or you could worship The Smiths, but it was against the law to like both – and I had just started on my second six-pack of beer.

I picked up the receiver and burped loudly into it. 'Yes?'

'Is that Mick Wall?'

'Yes.'

'Hi, Mick, this is Jo from Geffen Records.'

I'd never heard of her.

'Yes?'

'Does the name Jimmy Page mean anything to you?'

'Fuck off,' I said and hung up.

I looked around the office trying to seek out the culprit. One of the girls pretending to be on the phone, maybe, put up to it by Krusher.

At the time, the Zep thing was a running gag. I had taken to checking into hotels as Jimmy Zep or Robert Prance. If Krusher was in the pub across from the office I would phone and ask to speak to Mr Magus-Page. Just for the fun of hearing the Irish landlord yelling around the room for Mr Magus-Page. Oh, how we tittered.

Once I rang Pete Makowski and pretended to be Ritchie Blackmore on the phone, warning him that one of the Japanese groupies I'd fixed him up with when he'd last been out on the road with Rainbow had the clap and that he should get it checked-out immediately. I didn't even put on much of a voice, he just believed me. Then I burst out laughing. *Only me!* Boy was he pissed off. Didn't see the funny side at all. That was me now, with this stupid have-you-heard-of-Jimmy-Page thing.

Now I understood why. But the phone rang again. Same voice on the line, same enquiry.

'Look, who *is* this? I'm really busy and don't have time for this shit.' I had another slurp of beer. Lit a cigarette.

Turns out it really *was* someone called Jo, who really *was* from Geffen Records and she really *did* want to know if the name Jimmy Page meant anything to me. Which still seemed like an incredibly ignorant question, rude even, seeing how I was the star writer on the world's most Zep-friendly rock magazine. *Don't you know who you're dealing with here, baby?*

Those thoughts instantly vanished from my mind, though, as she spelled it out. Jimmy was about to release his first solo album, *Outrider*. And he was a fan of my show on Sky and—

'Wait. He watches the show on Sky?'

'Yes, apparently he never misses it. And . . .'

She wanted to know if I would help put together what is known as an EPK – Electronic Promotional Kit – to go with the record. Knowing there would be hundreds of requests for interviews from around the world, and that Jimmy would refuse them, she'd suggested instead he do a series of interviews with one person he felt he could get on with – one for all the press, one for all the radio. And he had asked for me.

What did I think?

I still thought someone somewhere was pulling a fast one. Or that this was an elaborate way of paying me back for some perceived slight. Something I'd written or said that had caused

Jimmy Page to hatch a plot to have me kidnapped and killed. I racked my brain trying to think of something I'd done but there were too many possibilities . . .

I was still thinking about it a few days later when the limo pulled up outside my flat in Ealing to take me off to the Sol, Jimmy's own studio by the river in Berkshire. I sat in the back, smoking a joint, wondering what I'd let myself in for this time. Unlike 90 per cent of the artists I now interviewed, I had actually been a paying Zeppelin fan as a teenager, had literally bought the T-shirt. Their album *Houses of the Holy* had been one of the first I'd ever saved up to buy when I was fourteen. And unlike so many of the artists I had most loved as an earnest album-collecting kid – Rod Stewart, David Bowie, Elton John – I had grown to appreciate my Zeppelin albums even more as I'd grown older. It was the blues that ran in the music's blood, I'd decided. It was timeless, unimpeachable. And it continued to grow on you like mould. There was no escape nor desire to flee, like there was when I happened upon some old Bowie nonsense from *Ziggy Stardust* or Elton overdoing it as usual on *Goodbye Yellow Brick Road*. Just an ever-growing appreciation of how deep underground those roots ran.

As the years had stumbled by, my mind had begun to allow Zeppelin to occupy the same elevated plain as Hendrix and the Stones. Not quite Dylan or The Beatles, obviously – Robert Plant's lyrics would always be Zeppelin's weak point, which is one of the reasons (but only one) that Robert would never be comfortable revisiting most of that stuff in the future – but high enough into the exosphere to belong with the immortals. For their music, their depth, their fearless disregard for rock orthodoxy, for their whole we-are-your-overlords vibe. Somehow, at their best in their earliest, most potent days, they had found the key to stealing your soul then selling it back to you – at a certain price.

At no time on this long musical journey had I anticipated actually sitting down with Jimmy Page, the dark master, and discussing any of this. It was one thing to sit there for hours on end putting up with Jon Bon Jovi telling you how his latest album was the best thing he'd ever done and how the new tour was going to be their best ever, your face aching from the effort of continually smiling as you played along, but quite another to sit down with a gen-u-wine rock god, and somehow *not* look and talk like the gurning awestruck fan you were, and would be desperately trying to conceal.

I was still thinking like this when he walked into the room.

'Hello, I'm Jimmy. Pleased to meet you.'

I followed him into his studio where I sat next to him while he played me the *Outrider* album. Loudly.

I'd asked for some beer. If we were going to sit and dig the new album, some beer was the absolute minimum requirement, surely? Jimmy's manager had asked what kind of beer I wanted. I said, Pilsner, half-expecting him to say they only had Budweiser or something equally disappointing. But within moments of sitting down in the studio a cold-tray with twelve cans of Pilsner lager embedded in ice appeared at my side. I noticed a similar tray being laid down on Jimmy's side of the desk, but that had only Kestrel lager on it. The alcohol-free variety.

If this was what he had to do to take control of what was left of his life, I was glad for him. But sad for me because I'd've loved to have known the black swan with the glowing red eyes that sailed the unchartered rock seas of the seventies. The one with the largest private collection of Crowley artefacts in the world – including the master's haunted old dwelling in Scotland, Boleskine House. The one with the wands and the whips and the heroin on ice. You know the one.

I'd thought about skinning up but seeing the Kestrel I thought better of it. Maybe Jimmy had been into rehab and was off everything. I grabbed a cigarette instead. Offered him one and lit it for him.

In truth it was a fairly boring meeting. It soon became clear the album lay in the not-bad category, which is about as bad as it gets for someone of the calibre of Jimmy Page. It was a ragbag of guest vocalists and players, though all in a fairly consistent sub-Zep style: John Miles – he of the 'music was my first love' hit from the mid-seventies – sang a couple; Chris Farlowe – he of the horse's face and 'baby, baby, baby, you're out of time' hit from the mid-sixties – sang a couple. Even Robert Plant sang one, 'The Only One', which *really* brought home the second-hand-Zep thing. And there were a couple of instrumentals, nice enough, but nothing you'd be able to remember the next day. The only track that really made your hind legs stand up was a version of the old Leon Russell chestnut, 'Hummingbird', sung like a trooper by Farlowe and featuring Jimmy somewhere maybe 70 per cent close to his shape-shifting best.

Of course, I didn't say any of this to Jimmy, who sat there waiting for my reaction. I just told him how great it all was. Like you would an anxious child. What else was I supposed to do? Eight years before he'd still been in Led Zeppelin, master of his realm if way too much out of control. For years he'd been completely off the radar, missing presumed floating face-down in his own private swimming pool. The last thing I wanted to do was *discourage* him.

Even the two so-so albums he'd made in the mid-eighties with Paul Rodgers, under the guise of The Firm, had only under-lined how dissipated he'd allowed his once-boundless talents to become. Then came that weird Live Aid performance . . . I'd been there for that one, standing at the side of the stage at the

JFK in Philadelphia watching it with Ozzy. Nowhere near as dreadful in the flesh as it has since been portrayed as, standing there twenty feet away from them as they rip-roared through 'Whole Lotta Love', it wasn't a misfiring Phil Collins on drums you noticed, nor the whistling feedback or fat-fingered solo from Jimmy on 'Stairway To Heaven', it was the *ascension*. The *invocation*. The different way the air suddenly moved inside the stadium.

I'd spent the whole day seeing heavy hitters like Jack Nicholson standing around jawing to people like Bob Dylan. David Crosby shaking his head sadly as Ozzy told backstage TV crews that Black Sabbath would be opening their set with 'Food, Glorious Food'. Ronnie Wood pretending not to be so coked up his lid was virtually flapping open as Tina Turner pretended to be interested in whatever he was babbling away to her about. No one batted an eye. But when Zeppelin came on the backstage area virtually shut down as everyone rushed to the giant screens set up about the place, to stand and gape as the ghost of the now dead behemoth rumbled back into a shadowy half-life.

The way the late seventies had been blown apart by punk and the early eighties had abandoned it to ridicule, with its spastic anti-dancing and po-faced groups stood like gloomy sentinels at their keyboards; the way good old-fashioned *fucking* had become convoluted and ultimately denigrated by AIDS; the otherwise wonderfully sexuality-questioning Boy George and his deplorable statement about preferring a cup of tea to sex, a joke that everyone took too seriously . . . there had been a lot of us lost to loathsome drugs, to desperate concealment of our true natures, to waiting for the bombs to stop dropping before we dared stick our dicks above the rubble once more. Jimmy had been a high-profile casualty of all that, but hardly the only one. And I felt for him.

In the course of our conversations I'd asked him about those 'lost weekends', and he admitted there had been years when he hadn't even *touched* the guitar. 'Then one day when I did finally ask my roadie to go and get the guitar out of its case, it wasn't there,' he told me.

'Someone had stolen it?'

'Well, they'd borrowed it by mistake,' he smiled. 'We got it back, though.'

We got the EPK done and then he came on to the Sky show as my guest. We filmed the programmes at ten in the morning, but when I arrived he was already waiting for me in the dressing room – with two big trays of ice-cold beers: Pilsner for me, alcohol-free Kestrel for him.

Of course I asked him all those things they are still asking now, twenty-five years later, and he was giving the same answers he still gives now as well.

Would he ever reform Led Zeppelin on a permanent basis?

'You'll have to ask Robert.' Snigger. Wink.

Had he ever read *Hammer of the Gods*?

'No. I read a bit of it, but it was all a bit sensationalist, wasn't it?'

I found out later he'd read every word and hated it. Blamed Zep's old tour manager Richard Cole for, as Jimmy saw it, shooting off his big mouth.

I never asked about the magic – or magick, as Jimmy would have it. I knew I wasn't nearly well versed enough on the subject to go there. One day, though, as we sat together waiting for them to set up the recording equipment for the radio interview we were doing for his *Outrider* EPK, he asked about some of the jewellery I was wearing. I was then into my full-on hard rocker phase, always in a black leather jacket, desperately tight sawn-off T-shirt, overripe cowboy boots and fucked-up jeans. I had a skull earring, a huge solid silver American bald eagle ring on one finger, another large, gold skull ring on another finger. All bought from the Great Frog in Soho. This was back when they only had the one shop, long before you could find a Frog in New York or LA. Back when they only did silver. My gold skull ring had been a special commission, which I'd paid through the nose for. This stuff still meant something to me back then, and I was happy to let Jimmy have the password.

'What do you think of this?' he said, in return, stretching out his hand to show-off his own prize gold ring: a serpent swallowing its own tail. All these years and lifetimes that have passed since I might have remarked how, in occult lore, the serpent was originally an angel with arms, head and legs, who forfeited them for tempting Eve, and though he remains immortal, is doomed to repeatedly suffer the pain of being reborn and dying, or, as it were, devouring his own tail.

But I didn't know that then and didn't know how to respond. I just mumbled some inanity about it being cool, or whatever. I sensed I was being put to the test somehow, and had failed spectacularly. It wasn't until many years later, when researching my Zep biography, *When Giants Walked the Earth*, that I was able to dig deep into Jimmy's lifetime interest and active involvement in, as he would always characterise it to me, 'alternative religions'. By then it was too late, though, to have any kind of meaningful conversations with him about it. All I could do was put into the book what a huge influence this had had on his life and career, particularly in the Zeppelin days when, like Crowley, it was all about affecting a successful outcome, as the indoctrinated might put it.

Another time, during a visit to his home in Windsor, the Old Mill House – the same house where Zeppelin drummer John Bonham had choked on his own vomit and died in 1980 – Jimmy had reached over and flipped open a special secret control panel in the arm of a couch. It was like something out of James Bond. The facing wall slid back to reveal four large paintings.

'Are you interested in . . . this sort of thing?' he asked, standing there avoiding my apprehensive gaze.

I walked over, got up close and peered at the artworks: thick splodges of oil on dark, antique canvas, what appeared to be a series of bodies twisted in torment, as though in hell. 'Weird,' I said, not knowing what to say. 'Heavy . . .' I turned to him, waiting for some explanation, but he merely stood there with a thin smile. Again, I sensed I had disappointed him with my inadequate reaction. Like an old medieval monk wrinkling his nose in disapproval at a hopeless novice he'd once had high hopes for.

He took me for a partial tour of the house and grounds. His then wife, Patricia, was there with their new baby son, Patrick. It was all cheerfully domestic and so at odds with his public image I couldn't get my head around what was actually going on. I wasn't far enough down the road to realise there was no separation in these things. That all was one, black *and* white. Or, as Jimmy liked to put it, 'Light *and* shade.'

'There's an electric side to me,' he told me, 'and an acoustic side.' Then added, 'You've only ever really seen the acoustic side.'

Was he challenging me to try to see more? Or was he just an old dog scratching at new fleas?

After it was over, though, we stayed in touch. Or rather, he stayed in touch. I was still too blindsided by who he was to consider calling him up, suggesting a night out, as he now did with me.

It was strange. He rang one day to ask if I fancied going to see Alice Cooper, who was doing a 'secret' gig at the Marquee. I hadn't imagined that sort of thing would appeal to Jimmy, but he seemed desperate to get out and about again, on the scene.

He picked me up that night in another chauffeur-driven limo, a white one. Inside, he and Patricia were making short work of a bottle of champagne. Or maybe it was just her, he was so bubbly and excited it was hard to tell if he'd started drinking again or was just delighted at having a night on the town. I got the impression he hadn't been out much lately.

When we got to the Marquee, he led the way to a spot near the front of the balcony, oblivious to the nudges and stares from the people he pushed past. It was hot and crowded in there that night, you could hardly breathe, yet Jimmy and Patricia stood there rocking back and forth like true-blue Alice fans. I stood on the other side of him, somewhat uncomfortable. I hadn't shown my hand so unselfconsciously at a gig for years. I rather wished he'd calm down.

I felt something suddenly. Like the first drop of rain. I looked around. Nothing. Then there it was again, heavier this time. Like someone was . . . throwing beer at me!

I spun around, pissed off. Then saw who it was – Lemmy! I threw him a look, like, what the fuck?

He raised his ogre eyebrows at me, nodded his head, agitated. I realised he was nodding at Jimmy, as if to say, look who it is!

'I know!' I mouthed. 'You want me to—?'

'Yes!' he nodded furiously.

I tapped Jimmy on the shoulder. He stood still for a moment and I yelled in his ear. 'Jimmy, do you know who Lemmy is?'

'Yes, why?'

''Cos he's standing behind you. Can he say hello?'

'Yes, great!' he beamed, like some speed-blurred Motörhead fan.

I turned around, grabbed Lemmy by the arm and dragged him over. Put him next to Jimmy and left them to it. I needed a line . . .

Jimmy was always asking about the current generation of rock bands that he'd seen on my show. What were Whitesnake like? 'Are they any good live or is it all smoke and mirrors nowadays?' What about Iron Maiden? 'Are they serious about what they do? Some of it seems a bit . . . silly, to me.'

He liked Def Leppard, then in the prime of their career, and regular guests on the show. 'I really like that guitarist,' he said, 'the one with the guitar hanging down to his knees.'

He meant Steve Clark, who had of course copped most of his moves from watching old videos of Jimmy in Led Zeppelin. When I told the band about this they all laughed and began goosing Steve about it, writing 'Jimmy's favourite' on his laminated backstage pass and asking him when he was joining the Magic Circle. Steve took it more seriously, and would come and whisper to me about maybe arranging a meet with Jimmy. I promised him I would look into it then never did. Not intentionally, I just had it in my head as something to do one day. Then Steve died of an overdose; Jimmy's favourite had gone on ahead, would catch us later, after our own shows were over.

Another time, I asked him what he'd made of the recent Whitesnake video for their hit, 'Still Of The Night', a bastardised MTV-sized version of 'Whole Lotta Love', with its clip of guitarist Adrian Vandenberg running a violin bow across the frets of his guitar.

He laughed. 'I nearly fell off the bed when I saw that! It was obviously a fake, but what are you gonna do, you know? I just thought it was funny.'

He seemed remarkably at ease with the new wave of impersonators who had scrambled to fill the Zeppelin-shaped hole the eighties was left with. But then Jimmy had hardly been slow at 'borrowing' from his own influences in Zeppelin. Maybe that was it. Or maybe Jimmy just didn't give a fuck.

He'd lived his life 'so far over the rainbow' these past twenty years it was almost impossible to guess where his head was at.

By the mid-eighties, outside of rock and metal circles, Zeppelin were as unfashionable as it was possible to get. Dismissed by 'serious' critics in their heyday, demonised in the wake of punk, openly laughed at in the aftermath of their grisly demise, the idea that one day Led Zeppelin would be considered one of the coolest rock bands of all time could simply not have been conceived of.

None of which seemed to bother Jimmy one bit. What bothered Jimmy was the sense that he was missing out. Like that hermit on the cover of the fourth Zeppelin album with the bundle of sticks on his back, Jimmy had been treading his own fearful path for so long he appeared to have run out of road.

'I go and see Eric play when he does his yearly thing at the Albert Hall,' he had told me when I asked him if he ever went out much on his own these days. He was only forty-four when we met yet he seemed to have not gone past Go for a very long time. Smack will do that to you, though. Time doesn't stand still, but you do. And when you finally unfreeze, as Jimmy finally had just a few years before, it was hard to find your way on to the right timeline.

Having been there myself, I felt for him. But it was still not a conversation he was willing to have in full just yet. At one point during the EPK process a major exec from Geffen's LA offices had flown in to do some handholding. She casually mentioned how she'd been strung out on gear herself in the past. I had nodded along, making it clear I was no third-party virgin either. Jimmy got the message but clammed up when it was his turn. He really didn't want to talk about it, acknowledge it even.

I tried another tack and asked him about his regrets. He told me he didn't have any. 'No, I don't regret anything, really.' The

coke and the smack, the booze and the dabbling with darkness
. . . 'that was what fuelled us, you know?' He hadn't gone looking for trouble, he insisted. 'Perhaps it was the other way round
and the darkness found me.'

I found it hard to swallow. If drug addiction had shown me
anything, it was that it was nobody's fault but mine, as the Zep
song went.

Jimmy didn't see it like that. 'If John hadn't died we'd still
be going today. We'd probably have gone on to even bigger
and better things. We were ready again for a new chapter. We'd
turned a corner and things were looking good again.'

For someone who had once carved sonic sculptures with his
music, who was able to move the immovable with such ease,
such daring, he seemed painfully full of self-deception.

And what if Bonham had died after the second Zep album,
just as they were starting to climb their stairway to heaven,
would they have quit then? 'Yes, it would have been the same
thing,' he said. Zeppelin, he said, 'comprised these four elements,
and once one of them was gone, the whole thing was gone.'

At which point, it dawned on me this was not about finding
a common ground to explore the truth, this was about being let
into Miss Havisham's ruined mansion, all the clocks stopped
at 23 September 1980 – the day Bonzo checked out in one of
Jimmy's plush guest bedrooms – and being expected to keep up
with the narrative that had been running inside the old lady's
head all these years, the explanation she gave herself for the
tragedy that had befallen her. In this case, not the actual death of
John Bonham, but the much earlier expiration of Led Zeppelin,
dead from the waist up since the day Jimmy lost control of his
many addictions, and Bonzo then Peter Grant followed.

I actually felt a little sorry for him. Him in his grade II listed
eighteenth-century country mansion; me in my one-bedroom

London loft with the slanted ceilings. Mostly, I could feel his neediness – to get back in the game, to be back on the cross, to get back to where he still believed he needed to be. But Robert was never going to agree to that. Robert, who would spend the rest of his life trying to live down Led Zeppelin, even after they became fashionable again all those years later. Robert, who would never quite forgive Jimmy for . . . well, everything.

As time went on, we stayed in touch. His manager asked me to help him find Jimmy a new singer to work with, but everyone I suggested had to agree to come to an audition without knowing who it was they were auditioning with – which meant no one I discreetly approached would agree to come. One was Neville MacDonald, the singer of a group called Skin. I had seen the band play a couple of times and Neville had a voice like a young and still hungry Paul Rodgers, and long, golden, Robert Plant locks, circa 1973. I thought he might be just what Jimmy was looking for, but when I made a couple of phone calls it was made clear that Neville, who lived in Wales, wasn't going to come all the way to London without knowing who it was he was being asked to perform for.

There was also a black singer with a lion of a voice and a heavy onstage presence, but when I suggested him Jimmy's manager didn't even bother to get back. It didn't matter. He would soon find what he was looking for when Geffen's chief guru, John Kalodner, successfully paired him up with Whitesnake singer David Coverdale.

I still saw Jimmy, still went out of my way to treat him right whenever I could, a relationship that lasted, on and off, right up until 2008, and the publication of my Zeppelin biography, *When Giants Walked the Earth*. Things were never the same after that. He did an interview with *The Times* shortly after publication, in which he was quizzed on his views of the book and in which, predictably, he claimed not to have read it. A few months later, however, bumping into him at a *Classic Rock* awards show in London, he leaned over and whispered in my ear, 'I just want to say I think you gave Robert a really fucking easy ride.'

It wasn't true. I had simply come to the same conclusion as Robert, while working on the book, that Zeppelin should never get back together. The famous O2 show in December 2007 had confirmed that view in my mind. As I wrote then, it was like viewing the ruins of an Egyptian temple: a grand spectacle, fascinating to behold, to try to imagine what it must have been like once upon the long-ago, before history overtook them and the sands just blew it all away. But it told you very little of what it was like to have lived there, back when the world was still young and believed it would live for ever.

13. Le Mondrian

Billy was hanging out in my suite at the hotel. It was way past three but he had all this coke and I was fucked if I was going to let him shoot off too quickly.

He kept glancing over at the bed where she lay. My *Playboy* Playmate of the Month. Miss Moon in June. She was tired, she said, wanted to go to bed. My bed. What was I waiting for?

I knew I was a fool, should have gotten this guy out of the place and gone over there and stroked her better. But I couldn't help it. Nights like this just lasted for ever, I was fairly sure. LA seemed to be full of pretty girls who liked to sleep in my bed sometimes. Often they mistook the hotel suite and the back-stage passes for fame and fortune, and LA was all about fame and fortune and how to hook into it. Sleeping in some guy's bed was viewed as a minimum requirement to getting closer to that magic formula. Like the Marilyn Monroe lookalike who followed me into the toilet at a showcase gig at the Roxy for Marillion. She was dressed to look like Marilyn in the white dress blowing up round her waist in *The Seven Year Itch*, and damn but you couldn't tell her from the real thing. Except that Marilyn was dead and this babe had her left leg lifted right up on my shoulder.

Sometimes it could be they just loved my cute English accent. These two non-blondes from Sony Records spring to mind. Pam and Jan, Lynne and Kim, Nicky and Vicky, something and nothing. I'd been by their office that afternoon, where they worked in promotions, blagging albums and spreading the good word. They both made such a fuss you'd think they'd never met anyone from outside LA before. I gave them the I'm-in-town-all-alone trip and they offered to come by the hotel that night and hook me up with some Wowie Maui, the best weed you could get in town at that time. We all sat in bed together smoking it.

Sometimes it was like they actually liked me for me. It was hard to tell. LA was party central, everybody was high on love and seven-day-weekends, dude.

On this occasion, with my green-eyed *Playboy* girl, I was in town with Iron Maiden. They had been playing the big enormo-dome out in Inglewood. Two nights. Sold out. Afterwards we had all gone to the Rainbow, as you do. I'd taken Lolly with me. She really was a babe, but with brains too. She'd only just had her photo-shoot in *Playboy* published and she was so proud she took copies of the mag with her everywhere she went.

She had plonked herself down between me and Steve Harris, at one of the half-moon band tables, at the back. She opened the mag to the centrefold, where she lay in all her splendiferous glory. Steve looked across at me, like, 'Is she for real?'

I just smiled. What else could I do? This was a new one on me. As long as Steve didn't want twos-up, which I knew he was fond of, I didn't mind. It didn't matter if I did, anyway. Lolly was her own person, not like the other girls from Hef's mansion.

'Yeah, very nice,' Steve told her. 'Very nice indeed.' He looked over at me again, like, 'Are you fucking her?' I nodded. Which wasn't strictly true. But we were close.

Then later that night, up in my suite at Le Mondrian – the hotel David Coverdale had secretly sunk money into, hence all the videos from Whitesnake's *1987* album being shot in *his* suite there – sitting talking dreadful coked-out bollocks with Billy, I knew it was now or never with Lolly, but I just couldn't drag myself away from the table.

The truth was, and still is, I preferred raging conversation, torrid tales, fireside stories of fuck-ups and furies, with grown men, often older, or simply more worldly, who had *lived*, who had walked through the fire and come out smoking a cigar and laughing through their blackened teeth, than I did getting on down real slow and easy with the ladeez. There was something wrong with me that way, and I tried to fight it and sometimes even won, but not often. Or not often enough, now I look back on it.

Billy was telling me all about how stoopid and unfair it was that Steve Harris had won bassist of the year in some instrument magazine. Billy worked as a roadie but was also a high-functioning musician himself. 'I mean, come on, man! Even I can play bass better than Steve. I mean, he has his own style and he's famous, of course. But when it comes to actually playing the bass, well, I mean, come on, it's just so fucked up. The only reason he's won bassist of the year is because he's in Iron Maiden. That's all it is!'

There was nothing wrong in what Billy was saying. There wasn't much right to it either. *Of course* Steve had won because he was in Iron Maiden and was famous. Who did he think voted in these things?

He had a *lot* of coke, though, and I wasn't about to start arguing over some minor clause in the contract. It all seemed fairly straightforward to me. Magazines were magazines, who cared what they said or thought or pretended to think or say? I'd stopped buying music magazines the same time my tastes in music began to broaden, when I left school at sixteen. Just because I was now writing for them hadn't changed that one bit. I knew where to go to find the best music, and I knew where to go to find the best music writing. If the two coincided, which sometimes they did, that was just lipstick on the nipples. But Billy was a 'proper' musician and, like all 'proper' musicians, he didn't get it. He thought music magazines were about music. It's a mistake people still make to this day.

All very well, up to a point, especially if that point has been dipped in the purest Bolivian nose candy. But now I was getting restless. It was getting light outside and I wanted to go and gently wake my little bunny honey.

But Billy was in no hurry to leave. I ran through my act, yawning, fussing, making the well, gotta go now noises, you do. He caught on but somewhere far off in his tiny musicianly mind he was still harbouring fantasies of joining me in a little ménage à trois. Well, no way, hozay.

He was still jabbering about bassist of the year and fucking rock stars and it all being not fair and whatever as I nudged him out of the door. Finally. I went back to the table, slurped down the last of the wine then crept over to the bedroom and its king-sized double bed. I nestled myself on the edge next to her pillow and leaned over, did a little wine burp in her ear. Oops, sorry!

'Lolly,' I whispered. 'Are you awake?' I shook her, just to make sure I got the right answer. No response. I shook her harder.

She came to with a start. 'Uh . . .?'

'It's me. Just wondering if you're awake.'

She turned over to look at me. She had LA eyes – all cool and unimpressed – and long, red Texas hair. And a big New York brain, which she wasn't afraid to use on me. 'Well, I am now.' She lifted her head. 'Is he gone?'

'Yes. I had hell getting rid of him but he's gone. There's just us.'

'Are you coming to bed?'

'Yes, but . . .'

'What?'

The coke gave me the courage.

'Listen, we keep going to bed. We keep kissing. But we never fuck. Just so's I know, are we *ever* going to fuck?'

'Sure,' she said. My face lit up. 'You have to have a shave first, though.'

I touched my chin. About a week's growth.

'And brush your teeth too. Your breath smells bad.'

No problemo. I went into the bathroom and closed the door, trying not to appear in too much of a hurry. Once inside, though, I got to work fast. Too fast. I cut myself with the razor so badly the blood wouldn't stop running down my face. As I brushed my teeth the blood mingled with the toothpaste and I had red foam drooling off my chin.

I did my best to stem the flow, but it was no good. I came out with a swatch of red – getting redder – tissue stuck to my face. She was lying there waiting for me, also trying to be cool but it was plain neither of us were.

I had known Lolly off and on a while. I couldn't think of her as a *Playboy* model. She wasn't one of those chicks who exuded that kind of aura, who relied on their sexuality to get by with men. She hid it all in plain sight, and most people – me included when she first told me – simply didn't believe her, thought that maybe she'd gone temporarily insane when she mentioned she had done a photo-shoot for *Playboy* and blah, blah, blah.

I had a different kind of hard-on for her. I had wanted her since the time she'd simply walked up to me one evening and kissed me so deeply and passionately I felt my own nipples go hard. She had been in a bad way then, had been thrown by a boyfriend. Men were always pissing girls like Lolly around. She was too smart for them and always made them pay, and that just made them fuck her around even more. Guys in bands, especially. Well, duh.

That time I had been her knight in 501s. As time passed, though, and she found her feet, she had been careful not to allow me too much oxygen. She always liked to hang out, coming to the show, even staying at the hotel with me, wherever that might be. But the closest I had come to anything more had been lying there on my side, sweating and unable to sleep, just staring at her immaculate bell-shaped arse lying next to me. The last temptation of Christ. The gateway to hell. The place of dark roads and empty sorrows. The hard rock café of mortal dread and delicious sin and no let-offs, ever. All the places I wanted to go and be seen and be torn apart by. Again.

Lately she had begun scoring little bags of weed for me. I was still in my the-best-writing-is-done-stoned period, and was always short of enough dope. Lolly to the rescue! We would go out for dinner at this cool Italian place on Melrose and they would treat us like a dating couple, but somehow things had not moved more in that direction. I would have suspected her of using me to get close to rock stars, which I was used to, but Lolly didn't need me for that. She had her own thing going on.

It didn't occur to me that she might be hung-up on the fact I had a so-called girlfriend back in London. Well, double-duh! (Not Maria, who had split from me the minute she found someone else who didn't know how he was making her feel, but a stick-thin lady beetle whose name I could never remember whenever I was away, which was now most of the time.)

I approached the bed as calmly as I could, which was not very calmly at all. We kissed, but it felt forced. I spoke sweet words to her, told her how beautiful she was, how wonderful her hair was, her eyes, her delicious body . . . she'd heard it all before, of course, but what else was there to say? I moved down to her breasts, now *Playboy* breasts only they didn't look like that up-close. They were proper woman's breasts, one a little larger than the other, maybe, one here and one there. I began kissing them, gently at first, then hard, nibbling, teasing, licking, tickling.

Not much response. Just . . . resigned, it felt like. In desperation I moved down to her belly and her thighs. Trying to take my time. Failing. In a hurry to get down to the holy of holies, where I knew I would rule. I had always been good at going down on girls. When all else failed – you came too soon, you couldn't get it up, you were on your second or third go round and needed something different – I knew I only had to go down there, perform my tricks, taught to me years before by an expert in the field, a teenage goddess with many more years' experience than me, and all would be well in the world.

I went to work on Lolly, in the confident knowledge that now I was in charge and that when she came, finally – I didn't care how long it took – she would be mine. It was a done deal.

Time slowed to a crawl. It was good down there but not that good. I had her world-beating arse in my hands, my bloody mouth on her pussy, I had been oh so gentle, smooth, kind, then rough, terrible, vengeful. I had beseeched her with my tongue, gouged her with my nose, rubbed my soft shaved face this way and that along the length and breadth of her. Kissed her on the lips sweetly and bitten them, just tiny prods with my newly scrubbed teeth.

Still nothing. Nothing real. Some appreciative noises but no real encouragement . . . I could feel the sweat running down my back, my neck starting to spasm.

Finally, she said it. 'Wait, wait,' she whispered.
'What?'
'What about your girlfriend?'
'What?'

'What about your girlfriend? Don't you love her?'

I tried to ignore her, make the question academic. Something we could talk about if we really had to after she had come, if she was ever going to fucking come. I forged manfully ahead but I could feel the moment drifting away.

She kept on. 'But don't you love her? Your girlfriend in London?'

'I don't care about her!'

'Yes you do. I know you do!'

It was too much to think about and do this. I gave up. Moved back up to the pillows and rolled over on my back panting, waiting for the room to stop moving.

She lay there on her side, looking at me. I had no idea what she was thinking. The battle was over. I had lost. I should have let Billy stay, snorted all his coke. I should have done something I didn't do, but I didn't know what. Born wrong.

I was pissed off, frustrated yet secretly relieved in some weird way. It meant I didn't have to keep trying so hard. I turned my back on her and punished her by pretending to fall asleep. But the coke wouldn't let me off the hook, and I just lay there until finally I heard her snoring. She was a cool chick, and she'd been right, of course. It didn't feel right being so wrong, though. How did the rock stars get away with it? One of Rod Stewart's people told me once that if Rod did a tour of ninety cities, then 'by end of it, he would have fucked ninety chicks, maybe more'. How did guys like that cope? All that action, it must have taught them something the rest of us would never know. Something the chicks understood and the rest of us would never be able to fake. Spot you coming a mile off . . . I mean, Lolly hadn't even grabbed my cock or made much of a play of getting *my* rocks off. I grew more pissed off. What else could I be under the circumstances, really?

Later that morning as we were having brunch together by the pool she said to me, 'Do you wanna do something tonight?'

'Like what?'

'Do you wanna go to dinner? How about you call Slash and I'll call my girlfriend, Francesca? She's a *Playboy* model too and she absolutely *loves* Slash. She'd *die* to meet him. We could double date?'

I said I'd think about it, call Slash later, let her know. But I knew he'd never come. The last time I'd seen Slash he'd been so strung-out on smack he'd lost all interest in anything else, except maybe the guitar and his damn snakes. For Slash, *Playboy* chicks were hard work, old news. Dinner, talk, you had to be in the mood. Now, porno chicks, that was more his scene. You didn't need to do anything there except show up, get high and lay it down. I began to think Slash was on to something.

14. **Diamond Dave**

Word backstage was, things were getting *heavy*.

So heavy, the rumours had reached right across the Atlantic that year: off stage singer David Lee Roth and guitarist Eddie Van Halen were fighting all the time. On stage they were barely speaking. Nobody really knew why, though.

On paper, 1984 was shaping up to be Van Halen's best year yet. Their sixth album, which they'd cheekily even named *1984*, had become their first to go to No. 1 in America, and was now a big hit around the rest of the world, too. They'd even had their first globe-straddling hit single that year with 'Jump', a song so obviously classic that it felt like it had been around for years, yet was so new-sounding, with its swirling synths and vocal harmonies, that some rock fans had turned their backs on it the first ten times they'd heard it pumping out of their radios. But then came that eleventh time, baby. . .

Now here they were that summer in England, about to hit the stage as 'special guests' – that is, second on the bill to AC/DC – at the 1984 Castle Donington Monsters of Rock festival.

Like everybody else in the VIP area that day I couldn't wait to catch a glimpse of them, to sneak by and say hi over a beer and a toke or two. And, like everybody else in the VIP area that day, I was astonished to learn that Van Halen had their own VIP-area-within-the-VIP-area set-up, that you needed even more special passes to get into.

What the fuck was this?

Not even the famously reclusive AC/DC had that kind of deal going on backstage. Indeed, although the Young brothers and their slaves didn't arrive at the show until late in the afternoon, once they did so anyone could go up to singer Brian Johnson and ask what it was he was really hiding under that flat cap of his.

When I was finally ushered through the various fenced-off sections into the mini-trailer park that was the Van Halen back-stage area, the division between David Lee Roth – outrageous frontman, unabashed showbiz entertainer and all-round crazy motherfucker – and Eddie Van Halen – introspective musician, hater of what he called 'circuses' and all-round motherfucker in his own right – was obvious.

Stretched out between various campervans serving as port-able dressing rooms, were Diamond Dave and his personal trainer, huffing and puffing, engaged in a complicated series of calisthenics that looked positively Olympian. Meanwhile, seated, drinking and smoking in the contrived darkness of his own campervan – scarves draped over lamps, blinds down on the windows – was Eddie and his drummer brother, Alex.

'Hey, man, grab a seat,' said Eddie, offering me a limp hand-shake. Alex just sat there and grinned, working on his beer. Across the way you could hear Michael Anthony whomping away on his bass, warming up, fucking around, whatever.

'What's happening?' I asked.

'Nothing,' giggled Alex. 'Relaxing before the show,' smiled Eddie. 'It gets pretty hectic once the show starts, so before it we just like to lay back a little, you know?'

I nodded to the door, on the other side of which Roth and his trainer were still hard at it, whooping and high-fiving.

'Is that Dave's way of laying back before a show?'

'Uh . . . Dave has his own way of doing things,' said Eddie, still smiling but his eyes coming more into focus.

'Kind of like on stage,' I said, thinking of the whirling dervish Roth became once he hit the stage each night.

'Yeah, kind of,' said Eddie, the smile slowly melting away. 'He's always got his own way of doing things . . .'

You could say that again. The first time I had seen Van Halen perform live had been when they'd opened for Black Sabbath in London in 1978. Dave's ability to seemingly levitate on stage – the living embodiment of the catchphrase used to sell the Christopher Reeve *Superman* movie, also released that year: 'You will believe a man can fly!' – had made Ozzy's plodding stoner look imbecilic by comparison. The whole razzmatazz of the Van Halen show – shamanic frontman; aurora borealis guitar player – had made Sabbath look and sound horribly dated suddenly. It seemed no coincidence that Sabbath and Ozzy had split soon afterwards.

Musically, though, Van Halen had always belonged to Eddie. Granted, Alex was a superb powerhouse drummer, while Michael was the opposite of the clichéd 'quiet man' bassist, providing personality-filled backing vocals as well as booming bass. But it was Eddie's from-the-future guitar stylings that became both the sound of Van Halen and the signature rock and metal sound of the eighties, as every other Sunset Strip shredder struggled to keep up with him.

'People say we like to put on a show,' said Eddie. 'And we do, we have to, the places we play. They're so big it's not enough just to stand there and play. But it's always the music that comes first. At least, for me,' he added, thinking perhaps of the larger-than-life character working up a sweat outside the door. 'I didn't get into a rock 'n' roll band so I could join the circus,' he said, pointedly. Was he saying he thought of Roth as a clown?

I wish I'd thought to ask him that at the time, but back then, with Van Halen then the biggest rock band in the world, it simply didn't occur to me there could be that much discord in the camp. Yet it was all there, festering away in the background like a bad smell coming from the kitchen. A smell of burning . . .

Before I could really notice, however, Dave's trainer, or body-guard, or whatever he was, stuck his head around the camper door to inform me my presence was required elsewhere.

'Dave's kind of wondering where you are?' he said, looking puzzled by my apparently weird fascination with talking to the Van Halen brothers.

'I thought he was busy,' I protested. 'Doing his . . . thing.'

'No, he's in his dressing room waiting to talk to you.'

I followed him the ten yards or so to Dave's 'changing room', an identical campervan to the one I'd just left. Roth, who'd apparently just showered, was lying outside on a low plastic couch, hair tied back in a ponytail, eyes resting behind huge aviator shades, the arms dangling by his side bulging with mountain-climber muscles.

He sprang to his feet as his 'assistant' introduced me. 'Well, well, well! What have we here! Man, I *love* the magazine you work for!' He was bouncing up and down on his feet like a big over-excited kid, that by now familiar look of utter astonishment on his face.

'And I just love DONINGTON! Yeah, baby! Don-ing-ton! I mean, we have shows like this in the States but we don't have the *roots*, you know what I'm saying? The *history*! The *blood*! I mean, this is where it all comes from, right? RIGHT? The Beatles, the Stones, The Who . . . I mean, COME ON!'

I searched for something equally excited to say, but all I could manage was a feeble, 'Yeah.'

He seemed to understand. He'd been through this a thousand

times before. Knew the words backwards. I was still just trying to hum along.

'I tell you what, though, man, when we walk out on that stage today, that will be *something else*! 'Cos when we hit it, it's *circle the wagons time*, you know what I mean? I mean, like ZAP! POW! Bang fucking bang, baby! You looking for trouble? Well, I'm here, baby! I'M HERE!'

While he was cackling with laughter I managed to squeeze a request for a quick interview. But he was having too much of a good time for that.

'I can't right now, man! I'm just too *busy*! But we *will* talk. Later, after the show, right? Right now, though, I gotta catch me some rays. You know what I'm saying?'

With that he sprang back into the prone position on his plastic sunbed, and I was led away to the perimeter of the Van Halen VIP area, back out into the general population of lesser leading lights like Malcolm Young, Ozzy Osbourne, Gary Moore and various members of Mötley Crüe.

I never did get my after-the-show interview with David Lee Roth at Donington that day. For despite putting on what many there agreed was the second best set of the day, after AC/DC's, I found out later that Dave and Eddie had been spitting bullets at each other as the band left the stage. Over what, it seemed everyone had given up guessing, by then.

As Roth would tell me some time later, 'Man, we were not going through happy times. Everything was going wrong between us. We were barely talking. The most fun I had all day was actually being on stage, and even that was a little strained. I remember one particular point, I was starting to get into a number and really fly. I glanced over to the side of the stage and I saw this female photographer with her back to me bending over, searching around in her bag for something.

'Man, I was already working on my high, trying to get into the set, and then I saw this cute little ass wiggling at me and I just went for it! I ran right over to one side of the stage and got down on my knees and planted a kiss on that sweet little butt. And do you know what she did? She spun around like someone had just kicked her in the ass and hit me – whammo! – straight in the jaw!'

He roared with laughter at the memory. Lit another joint. 'And that chick packed a wallop, man. It almost knocked me off my feet! I thought, "Jesus, this day is doomed . . ."'

It was a sad but typically crazy end to the story of a band that, in its music and its message, had appeared to offer so much zest for life throughout its brief but dazzling career.

But then as Roth told me, 'Life is far too important to be taken seriously. Same with music and setting people free. All we ever wanted to do in Van Halen was show people a good time. I mean, a *real* good time! And most people responded to that. The only ones that ever had a hard time with it were the goddamn critics. They just couldn't figure us out at all.'

It was true. They couldn't see past the hype. Couldn't get over Roth's wild, lion's mane of blond hair, the two Van Halen brothers' deeply fucked-up feel for partying, or the fact that Michael Anthony looked like a trucker but played like an angel. They felt uncomfortable with the knowledge that the band came from Los Angeles, where even the palm trees were fake. Alice Cooper – Roth's biggest inspiration going into Van Halen – at least made the girls cry with his snakes and his chopped-up dolls and painted black eyes. Van Halen looked like they'd rather spend the night playing dress-up with the girls and sharing sex tips.

In short, there was something superhuman about Van Halen that made the rest of the male population cower in a corner. At least until they heard that damn *Van Halen* album and realised they had just been propelled far into the future, where one day all hard rock and heavy metal bands would look and sound like this. Or at least try their hardest to do so. The shock release of *Van Halen* didn't just sound the death knell for seventies rock as we knew it, it marked the actual arrival of the 1980s – two years early. Zap! Pow! Bang fucking bang, baby!

But if Eddie was the wellspring, in terms of the ratcheted-up, Hollywood-after-dark sound of Van Halen, the key to their destiny was all down to 'Diamond' Dave.

Born in Bloomington, Indiana, in 1954, the son of a millionaire eye-surgeon who moved his family to a 14,000 square-foot estate in Pasadena, California, Roth grew up an over-entitled, hyper-confident, intimidatingly intelligent young man. The fact that he was blessed with good looks, a talent for martial arts and a gift for speed-reading a book a day made him an extremely alluring prospect to the female population of Southern California and an extremely alarming one for its male population.

It didn't matter that he didn't have much of a singing voice and could never abide learning to play an instrument, the teenage Roth had already decided what he wanted to be when he didn't grow up: a rock star. Not just any old rock star, either. But, as he put it, 'The heavyweight champion of the world rock star!' The fact that he had to wait until he was twenty-three before he achieved his goal seemed to Dave like maybe he'd been slacking. No matter. He simply blamed the more 'relaxed' attitude of the guy he'd teamed up with to help him achieve his ambitions: a puppy-faced LA guitar-savant named Eddie Van Halen, who was a year younger than Dave but about a hundred years older in street-dog years.

Eddie was an Eric Clapton and Cream freak, who envisaged himself playing slow, soulful blues and acid-tinged jazz-rock.

'I just wanted to jam, man,' he would tell you. 'Sure, you would have verses and choruses, but that was only to get you into that space where you could just wail on the guitar.'

But then Dave showed up with a keg of beer, a pocketful of high-grade weed and suddenly all bets were off. Just 'wanting to jam' would never be crazy-from-the-heat Diamond Dave's idea of a good time. He liked rock with a capital 'R'. Loved good time blues and soul. Longed to put on a show in which he was the most glittering star. So while Eddie and Alex and their other new friend, Michael, would practise every day on their instruments, Dave would be driving around town with the radio blaring Top 40 hits, scheming and dreaming how he was gonna make it one day.

For the next five years Van Halen, as Dave always insisted it was his idea to call the band, played every titty bar, glam-rock hellhole and backroom set-up the neon-gorged streets of Holly-wood had to offer.

'We didn't care where we played,' Roth would tell me. 'Didn't care *where*, didn't care *when*, didn't matter *what*. Some nights we would play six or seven shows in two or three different joints. Straight out hard rock in one joint, soul and R&B covers in an-other, Top 40 shit in the next. By the time we'd signed a record deal we had a set of about four hundred songs we'd learned. We felt like we could do anything. And we could!'

So bizarrely accelerated was their success – *Van Halen* eventually sold over twelve million copies in the US alone, followed by four multi-platinum albums in four years – the critics never had a chance to make their minds up about them first. Something guaranteed to fuel animosity in those days when critical approval was nine-tenths of the law. The fact that Van Halen achieved all this while at the same time ap-pearing to have more fun than any 'normal' people had a right to, made critics even more antsy about their rapid ascent to stardom.

Even the astonishing success of the *1984* album – the high-water mark of a career already bloated with overachievement – was only grudgingly given its due at the time it was riding the world's charts like a bronco. Previously regarded as something of a joke, of having no respect, of being somehow fake, when Van Halen proved them all wrong with bona fide future rock classics like 'Jump', the critics still found something to quibble about.

I couldn't understand it. What was wrong with a little razza-matazz? Getting het up about whether a rock artist was fake or not . . . were they joking? Like Led Zeppelin and Black Sabbath had been *real*? What was wrong with these rock stalwarts who couldn't see the funny side? Personally, I couldn't wait to meet them, to hang with Dave, to write about them like I knew something. Fake? FAKE? That was my middle name! I couldn't give a fuck what some prissy little tosser on the mainstream music press who had never left home thought about anything. I had met these people. They made me sick. Everything they'd learned they'd picked up from reading other writers on the same music papers. So Van Halen was fake and, uh, The Cure weren't? David Lee Roth was ridiculous but Morrissey wasn't? Well, I was a fake too, right down to my $100 dollar shoes and silver coke spoon. As fake as my pad in LA and my deep blue swimming pool. I couldn't wait to be even *more* fake. Anything just so long as I didn't have to pretend to still be at university, imagining I had the slightest clue as to how the music business really worked or what it's real core values were – including those of so-called revolutionaries like Joe Strummer and Johnny Rotten, both of whom couldn't wait to get to America and wet their beaks at the Hotel California.

'I don't read press cuttings,' Roth boasted to me when we did finally get to know each other. 'I weigh 'em! As long as the scales keep tipping in the right direction, I'm happy. Don't matter what they say, as long as they keep saying it.' More horse laughter.

By 1984, however, things had changed. Not just for Roth, who was fast becoming the most eligible rock superstar on the planet, offered solo deals (which he accepted), movie roles (which he accepted) and guest spots on TV and radio (which he also accepted), but for Eddie too. Fêted by Michael Jackson, who'd used Eddie's snarling guitar to sucker rock fans into buying his 'Beat It' single, he was now glorified by a whole new generation of guitar-stars who all bowed down as not worthy before his famously homemade 'Frankenstein' guitar, knowing that no matter how fast they 'tapped' they would never match Shreddy Eddie.

'Suddenly you've got these two giant egos trying to share the same dressing room and it was just never gonna work,' as one former management aid told me privately.

Or as Sammy Hagar would put it to me some years later, offering a unique perspective as the guy who finally came between Dave and Eddie, 'There's no singer on the planet that's not a leader and there's no guitar player in the world that's not a leader, either. And once one takes over the other guy starts putting out shabby work, says, "OK, I don't care any more, fuck it, this is your trip." And then the other guy takes over and starts being self-indulgent. It happens every time . . .'

Sure enough, by 1983, both Dave and Eddie had their own separate dressing rooms, as did Alex and Michael. They also had their own limos, as did, it seemed, their entire road crew and entourage, who needed twenty-two limos just to get them to and from the US festival in San Bernardino.

Moreover, there were now – wait for it – *musical differences* starting to come between them. Tired of never knowing whether people were laughing *with* him or *at* him, Eddie craved the one thing he didn't already possess: credibility. Whatever Van Halen did next, it would have to be taken seriously on a musical level, Eddie insisted. Especially now the band owned its own recording studio, 5150, opened for business in time for *1984*, now expanded to state-of-the-art proportions. For their next album, Van Halen would be able to take all the time they wanted to get things absolutely perfect, Eddie decided.

Dave, meanwhile, grew exhausted at the very thought of such an idea. His plan, he told anyone that would listen, which meant pretty much everybody except the rest of the band, was to go in, record a new album quick-quick-quick and get back out on the road at the first opportunity.

As he put it, 'The day fun stops being fun, that's when I'm outta here.' True to his word, by March 1985 he was gone. Taking most of 'the fun' with him.

On one particular occasion, at a show in Massachusetts, on an early David Lee Roth solo tour, I got a taste of exactly what this entailed. In Van Halen, everybody liked a smoke, everybody liked a line, no one was allowed to drink anything softer than Budweiser, Jack Daniel's was the fifth member of the band. But where Eddie liked to kickback after a gig, a guitar on his lap, hanging out with his stoner pals, Dave liked to keep the show going, never fully turned off.

Having showered, changed and wolfed down a lobster dinner, he would now be ready to 'get it on!' as he put it. Sitting in a room with him and his new 'Eddie-upgrade' – whiz kid guitarist Steve Vai – we were entertained by naked dancing girls, all strutting their stuff to the sound of the Average White Band blaring from a ghettoblaster.

As a guest, I received special treatment: one of the girls writhed and smiled in my lap as I sat there with a joint in one hand and a bottle of Jack in the other, Dave and Steve and some of their entourage all whooping along while the party got into full swing. I was hoping she wouldn't try to pull my cock out and give me a blowjob, or just squat on top of me and ride me like a pony. That might have been very nice behind closed doors, but not with an audience looking on. I'd never been into the kind of routine exhibitionism most rock musicians considered normal. Sharing girls on the road had always been considered normal. Orgies always a given. Francis Rossi of Status Quo once told me how in the early days of the band they would organise nights on the road when they would show old-fashioned porno films on someone's hotel room wall. 'We'd all sit there with our knobs out having a good polish,' he explained nonchalantly. Fortunately, there was to be no polishing this night on the road with Roth. Or none in public at least, thank God.

This, though, was hardly extravagant stuff for the mid-eighties, at a time when rock could be measured in the size and number of limos a band employed, the quality of the drugs they enjoyed and the number of sheer heart-attack babes they filled their dressing rooms with each night.

What made this different was that at one point, around 2 a.m., when people had begun to leave and the girls were putting their clothes back on, Dave decided it was time for our interview, and I found myself in a room with him, along with a plastic shopping bag full of champagne-quality weed, another smaller but no less bulging plastic baggie of Peruvian flake, several cases of beer and a bottle each of Jack Daniel's.

What resulted was the most fun, if most wilfully deranged interview I ever conducted. I say 'interview', but it really wasn't like that. It was like a scene from some weird movie where two guys are stuck in a spaceship going God knows where. When we emerged from that room nearly *twelve hours later*, it wasn't just the next day it was the next dimension.

I asked how he dealt with all the criticism over the years. People either loved him or hated him. Yet there was obviously a tremendous amount of thought that went into his performances.

'If they hate me it's because they don't *understand* me. Either we haven't had a chance to sit and get to know one another, or I'm screwing up on the transmission end. Or maybe they just don't like the changes I've been through with my music over the last ten years. But I never wanted to be a performer who stood for just one thing, one style, one set of moves and that's it. How boring! Nobody reading this right now wants to spend the rest of their lives doing the same thing over and over, so why should I?'

I mentioned how much I enjoyed the sheer athleticism of his performances on stage. Who else in rock did the splits on stage? Who else could make it seem like they were actually flying? This wasn't Kiss, where everything depended on lights and pyro, this was good old-fashioned stagecraft.

His face lit up. 'I remember when I was a kid going to see a production of *Peter Pan* with my sister, and here was this woman dressed as a man flying from one side of the stage to the other on the end of a wire, and I just thought this was the greatest thing I'd ever seen! There's a certain kind of character displayed in theatrics like that who appeals to me greatly. I don't mean like a cartoon character, I mean in the sense that there's some soul there, there's some heart in stuff like that. And I don't mind having a little bit of that same soul in my show.'

Where did he find his inspiration, though?

'Anything, man, anything that moves me. Sometimes it's a book, sometimes it's other things. You gotta remember, I'm not a natural anything. I got it all out of books, I got it all off a screen, I got it all off the radio, I got it all off other people and put it all together.'

I asked him to look into the future, and wondered whether there was ever going to be a David Lee Roth that could be a quiet, family man with a wife and kids, etc?

For once he didn't laugh. 'I surprise people a lot in that I actually spend most of my time by myself. I lived with a girlfriend for a couple of years, but we broke up about a year and a half ago. Before that I lived by myself for twelve years. And I do again now. And this is . . . how I'm happiest.'

Hence, he said, his passion for climbing mountains and going on jungle expeditions, something he'd been doing since Van Halen days.

'This is all introspective stuff, and I brood. A lot of times people are very surprised if they run into me on the streets. It can be very different from what they expect me to be like in public, or on a stage. I can be the most outgoing, public person in the world or I can be the most private dude you've ever come across. And I like both extremes.'

Could he adopt the Diamond Dave persona at the drop of a hat, when he wanted to, like Marilyn Monroe was said to be able to do?

'It depends. I mean, I know how to misbehave right on cue! That's the trooper part of it. But, luckily, I've managed to work most of my reality directly into the music, directly into the show, and for the people out there who are familiar with what I've been doing over the years, they know it's never been just one face I've worn, one approach.'

Even after we finally got back to the hotel he wanted to continue the conversation, trying to persuade me to come back to his suite for 'a nightcap'. I couldn't, though. By then, my night had been capped so heavily I thought it was stuck tight for ever.

Also, I was afraid. I'd been told on the quiet that Dave was gay, or at least bisexual. That he had recently begun picking up young guys on the road. That no one was safe. It sounded like the typical bullshit people say about rock stars – particularly infamous chick-magnets like Roth – to somehow get back at them, to drag them down in the surest way they know how. It also sounded like it could be true, at least to me. Either way, I wasn't taking any chances. If things had gone queer-shaped in his suite he'd have thrown me over his shoulders like a rag doll and there would have been nothing my skinny little English bod could have done about it, other than squeal like a stuck pig. Which might have just made him even happier.

I woke up later that day with what felt like an elephant shitting on my head – 'No wonder,' I thought, 'the rest of Van Halen were so happy to settle for the more down to earth Sammy Hagar.' After so long being caught in the razzed-up comet trail of Diamond Dave, Hagar offered a new, earthbound security. Suddenly, everybody in the band, especially Eddie, knew what was going on, not just pretending to so as not to seem dumb.

Sammy didn't have the razzle-dazzle of Diamond Dave in his heyday but at least he was more nearly normal. No one could keep up with David Lee Roth. In the end, not even Roth, whose solo career would stutter to a halt amidst band defections – notably that of Vai, who fled for the more staid Whitesnake – and the hair-metal-cutting arrival of grunge.

For a time, whenever Dave came to London I would get a call asking me to procure him some dope. Overused to sticky green California weed, he liked to get off on the big black lumps of hash then regularly on the dealer's menu in London. I would score him an ounce, maybe, then drift over to his hotel, where his 'guy' would meet me in reception, taking the gear off me and taking it up in the elevator to Dave. I was never invited up to share a smoke. Instead, I would be left in the bar, drinking alone or with one of Dave's 'people', waiting for the Rock God to eventually appear in full night-out regalia. The last time this happened we ended up all going out to Peter Stringfellow's club, where we were given a half-moon table right near the action, the dancing girls all over us. Stringfellow gave the DJ the nod and he spun 'Jump', which cleared about half the dance floor, until someone realised David Lee Roth was actually on it, dancing to his only real British hit.

I eventually got the message and said my goodnights. Caught a cab home. And wondered about the next time. Until one day there wasn't any next time.

The last time I really saw Dave was in 1990, when he was swanning around at a video shoot for The Black Crowes, who Dave's manager, Pete Angelus, had just taken on. The Crowes weren't famous yet, this was a video for their first single, 'Jealous Again', which would not be a hit. But someone at the label had pressed the button and they were being given the big budget treatment. Talking to them in the dressing room halfway through, I expected them to be grateful for all the high-level help they were getting so early in their career. But the brothers Robinson – singer Chris and guitarist Rich – who ran the group were seething with rage.

'I know he's supposed to be some big star,' said Chris, referring to Roth. 'But Van Halen didn't mean shit to me when I was growing up. I was more into the Stones and Muddy Waters.'

'Besides,' said Rich, 'his time's gone. It's our time now, he needs to get the fuck out of the way.'

When a few minutes later I heard them raging behind closed doors to Pete about getting rid of Dave, it was embarrassing. For all of us who stood there trying not to overhear, but most of all for Diamond Dave, whose shine had dimmed to almost nothing by the time Pete was forced to take him quietly to one side and tell him his presence would not be required for the remainder of the shoot.

I don't know what happened next. I didn't want to know. Stars like David Lee Roth aren't meant to become lost in space, growing dimmer by the day. That's one spectacle no one wants to behold.

15. **Out of Tune**

After the *Monsters of Rock* show finished on Sky in the summer of 1988, it took me a while to realise it was really over. Every summer for the past three years I'd been told the show would not be coming back after its annual fortnight's break – but every year it did. The money never changed, though – £100 per show, no repeat fees – and the contract they had always talked about offering me never materialised. But I had never cared. It was always just a lark that would end some day, no biggie.

When, finally, it did finish – in anticipation of the launch of Sky's new affordable satellite dish, and the arrival with it of twenty-four-hour MTV, thus negating the need for the channel to keep on making its own music programming – I was so busy working on other stuff that I brushed it off. The time had gone, the song was over – didn't think I had much more to say.

It wasn't until years later that it hit me what an opportunity I had missed. At the time of the show's ending, I was being approached by potential managers who told me what a 'natural' I was in front of the camera and how I should seriously think about 'branching out' into a broader chat-show format. But I just took it for granted and never followed up on any of the calls. There was also talk of a sitcom, pitched somewhere between *Morecombe and Wise* and *The Young Ones*. But I was in a black mood at the lunch to discuss it with the producers and sat yawning at all their ideas. There were promoters here and abroad that offered me live shows, big wads of cash in hand, but I couldn't grasp what it was I would do, other than pitch up and spin a few records. Surely people wouldn't pay money just to see someone they had heard of do that? The era of the star club DJ had already begun, but not in rock, and I just couldn't picture it.

The new London-based MTV also came a-calling, but when they asked me to audition I reminded them of the hundreds of hours of tape I had accumulated from the *Monsters* show, and pointed to the five thousand letters of complaint that came in when the show was cancelled. Basically, I told them to go fuck themselves if they thought, I, the great Mick Wall, would stoop to an audition. So they did.

Instead, my head was now in LA, where I'd been invited to front the launch of what was billed at the time as the world's first video-magazine, *Hard 'N' Heavy*. It was essentially an extended roadshow version of the *Monsters* programme but shot mainly in America, and the pay was ten times what I'd been earning at Sky. I was also now writing for a few of the American rock mags, had my own US bank account and social security number, and soon my own room with a view. I was *glad* the *Monsters* show had ended. That's what I told myself. I'd had *enough* of London. I wanted to live under that big-illuminated sign on the hill of dreams that spelled H-O-L-L-Y-W-O-O-D. Right beneath that big wonky 'H' . . .

My head was so over the hills and far away that when the *Daily Mail*, then the biggest-paying newspaper in Britain, asked if I'd be interested in writing their TV column, I actually found myself explaining that I didn't know much about TV. Sitting here writing this now, I still shake my head in wonder at that.

Here I was, having just spent the past few years presenting and helping produce my own weekly TV show, telling a newspaper that I didn't know much about how any of it worked. Didn't feel qualified to comment.

I was on the road to nowhere, a place I clearly felt more comfortable in than most.

I was about to make the move to LA a permanent thing when something came up that did appeal to me: my own weekly show on Capital Radio. I'd come of age, musically, with Capital, which had launched as London's first commercial music station in the mid-seventies. It was much groovier than Radio 1, in those early years; where the BBC led with nauseous windbags like Tony Blackburn, Dave Lee Travis and 'Diddy' David Hamilton, Capital brought us Kenny Everett doing the breakfast show, supercool Roger Scott in the afternoon, and at night that dandy of the underground 'Little' Nicky Horne and his 'progressive' rock show, *Your Mother Wouldn't Like It*.

As a teenager I had identified with Capital. In the staid, culturally barren environs of mid-seventies London suburbia, an American-style radio station with commercials was a great novelty. It sounded excitingly *young* at a time when the BBC sounded so repulsively *old*.

Over the years there had been a great deal of toing and froing of DJs between Capital and Radio 1, to the point where, by the end of the eighties, there was little to choose between them during the day. But at night Capital still kept its edge, with specialist music shows from David Rodigan (reggae), Charlie Gillett (world music), Peter Young (soul), Tim Westwood (hip hop), Alex George (jazz) and, until 1988, Alan 'Fluff' Freeman doing his exalted rock show. When Fluff was enticed back to Radio 1 that year it left a vacancy for a rock presenter at Capital.

Tipped off by an old pal at Sky, I sent in a letter and a video show reel. Imagining they would be inundated with applications for the gig, I hardly expected to hear back. But when the producer of Fluff's old show phoned and invited me in for 'a chat', I was in. I knew it before I'd even put down the phone. I saw myself as the natural choice, the heir apparent to old fogeys like Fluff; I saw myself building a career at Capital and felt like I'd just been offered a pension. Unlike TV, you could grow old disgracefully on radio. It didn't matter what you looked like, and you didn't depend on a roomful of technicians and producers to get your act up and running. You just turned up in a T-shirt with beer stains down it, fag ash in your hair, coughing and spitting and growling into the mic about whatever cool record you were spinning. And they would actually *pay* you for it. What a doddle!

That was how I imagined it anyway, until I got there.

The producer made it clear from the start that there was very little overlap between TV and radio presenting; least of all the way Capital DJs did things – what they called 'self-op'. Meaning you were on your own during a live show, no engineers, no producers, certainly no production assistants. Just you. These days, where everything in radio, as elsewhere, is run on computer, that's less tricky than it sounds. Simply a question of 'opening' the mic when you speak, pushing a fader up, and hitting the 'enter' button when you want to play the next track, with everything – music, ads, promos, news – already pre-set onscreen.

Back then it felt like trying to operate Doctor Who's Tardis. Although most of the tracks were now played on CD, a great many were still played on vinyl. This meant flitting about between two CD players, which may or may not work every time, and two record players, remembering to switch between 45 rpm and 33⅓ rpm depending on whether you were playing a single or a long player.

There was also the question of all the other stuff: mainly, the tape cartridges you had to load into a machine that contained the various ads that were to be played throughout the show. Plus, a vast selection of carts that I learned were called 'beds'. The beds were sections of music the producer had lifted from various records, lasting anything from 20 seconds to 90 seconds, over which I would do my 'speech' – the inane DJ natter expected of a top Capital Radio pro between records.

In order to learn how to do all this without disruption I would have to go through weeks of 'learning to drive the desk'. Which is exactly what it felt like: learning to drive a potentially dangerous vehicle. You'd dare not make a mistake. Not if you wanted to survive longer than your six-month contract, the standard issue for all 'specialist' DJs, as I discovered I was now categorised as.

Because of Capital's 'hot seat' policy of one studio, one desk, one DJ chair, which the DJs would jump in and out of between shows – hence the weird reality of the seat actually never going cold – you would never know if you'd actually mastered the ability to self-op your own show, until the big day arrived when you finally went live on air. So, a long, tense few weeks were spent sitting mostly alone in a small off-piste production room, pretending to do a show. Tapes of which would then be sent to the production team for analysis. Christ.

The switch from standing up before a two-camera film crew, with sound, make-up, lighting, and various production assistants and guests crowded into the studio with me, looking on as I performed my antics, lots of stifled guffaws and backslapping between takes, to suddenly finding myself sitting alone, talking bollocks to myself in a small, smoky room, trying to crack wise while at the same time finding something new to say about why I was playing 'Stairway To Heaven' or 'The Boys Are Back In Town' was an excruciating experience. Suddenly I had new respect for the gobshites who did this sort of thing for a living five days a week on daytime national radio. Suddenly I understood why Tony Blackburn always sounded like his arse was knotted so tight he could barely get the words out. Conversely, listening to someone like John Peel became equally unbearable – he was so laidback and in command, having mastered the dark art of sounding as though he really was in the room with you just chatting, I grew to hate the bastard. How did he do it? What was his trick?

It was the beginning of a year in which I grew steadily to hate the idea of having my own show on Capital. Nothing really felt like me. Nothing really felt under my control, not nearly enough, and I realised that far from finding it just an easy extension of what I had learned to do so easily on TV, this was a far more difficult, largely joyless task.

When we did finally 'go live', there was further frustration. Fluff's old show had been on Sunday afternoons. My replacement show would air as late as possible on Saturdays – midnight till 2 a.m. Sunday. It meant I had all day and night each Saturday to wind myself up to do the show. So no drinking, no dope-smoking, no going out and enjoying myself; no nothing, except sitting around for hours waiting to get to the studio.

I would arrive at around 10.15 p.m., go into the production office I shared with Charlie Gillett, make sure I had all the records and CDs I needed, along with the box of twenty-four beds, check the 'script' – the running order, with tracks, ads, promos, everything laid out on it, timed to the second – then, with about ten minutes to go until show time, I would find myself lurching to the men's loos to have a shit. Not just any shit either. This was a big, brown, smelly breakfast shit. I never went like that at night. Rarely even in the mornings. But now it would happen, just like that, every Saturday night at the same time, a few minutes before midnight. I had never realised they were being so literal when people talked about 'shitting it' or 'shitting bricks'. It could and did actually happen. It did to me, anyway, so twisted up inside and freaked out was I about working my own live show every Saturday night on Capital.

I would arrive just as Tim Westwood and his ever-expanding 'crew' were leaving the studio. This was always especially hard to take, as Tim seemed to be having such a genuinely fine time, slapping down big platters of black plastic-like slices of pizza on a hot plate and rapping gleefully over the top in his contrived, Noo Yoik meets East Anglia, suppressed-posh accent, bringing in a seemingly endless stream of guest voices, male and female. They were predominantly black, garbed head to toe in bling, and it was like peeking through the soundproof glass and seeing the best party you would never be invited to going on each week – before it was my turn to take over and the vibe fell straight back down to lonely, fucked-up zero. They would all be laughing and smoking and teasing and pleasing as they walked out, then I would walk in with my tense, over-anxious, no-way-I-can-do-this vibe, and that's when I really knew I was no good at this. That it was all a big waste of time. That I didn't even *know* who I was supposed to be kidding any more.

For the first few months, I was so concentrated on trying to get the mechanics right, I scripted my links, right down to tough-to-remember lines like: 'And that was Metallica, and this is Guns N' Roses . . .' Proper DJs did not script their links. They might bring in notes, do some background prep, but their words would come straight off the top of their head. It might have been

90 per cent drivel, but it was unscripted drivel, and it made me feel even more of a fool knowing I couldn't manage even that.

One afternoon, they took me into the studio to sit quietly and watch David Jensen do his afternoon show, to see how a real pro went about his work. I'd never met David before but I'd been a follower since his days as Kid Jensen, presenting his own highly credible shows on Luxembourg then Radio 1. Seeing him in the hot seat, his fingers whirring around the faders, dropping in carts and fading the ads in and out while keeping up an endless stream of burbling chat was a good lesson. It confirmed everything I knew. This wasn't for me at all.

I kept plugging away, though, reducing the amount of scripted links little by little, but still struggling to say anything remotely interesting or, God forbid, amusing. Every time I thought I'd made progress, I'd get knocked back again. Once, convinced I had cracked it, I didn't bother to write a script – then ten minutes into the show lost my cool and had to write stuff spontaneously on the back of the production notes. The bosses would lecture me: 'We don't want a guy who just says, "And that was . . . and this is . . ." – you have to inject some personality into it.'

So I would write longer links. Then they would tell me, 'Stop gabbing so much. Keep your links to thirty seconds, no one's really listening at that time of night anyway.'

Ah, fuck.

One night I turned up and for some reason my key wouldn't open the locked production-office door. With minutes to go before the show was supposed to start, I didn't have my script, my running order, none of my records and CDs, none of my beds and carts . . . *dear God, what was I going to do?*

I tried phoning the producer. But it was late on Saturday night and he was out, and this was before most people had mobile phones. Fucking fuck, fuck! Then I found the home number for Richard Park, the programme controller, a preening, self-regarding legend-in-his-own-lunchtime who liked to feel he could put the fear of God into his producers and presenters. Park was a joke to me. A walking radio cliché, with his tight little moustache and stripy shirts with white collars. But I knew phoning him at this time of night on a Saturday was an especially wrong thing to do. I was so panicked, though, I was ready to try anything.

As predicted, he was not pleased to get my call.

'So what?' he snarled at my predicament. 'Just go into the library and pull out some Deep Purple records or something.'

'I can't do that!' I bleated, squeaking with farts. (I hadn't been to the toilet yet.)

'Why not?' he barked. 'You're a DJ, aren't you? Play some records!'

He hung up.

I stood there trembling, not knowing what to do.

'Can I help?' I nearly jumped out of my skin. That time of night, after the Westwood mob had taken off, there was barely anyone else in the building. Who was this?

'Clair!' I cried. 'What are you doing here?'

Clair was a blonde, very striking, very muscular young production assistant of about twenty-five, whom I had gotten to know slightly because we both belonged to the same fashionable Covent Garden gym. But where I used the gym a couple of times a week, max, mainly as a good way of recovering quickly from hangovers, Clair was the real deal: in there pumping iron four or five mornings a week, before she went to work at Capital. You could see it in her long tan, thoroughly ripped body.

'She fancies you,' someone had said one day.

I'd thought it possible – Clair was always finding ways of stopping and chatting with me – but had shuddered at the prospect of trying to have sex with such a woman. This was one super-fit young woman, able to snap wimps like me in half with just a flick of her thoroughly tan hair.

Now, though, she became my angel of mercy.

'I've been helping out at Capital Gold,' she said. 'Cataloguing interview tapes. What's the matter? You all right, babe?'

I hurriedly explained that no, I was not all right. Adding the bit about Richard Park telling me just to get on with it and play some records.

'Why not?' she chirped. 'I'll help you. Give me a list of the records you want and I'll get them from the library for you while you do your stuff, OK?'

Oh, Clair! How I loved you in that too grateful moment. I babbled some names at her – Zeppelin, Purple, Sabbath, Guns – then ran for the toilets.

It turned out to be one of the best shows I ever did. Unscripted, full of 'that was' and 'this is', but made so much easier by the fact I didn't have any beds to talk over, very few ads carts to fire-up, and just stuck to CDs of obvious rock hits. Clair kept coming back from the library with more and more, and by half-way through we were both sitting back laughing and joking.

It was such a change of mood from what had gone before, and so different to the high levels of anxiety that accompanied my so-called normal show, I became quite delirious. We were sitting so close our knees were touching. Then we both got up at the same time and found ourselves facing each so closely it was almost harder not to kiss.

And then things really did hot up.

The fever was suddenly upon us. She had on summer shorts, which quickly fell to the floor. I yanked open the belt to my jeans and they followed. We had a Genesis CD on and I reached over and pressed the 'continuous play' button. No interruptions.

Then, suddenly, she was leaning over the console, her back to me, her arse pushing on to my cock. No foreplay. She was already sopping wet and I was already very hard. As I rammed into her I could feel the taut muscles of her tight, tan arse flexing and giving, then tensing again, like rock, as I slammed harder and harder.

I had never fucked anyone so incredibly hard and muscly before. It was a whole new thing. No flab, no extra flesh, just rock hard buttocks and a grip on her pussy like claw.

'Harder!' she screamed. 'Harder, you fucker! Hurt me!'

I did my best, standing on tiptoes now as I held on for dear life. We were both now hollering. Only there were no words left. Just the piledriver rhythm of the music we were making together, like pistons pumping until finally, finally, we both exploded like stars. I couldn't stop coming, my cock twitching and spurting as I let it out, her hips rolling and jigging as she collapsed across the console gasping for breath.

I fell back on the chair, my hurting cock still sticking up. Lit a cigarette. Life being never less than utterly ridiculous, I noticed the Genesis track now playing was 'In Too Deep'. I didn't say anything, just waited it for it to finish while Clair cued up the next track, something by the Rolling Stones. Then I opened the mic: 'And that was a special triple-decker from Genesis. Hope you enjoyed it. I know I did. And this is the Stones. "Brown Sugar" . . . for Clair . . .'

There wasn't much to say after that. Clair left soon after. She never spoke to me again. I didn't know what that meant, if anything. I could just as easily say I never spoke to her again. The truth was we'd done all we were going to do – and now it was done what else was there to say?

I had one last surprise, though, when I got home that night. As a beginner, still trying to learn a few tricks, I would routinely record each show, on a cassette playing inside the studio as I did the show. Then when I got home, I would roll an especially fat one, crack open a beer and sit and listen to the show.

This one held a special interest for me, naturally. I listened rapt at my utter cool playing tracks that Clair had only just brought in, making with the easy links and cool mumblings.

When it got to the bit where we played three Genesis tracks in a row, I sat there smirking – then suddenly horrified as towards the end you could hear Clair's voice shrieking, 'Harder, you fucker! *Harder! HARDER!*' Against a backdrop of grunts and groans, like someone trying to shove a piano up some stairs.

Jesus! We must have pulled down one of the faders while we were doing it. Then suddenly it was back to the music, Phil Collins crooning about 'playing for keeps' and being 'in too deep'. Then, just as I hoped we'd gotten away with it, my voice, unmistakable in its dishevelled glee, 'God that was so *fucking good . . .*'

Oh shit. I waited for Monday morning to come around and the phone to ring. It seemed obvious to me what would happen. The sack, surely. A horribly embarrassing scene, at the very least. I tried to prepare myself, have something plausible to say, but what? 'See, I was all sweaty and panicky and Clair was there and helped me and I was so grateful I just had to fuck her from behind, you know?'

But in the end . . . nothing. No phone call. No tittering the next time I went into the office. No nothing. And then it hit me. No one at the station ever actually listened to the show. Certainly not to the music, that's for sure. Least of all three Genesis tracks played back-to-back at 1.30 in the morning.

I had escaped. But into what? More late-night, early-hours shows no one listened to? I gave up scripting anything after that. I stopped having to run to the toilet before a show. Not long after that I stopped bothering to tape the shows too. They all sounded the same anyhow – better than before but of a piece, a sameness, like trees falling in a forest not even Buddha knows exists.

Then one Monday morning Richard Park's secretary phoned and asked me to come in later that day for a meeting with Richard.

'What's it about?'

'Oh, nothing. He just wants to talk to you about something.'

'At last,' I thought. 'Here it comes.'

When I got there I had to wait while Peter Young had a meeting with Park. Typically, Richard had a glass wall to his office so you could see in and out. I finally got an inkling of what was in store as I watched the stiff back of Peter Young, sitting there smoking and nodding his head while Park talked and talked, pacing around his office like a king in his throne room.

When Peter was finally let out, his face was pale. A generally jolly chap who could always be relied on for a choice word or two of inter-office banter, he looked right through me as I passed him on my way in.

I sat down and lit a cigarette of my own, and waited. It came. Change of programming policy . . . such a shame after the great start I'd made . . . advertisers so much more demanding now . . . bollock, bollock, fuck, fuck . . .

He concluded with a smile so thin you could count his teeth: 'I'm sure this will have been a great experience for you, that you will be able to carry forward in whatever you do next in radio.'

He offered me his hand. I took it. Limp. Like shaking someone's dick.

I found out later they called it the night of the short knives: Richard deciding to axe the specialist shows, in favour of round-the-clock Kylie and Madonna. There was bucks in them schmucks and, who knows, if I'd been him, a moneyed-up company man to the grave, I'd maybe have done the same.

Maybe.

16. Guns N' Fuckin' Roses

The first time I met Guns N' Roses was in Manchester, in October 1987, headlining a half-empty show at the Apollo. The *Appetite for Destruction* album had been released a couple of months before but, despite good reviews, sales had been slow due to an almost total lack of airplay. In America it looked like it was already dead in the water. In Britain, though, with its easier-to-access music press and smaller, easier-to-impress rock audience, the feeling was they still stood a chance. They had been over for some Marquee shows in the summer and the press had fallen over itself to get in on the action.

Now they were back for five shows at theatres, most of them, like the Apollo, with the balconies closed off. Axl was swaying like a cobra, the charismatic ringmaster. To his right Duff; a tall, bottle-blond whose clean-cut good looks belied his Seattle punk roots. To Axl's left, Slash, one boot resting on a monitor, firing off riffs with the gleeful abandon of a man pissing his name into the snow. Behind them, sweating and shirtless, Steven, Cleveland-born, but straight out of sunny, smog-assed California; the quintessential blonde himbo who likes to 'hit things and get high'. And then – last, as always, but not least – Izzy, who never really found a permanent place for himself on stage, ghosting around at the sides and the back, scaring away crows.

Together they were way more 'street' than current rock pin-ups like Bon Jovi and Def Leppard; yet not so extreme they frightened off the girlies, the way Motörhead and Metallica did. In fact, apart from the big hair, they bore no relation whatsoever to the more nonsensical forms rock had twisted itself into by the late eighties. There were no dungeons or dragons, no armies of marching men in their songs. In their place staggered junkies and sluts ('Mr Brownstone', 'Rocket Queen'), thieves and outcasts ('Welcome To The Jungle', 'My Michelle') – 'motherfuckers', one and all.

Even more intriguing, there were also tales of loved ones and lost dreams buried in that dark, chaotic set. 'Paradise City', with its chiming riff and adolescent yearning for a place where the *grass is green and the girls are pretty*' was instantly appealing, right up there with 'All Right Now' and 'Brown Sugar' as one of rock's most uplifting anthems. 'Sweet Child O' Mine' also suggested a submerged vulnerability not immediately obvious elsewhere: '*Her hair reminds me of a warm safe place / Where as a child I'd hide,*' intoned Axl.

It was this, more transcendent aspect to their music, which would enable Guns N' Roses to rise above the LA scene. Just as Nirvana would do four years later, Guns N' Roses eschewed contemporary musical mores in favour of what they saw as a more meaningful seventies mien; taking their inspiration as much from Bob Dylan and Elton John as they did from Led Zeppelin and the Stones.

'We didn't have any defined goals,' Slash explained. 'We just didn't want to be lumped in with the LA scene. We were the decadent seventies shit.'

Which is why, for example, in an era when most bands stuck out half-a-dozen formats of the same single in order to soak a baffled fan-base and jumpstart the charts, the first Guns N' Roses single, 'It's So Easy', was so spattered with fucks their own record company discouraged radio stations from playing it. It was a statement that said: this band is different. And 'different' was a quality in despairingly short supply right then.

Post-AIDS, post-Reagan, third-term Thatcher, rock had become a shiny, happy, big-haired thing that no longer needed drug dealers and groupies to sustain it. Stars like Jon Bon Jovi, Def Leppard's Joe Elliott, and even that notorious ladeez man David 'Whitesnake' Coverdale, were all married and drinking mineral water. Jon Bon Jovi was still claiming he'd never even *tried* drugs; most bands avoided the subject completely, whatever the reality behind the scenes. Instead, they were all now into working out (and cosmetic surgery, liposuction and hair-weaves). Marketing was more important than A&R; videos more 'market penetrative' than tours. Frankly, the whole thing bored me to shitting tears. I had not begun writing about rock to find myself discussing demographics with people too uptight to even take a drink.

Then came Guns N' Roses, moving towards you like a stinking wind. You might not like that smell but you couldn't deny it was the real thing, or whatever the realest thing now was. Standing in the dressing room after the Manchester show, it seemed like the clock had been turned back fifteen years. It wasn't just the way they dressed – the hats, bandanas and button-less shirts; the scuffed leather jackets, skull-and-crossbones tattoos and lurid, rock-crucifixion jewellery – it was the way they *were*.

'Hey, man,' said Steven, spying strangers. 'Where can I score some 'loods?' referring to Quaaludes, the drugs *du jour* for early-seventies American concertgoers; heavy-duty tranquillisers that made walking into walls seem fun.

'You can't get loods in England,' I replied.

'What!' he cried. 'You're fuckin' kidding me! What *can* you get, then?'

'Mandrax,' I said. 'Mandies. Or reds – Seconal. That's probably the nearest equivalent.'

'Cool,' he said. 'So how can I get me some red Mandies, dude?'

The guy was clearly on a mission. Then Izzy ambled over. 'Hey, man,' he drawled. 'I smell pot. Who has pot?' Someone passed him the joint and he clung to it like a drunk steadying himself against a lamppost. I turned to speak to Slash, the only one I'd actually been introduced to. He looked like he'd just stepped off the album cover: black top hat pulled low over a waterfall of dark curls, deliberately obscuring his soft brown eyes; holding tight to a Jack Daniel's bottle like a toddler clinging to its teddy.

'I bet you go to bed with that thing,' I joked.

'Sure,' he said, 'I like to wake up to it, too. It's the only way,' he paused and glanced around, '. . . I can handle *this*.'

I was introduced to Axl as we passed on the stairs. Utterly unlike the manically pumped-up, backcombed banshee who had just bossed the stage, up close he looked surprisingly small; his pinched, freckled face and upturned nose giving him a vulnerable quality the stage lights had kept hidden. He avoided direct eye contact, glancing at you warily when he thought you weren't looking. It was hard to believe this was the guy who had just been arrested for attacking a security guard at a show in Atlanta; had launched into an onstage tirade at the Paradiso in Amsterdam, three nights before, inviting Paul Stanley – who had apparently accused Guns, somewhat ludicrously, of ripping off Kiss – to 'suck my dick!'; and who had ripped the phone out of the wall and thrown it at the hotel receptionist before the show in Nottingham the night before. Controversy was becoming part of the act, it seemed. Despite the bullshit, it was clear Guns had something. I decided to keep in touch.

Almost a year after its release, *Appetite* entered the US Top 10 for the first time, propelled by heavy rotation on MTV of the new 'Sweet Child O' Mine' video. Their two scheduled appearances opening for Iron Maiden at the 17,000-capacity Irvine Meadows arena in LA should have been a glorious homecoming. Instead, both appearances were cancelled when Axl succumbed to 'voice problems'. The rumour-mongers whispered that there was nothing wrong with his voice; Axl simply resented opening for a band in LA he now considered smaller than Guns N' Roses.

Whatever the truth, the sudden break left Slash kicking his heels that weekend. Staying at the Hyatt House on Sunset, under the name Mr Disorderly, he invited me to join him on the Saturday. I arrived just as he was saying goodbye to his father, Tony Hudson. A well-dressed, soft-spoken Englishman who looked nothing like his son, Tony had been a successful album-sleeve designer in the seventies (check out Joni Mitchell's *Court and Spark*) who knew enough about the music business to be concerned about his son's impending elevation to its giddiest heights.

'He was telling me to keep my feet on the ground and stuff,' Slash said, as we crossed to the bar. 'I told him, I'm cool. I know what it's all about. I mean, look at me. T-shirt, jeans, boots, that's me, man. That's all there is. Besides,' he added, 'we haven't had any money yet. We just get these phone calls – yesterday it was 35,000 sales, today it's 91,000 sales. It freaks my ass out.'

He was, he said, most excited about the *next* album. The new songs would be 'even more angry and anti-radio' than on *Appetite*. 'To prove there's more to us than those bands whose roots go back, like, three years. The ones who bought the clothes first.'

The more I got to know him, the more I realised it was true: Slash really did belong to the seventies, back when it was normal for the lead guitarist in the world's biggest band to ride around in limos, out of their heads on cocaine and heroin, fucking honey-hipped teenage groupies. Instead, born fifteen years too late, he'd had to make do.

The first thing he said to me on the street outside the hotel was, 'Hey, man, I'm kinda trashed. I just smoked a foil.' A 'foil', in rock parlance, meaning he had just smoked some heroin.

'Oh,' I said, 'are you OK?'

'Yeah,' he drawled. 'Let's get a drink . . .'

I shrugged and eyed the already open bottle of Jack Daniel's he was carrying. It was midday. We made for the hotel poolside bar, where he ordered 'a large Jack Daniel's and a beer chaser' then took a hit from his own bottle while he waited.

We had just settled ourselves when half-a-dozen blonde girls in bikinis came running over. The oldest looked about seventeen.

'Oh, Slash!' she trilled. 'We love you!'

'Hey, baby,' said Slash grabbing her breasts and giving them a squeeze, 'I love you too.' She screamed with laughter, flung her arms around his neck and kissed him.

Later that day, we were sitting in the back of a limo on our way to a David Lee Roth show at the LA Forum. Joining us was a well-dressed woman writer from *Life* magazine.

'So, Slash,' she began, pen and notepad poised, 'what is it about Guns N' Roses that makes it different to other bands?'

'Shit,' said Slash, 'I guess we just fuckin' . . . you know . . . like . . . fuckin' . . .'

He took a long slow hit from a new bottle of Jack – he'd seen off the first one some time before – and stared out the window. The *Life* lady sat there writing it all down.

The limo pulled up at the gig and we all got out. Once again, a posse of teenaged beauties surrounded us. Slash hugged and kissed every single one of them – literally picking up one girl and swinging her around.

As we walked inside the venue, I asked him, 'Is it always like this for you?'

'Naw,' he shrugged, 'only every fuckin' day . . .'

It was that same quest for rock authenticity they all shared that led to incidents like Steven breaking his hand in a drunken barroom brawl when the band had opened for Mötley Crüe. Steven and Slash had also been involved when Nikki Sixx had OD'ed. Finding Nikki unconscious on the floor of his hotel room, the needle still sticking out of his arm, Slash said, 'Steven put him into the shower and I called the paramedics.' It was a close call: Nikki's heart had stopped beating at one point.

Then, in February 1988, halfway through their own West Coast tour, Axl walked out. Things had being going badly since he'd been arrested for trying to smuggle a Sten gun across the Canadian border. 'Axl was biting everybody's ass,' Slash said. Following another violent bust up at the hotel, Axl split. Meeting over. Three days later, though, he was back, after a lengthy heart-to-heart on the phone with Slash.

Acknowledging that part of the band's appeal laid in the notion that it might end tomorrow, Slash just shrugged. 'Actually, I'd rather it collapsed. I'd rather be as good as possible in the amount of time that you can do it, and do it to the hilt. Then fall apart, die, whatever . . .'

Three months later they were off the road, just as *Appetite* hit No. 1 in America. And that's when things went seriously fucking weird for all of them. The first Izzy knew about it was when he woke up hungover a year later in Phoenix county jail. His lawyer had to fill him in on the grisly details. He'd been arrested at Sky

Harbor airport the day before for 'making a public disturbance'
on a flight from LA – pissing in the aisle, telling a stewardess to
go fuck herself and smoking in the non-smoking section. The
charges were dismissed in a press statement simply as 'Izzy's way
of expressing himself' but the damage was done. With a 'prior'
for possession, Izzy was put on probation and ordered to seek
professional help, including weekly urine tests for a year.

'That was my wake-up call,' he told me. 'That was the point
where I said, "This has got to fuckin' stop." I didn't wanna wind
up dead or, worse, in prison.'

It wasn't easy. 'I'd been straight for a long time before some of
the others even noticed. They'd offer me a line. I'd say, "Uh, no
thanks, I don't any more, remember?" But these were, like, the
only friends I had. Those first five years we were together, the
band was like our little family. Dysfunctional as hell but everybody had each other, you know?'

Slash's turning point – in terms of smack – came just a few
months later and, bizarrely, also involved a strange trip to Phoenix. Slash had followed the band's tour manager Doug Goldstein
to an exclusive luxury resort where he was vacationing. 'This
was when I was in my worst drug period – and actually what
ended up getting me to clean up,' he explained. Doug was getting in another round of golf when suddenly a squad car full of
cops showed up. 'We've got a naked guy in handcuffs,' they told
him, meaning Slash. 'He assaulted a maid.'

'I'd smashed up my room,' Slash explained. 'There was glass,
I was all bloody. I'd showed up in Phoenix the night before. I'd
done all [my drugs] and mentally had a trip-out scene. I took
off running naked out of the shower – went through the glass
shower windows. Ran out naked into the resort, into one of
the rooms, ran over this maid and kept running. It was a big
scene.'

Narrowly avoiding arrest, he flew back to LA and checked into a hotel. 'I passed out and woke up to what they call an "intervention". I ended up going for the first and only time to rehab, which lasted for all of about three days. I said, "I'm not *that* fucked up." So I got out and took myself to Hawaii – on my own this time – and dried out. I've never had that serious a problem since then.'

For me the weirdness only really began in earnest six months later. In the time I'd known them I'd abandoned London to become a *habitué* of the LA scene. While the immediate after-effects of their success had appeared to all but crush Izzy and Steven, Slash and Duff, at least whenever I ran into them, still looked like they were having a so-called good time. Axl, meanwhile, hadn't changed so much as been let loose. With the means to now do as he pleased, that was exactly what he appeared to be doing. None more so than on this particular evening, sparking the incident which would lead to him later exhorting me by name to 'Suck my fuckin' dick!' on one of the most vitriolic songs ever spat out, 'Get In The Ring' from *Use Your Illusion II*.

The whole thing hinged on an interview I had done with Axl at his surprisingly modest LA apartment late one night in January 1990. It was around midnight when he phoned, raging about something he'd just read in *Kerrang!*. He wanted me to go straight to his apartment to talk about it – on the record. I threw on some clothes and jumped in the car: twenty minutes later I was outside his West Hollywood apartment.

I pressed the doorbell. When he answered it he nearly yanked the door off its hinges then stormed off down the corridor. I followed him into the lounge and tried to say hello but he was already in full flow. Standing there in crumpled T-shirt and jeans, a big red beard covering most of his tiny freckled face, raging about Mötley Crüe singer Vince Neil, who had been 'saying some shit' in the press – specifically, Vince's claim to have punched-out Izzy for 'messing' with his wife, a former mud-wrestler from the Tropicana. Axl said this was 'bullshit'. And now Vince must pay.

'Guns or knives, motherfucker,' Axl snarled. 'I don't care. I just wanna smash his plastic face.' This last was a sarcastic reference to Vince's then recent, supposedly hush-hush, cosmetic surgery.

Axl ranted on about Vince for another half hour or so then settled down long enough for us to tape a longer interview. When that was finished, I set up a different tape-recorder and we did something for my Capital Radio show. When it was over we shook hands and said goodbye.

Behind the couch on which he sat, hunched up over his Coke can and cigarettes, was a huge bay window, through which you could see the flickering lights of LA. Before us sat a rather grand-looking marble coffee table. He ran his hand over it lovingly. 'Third one I've had,' he said. Oh? What happened to the other two? 'I smashed 'em.' Oh . . .

The first hint of trouble I had was after the story ran a few weeks later and the band's PR phoned to ask for a copy of the tape so they could run it in the States on a special Guns N' Roses phone-line. My suspicions immediately aroused – of all the interviews I had done with Guns N' Roses, why would they want to run that one? – I asked for the number of this 'special phone-line'. That's when the back-pedalling began. She said she'd get back to me. (There was no phone-line.)

She did get back, a few days later. This time, though, the approach was more direct. Axl would 'really like' a copy of the tape, she said, because – well, how could she put this – 'He doesn't think he really speaks that way.' What? 'You know, that he would . . . say . . . those things.'

I still didn't quite get it. 'Axl doesn't believe he *said* those things?' I laughed. 'What does he think happened then? I made them up?'

Silence as the awful truth started to dawn.

'But I even checked with him first!' I cried, suddenly recalling how I had done just that. Worried by how harsh his statements concerning Vince had looked on the page, I had spoken to Axl on the phone and read him what I had, just to see if he still wanted to go through with it. I still recall his defiant laughter. 'I stand by every fuckin' word, man!'

'Yes,' she said, 'I know. But if you could just send him the tape . . .'

'No,' I said. If Axl wanted to call me and talk about it, that was fine. But I wasn't sending any tapes. What for? To prove I wasn't *lying*? After all we'd been through? How dare he! I slammed down the phone.

To be called a liar was bad enough. To be branded a liar by the person whose 'truth' it is you have been trusted to convey was almost unbearable. Was this actually happening?

I've now lost count of the times I've been asked over the years how my name ended up in 'Get In The Ring'. I never know what to say. Just like all the email and letter haters – long, fuck-spattered screeds in angry Caps Lock or handwritten red ink that I still, rather astonishingly, occasionally get today, a quarter of a century since the song first appeared – most people have already made up their minds. It was obvious: somewhere down the line I had upset The Man and fucked-up my LA privileges. All the proof anyone needed was contained in that part of the song where Axl claimed I and three others – Bob Guccione Jr of *Spin*, Andy Secher of *Hit Parader* and some unnamed hack at *Circus* magazine – were guilty of *'Rippin' off the fuckin' kids . . . Printing lies/Starting controversy . . .'* Crimes for which we were invited to *'Suck my fuckin' dick!'*

Did we deliberately 'print lies'? Well, I can't speak for the others, but I certainly never set out to do anything except tell the story of Guns N' Roses as it unfolded around me. The band fights, the drugs problems, the model girlfriends and estranged wives, the cancelled shows and bloody riots, the two dead fans, trampled to death in the mud at Donington in 1988. What was there left to make up? You had to work fast just trying to write it all down.

Couldn't I have cleared the whole thing up, though, by simply sending him the damn tape? Maybe. But this was LA, at the height of its heavy metal insanity, and Axl was then the craziest – not to mention, richest – lunatic roaming the asylum. By then the whole band was out of control: Slash, Izzy and Steven were all deeply into cocaine, heroin and anything else they could get their shaky hands on, while Duff's marriage break-up had precipitated his own slide into drug-and-alcohol-induced hell.

There was more ailing Axl, though, than the usual nasty habits. Axl was the sort of guy who believed in conspiracy theories, talked of seeing UFOs and took it as read that everyone was out to get him. The sort of guy who liked to handle weapons; posing on the cover of a magazine with his sawn-off shotgun. The sort of guy who would complain of suffering a 'chemical imbalance in the brain' one moment, then boast of 'long weekends' on smack the next. The sort of guy who continually threatened to quit not just the band but 'the whole fuckin' business' if he didn't get his own way. The sort of guy who, in short, you wouldn't put anything past, and though it sounds absurd now, I actually feared he might try to doctor the tape in some way. How else could he prove he was right, because it was all there?

Over the next few months, however, it all appeared to die down and I did my best to forget about it. Then, almost exactly a year later, I had my next – and last – meeting with Axl, and I realised this was never going to go away.

By coincidence, we were both staying at the Sunset Marquis. He must have seen me check-in because within moments of getting to my room he was on the phone. 'We need to talk,' he said. I had just got off a twelve-hour flight from London and was still horribly jetlagged but, at his insistence, I agreed to meet him in the hotel bar. When I got there he was accompanied by three of his entourage: Del James, Axl's half-brother Stuart, and another kid I didn't recognise. They eyed me sternly as I sat down. Then it began.

'I heard you're writing a book,' said Axl, sitting next to me but speaking in profile, his eyes staring down at the table.

It was true. What of it?

'I heard it was a book about Guns N' Roses,' he continued.

True, too. An enlarged collection of my various features on the band. In other words, nothing they hadn't already read before.

'I don't care what it is,' snapped Axl. 'I don't care if it says we're the greatest band in the world, or if it's just a bunch of old shit – if it has our name on it, I will track you down . . . and I will kill you.'

I stared at the side of his head. At which point Del waded in with some story about some other dude who had once 'crossed' them. I don't recall what happened to him – Del was always a terrible storyteller and my mind was too busy reeling from what Axl had just said – but I got the picture.

I sat there, wondering how best to respond. What was my crime anyway? Re-publishing old stories? Then it hit me: Vince. Was there something he would rather I didn't reprint in the book, I asked?

Now he did look at me. 'I don't give a fuck what it says or

doesn't say,' he scowled. 'I just don't wanna see any book by you with our name on it – or else.'

'All right,' I said.

'All right,' he said. Then they all got up to leave.

I admit, I was rattled. My first reaction was to cancel the book. Then I got over the jetlag and the righteous anger kicked-in. I spoke with a lawyer friend who told me what Axl had done was not only insulting but illegal, and offered to take action against him. I decided against that but did decide to go ahead with the book. By then it was clear Axl's bark was worse than his bite. Just a few nights later, he had already changed his mind about what he was going to do to me.

He rang at about 2 a.m. As if bringing the whole sorry saga full-circle, he said he'd just been reading 'some shit' I'd written in *Kerrang!* about the band's appearance a few weeks before at the Rock In Rio II festival in Brazil, where I had disparaged them for preventing support band Judas Priest from using their pyrotechnics; for forcing journalists and photographers to sign prohibitive contracts; and for surrounding themselves with bodyguards and generally forfeiting the down-to-earth, open-door policy that had won them countless friends in the early days – replacing it with an increasingly isolationist approach that alienated old faces and generated new enemies. Mine was hardly the only report from the festival that highlighted such deficiencies. Nevertheless, it was me that Axl chose to take umbrage with personally.

'I've just got one thing to say to you,' he said. 'See you in court!' Then he hung up, presumably with a slam. Needless to say, I never heard any more about it. Or rather, I did but in a quite different courtroom: that of a song.

I first heard about 'Get In The Ring' when Duff – who wrote the original version – told me about it excitedly at a Christmas party in 1989. Originally called 'Why Do You Look At Me When You Hate Me?', it was the Sid Vicious-worshipping, Seattle punk, Duff, who was to have sung it. He gave me a drunken verse or two and it sounded like a bad impression of Sid doing 'My Way'. When, a year later, Axl's bonnet was buzzing with so many bees he co-opted the song for his own purposes and re-titled it 'Get In The Ring', I'm told Duff was not exactly thrilled; his big solo moment gone.

Because my book, *The Most Dangerous Band in the World*, was published around the same time as *Use Your Illusion II*, it has always been assumed that the song was in direct response to it. Not so. While Axl was doubtless aggrieved to find me publishing a book he had every reason to believe he'd frightened me out of doing, it's pretty clear now that the crux of the matter comes back to that ill-starred interview he gave about how he was going to 'kill' Vince Neil.

But then, as so many others and I were to discover, push the right buttons and Axl was ready to 'kill' anyone: me, Vince, his wife Erin (who quickly divorced him), eventually even his own band, all of whom would be gone within the next four years, leaving Axl to soldier on with an endless parade of trumped-up session men, maintaining the Guns N' Roses legend in name only. Or, as the man said, printing lies, starting controversy . . .

As the years zipped by, and everybody cleaned up their acts, I became reacquainted with all the other members of Guns N' Roses, most especially Slash, who remains a pal and someone I work with from time to time, to this day. But Slash gave up talking much about Axl, having been asked to explain the unexplainable too many times, referring only to 'the old band' when he had to. It is no secret that they would all happily reunite with Axl behind a reformed 'classic' line-up of Guns N' Roses, but only on condition that Axl come down from his ivory tower

long enough to actually turn up on time and do the work –
which practically guarantees it will never happen.

'At some point,' Slash told me, 'I just lost Axl. Everything was
so out of control, then suddenly we came home and everything
just kinda . . . stopped.'

At that point, Guns N' Roses album sales stood in excess of
35 million in the US alone. A million more than Bob Dylan had
sold in his entire career. Even Zeppelin had taken four albums
to reach that sort of plateau. For the Guns N' Roses guys it had
all happened with just one record. Little wonder they had such
trouble hanging on to themselves.

It would be fifteen years before Axl finally came back with a
Guns N' Roses album all of his own – minus any of the other
original members – during which time the story of Guns N'
Roses had gone from being about one of the finest bands of their
generation to a weird tale of an angry guy living like a recluse
at the bottom of a well somewhere, issuing instructions to loyal
minions, some of whom now privately questioned his sanity.

Talking to Izzy, a decade after he'd been the first to bail out
in 1991, I asked for his take on why things panned out the way
they did. As the one who had known Axl since school, and had
been his only real friend in the band during those crazy years,
surely Izzy would be able to offer some insight?

He shrugged, smiled wearily. By the end of his time in Guns
N' Roses, he said, the band had 'become like the *Jerry Springer*
show. Everything was so magnified. Drug addictions, personali-
ties, just the craziness that was already there anyway.'

The reason he left, he said, was because 'I couldn't relate
to Axl any more'. Post-world domination, post-heroin, post-
everything, Axl had been transformed from the awkward,
'embarrassed', small-town hick with an 'authority problem' who
Izzy had befriended in their teens, into an increasingly blinkered

megalomaniac, issuing contracts for journalists and photographers to sign. He even started to thrust bits of paper in front of his own band.

'This is right before I left,' Izzy told me. 'Demoting me to some lower position [and] cutting my royalties down. I was like, "Fuck you! I'm not signing that. I helped start this band."'

The key to Axl's mania, Izzy thought, lay back in Lafayette, with a kid who 'got nothing but shit' and 'never got no pussy at school'. Now he had 'the chicks lined up, [he'd] got money, people . . . and the power went to this guy's head. He became a fuckin' monster! The control issues just got worse and worse!'

Izzy would return briefly, for five dates in Europe in 1993, including two nights at Milton Keynes Bowl, in May, after his replacement, Gilby Clarke, broke his wrist in a motorcycle accident. 'But Duff and these guys, man, they didn't even recognise me. It was really bizarre, like playing with zombies.'

When it was over he didn't even say goodbye. 'I thought, they don't even know I'm here, what's the point in telling 'em I'm leaving.'

As for my own failed relationship with Axl, it has become the most bizarre of my professional life. Any rock writer from the days when rock journalism still carried real heft (unlike now, where the Internet has cut out the need for middlemen communicators like *Kerrang!* and their ilk) ran the risk of offending the musicians they wrote about. Anyone who didn't wasn't really doing their job. And I have had 'run-ins' with a great many, but almost always we have patched up our differences to fight another day. (Axl wasn't even the first to put my name in a song, that dubious honour went to Gary Numan, in the title track to his 1979 album, *Replicas*, after I'd given a bad review to his previous album.)

With Axl, though, the situation has remained surprisingly toxic. When he arrived to tour the UK in the summer of 2006, I was warned by a still friendly face working for him that Axl had issued a list of names to security to watch out for every night of the tour, with my name top of it.

'So if I show up at the London show, for instance, and some eagle-eyed security guy "spots" me, what are they supposed to do?' I asked, mildly amused.

'Throw you out,' they said. 'I suppose . . .'

'You suppose?'

'Well, I assume that's all they would do. I suppose Axl might have given them different instructions.'

'Such as?'

'Well, you know . . .'

The irony is that I doubt Axl would even recognise me today. The further irony is that you couldn't drag me to a so-called Guns N' Roses concert these days. I admired the *Chinese Democracy* album 'they' finally released in 2008 – or the first Axl solo album, as it might more accurately be described – but not enough to want to see Axl faking his way around the stage with a bunch of hired hands. If Mick Jagger formed a group tomorrow with a bunch of session men and put it out as the Rolling Stones, would anyone buy into it?

An Axl Rose solo show – now that would really be something to see. He has the talent, he has the story, he has the personality. He really doesn't need to hide behind the sunglasses and big production any more. He should come out, show his audience what it really means to be bad-ass and brave, to be honest and human. To still be better than the rest.

If you're reading this, Axl – and I know you read almost everything written about you – what would really work too would be if we got together and did a Frost–Nixon and spent a few days filming a proper 'Get In The Ring'-style interview. Not in any real combative sense, though there would be that about it too, if you insisted. But something for the people to really enjoy and think about it. Something like an actual conversation between old friends/foes now old enough to supposedly know better. Come on, we've both lost our hair, we just have different ways of dealing with it.

Right, Axl?

17. My Friends Call Me Philip

An odd thing about becoming involved in the rock biz is how few of my former rock heroes I have actually gotten to work with over the years. I meet people these days in their twenties and thirties and they talk about Iron Maiden and Def Leppard, Guns N' Roses and Metallica the same way I once might have talked about David Bowie or Roxy Music. Yet for me the Maidens and Leppards, Roses and Tallicas meant nothing, as a fan. For a start I was older than all of them, or about the same age in the case of Iron Maiden. I'd even been in the business longer. There was no thrill in meeting them the way there was when I met Jimmy Page, or Ozzy Osbourne. Or, finally, David Bowie and Bryan Ferry.

Even then, by the time I got to meet those people I'd been around long enough to downplay it in my mind. It didn't trip me out. Not like the way it did when I got to know Phil Lynott and Thin Lizzy.

There had been the time with Pete Makowksi, when I was just eighteen and stood shyly behind him as he rapped with Phil, and was appalled when Johnny Rotten, whom I'd never heard of, came over and started moaning about being bored. I could not have guessed that a couple of years later I'd actually be working with some of these people.

'My friends call me Philip,' he had told me the first time we met, and of course I was deeply flattered that he might think of me in that way – though I never did hear anyone else call him Philip, not that I recall anyway.

We met because *Philip* was always coming to Wild Horses gigs. Robbo had still been in Lizzy when I'd first met him, now he was co-fronting Horses with Jimmy Bain, who were managed by the same Lizzy team.

Robbo was only a couple of years older than me and he was always delighted with my constant pestering for Thin Lizzy stories. It gave him a chance to relive recent glories. How Robbo had come up with the riff to 'Don't Believe A Word' but Phil had not credited him for it. How the Mafia ran the band's record company in America. How Phil had hit him in the face so hard one time he thought he'd never talk again – 'Fingers like fucking bananas!' Times he must have known that, even then, would probably never come round for him again.

As the band's PR, it would be my job to make sure Phil was made a fuss of whenever he showed up at the shows. But Phil could take care of himself. We were standing at the bar of a pub one night before a gig and he said to me, 'Look, you go over there and grab a table, give me a bit of room, awright?'

'Well, if you're sure . . .'

'I'll be fine, wait and see.' He winked at me.

I picked up our drinks and carried them over to the nearest table then sat and watched for whatever was supposed to happen next. As I sat down, I saw Phil stoop down, shoulders hunched, as though he was in pain. He pulled his jacket collar up, as if to shield from the wind. He spread his hands across the bar and lowered his head, as if deep in thought, and remained in that shape for a couple of minutes.

Then it happened. First one girl, then two then three, gently wafted over to stand either side of him, one with her hand placed on his back, as they leaned in and asked him if he was OK? If there was anything they could do for him? I heard him respond in his low Irish brogue, 'Naw, it's awright, girls, just gorra lot on me mind, you know? Wi' da band and all . . .'

I burst out laughing. The tricky bastard. It was all a game. Within minutes he and the girls had joined me at the table, where they did their best to cheer Phil up. Twenty minutes later he had disappeared with one.

'Where's Phil?' the other two kept asking.

'Don't worry,' I said, having not a clue where he'd gone or if he was coming back. 'He'll be back. Let me get you another drink . . .'

Then here he was, along with the girl he'd vanished outside with. The sweat trickling down his face. An hour later he'd disappeared with another of the girls. This time, though, we all knew where he'd gone and what he was doing.

The first girl was upset. 'How *could* he? I thought we were going to spend the night together. Until that slag got her nails into him . . .'

Then he was back again, second girl in tow. No apologies, no explanations, just a lot more sweat on that dark, unfurrowed brow.

'I can't help meself,' he would tell me later. 'I tell meself, "Not tonight, I need a fookin' rest." But they come along, and what can you do?'

Phil was a man's man, the leader of the gang. And Thin Lizzy really did look and act like a gang. Whenever someone would apply for a gig as a roadie, they would be questioned a little on their previous experience, their technical knowhow. Then, if fit for purpose, they would be passed along to Phil, who would take one look and go, 'Can ya fight?' Any hesitation, any doubt whatsoever, and they were out. Thus everyone on the road with Lizzy was a 'character', to say the least. It was beholden upon you, as the skinny PR kid, to keep up the way Phil wanted.

Somehow, I had stayed in touch with Phil, even after Lizzy had split and he'd gone solo. At first, we were both still on the gear, but at the stage where you never mentioned it, not even to a fellow junk vampire, lest they suck you dry of your own unsteady supply. I was a writer again by then and he would sit there in his new publicist's office, sniffling and croaking away, sweating buckets and going through the motions, talking up the last couple of really not very good Lizzy albums, like the half-arsed *Chinatown*.

The last time I actually spoke to him though was at the end of 1985, and our situations were different. I had been clean, if not particularly serene, for over two years, but he was still deep down in the devil's hole. You could see it a mile off. Not just the permanent night sweats and heavy sniffles, but now something else, the thickening of the jowls, the stoop no longer faked but deadening. The eyes forlorn and full of the pain of trying to hide it all away somewhere not so secret any more.

As well as writing, I was now appearing on the *Monsters* show. Phil was our guest that week and the two of us sat in make-up together watching the monitors, waiting for our turn to go on.

I don't know why, it must have been his sombre mood, but I began to babble about regrets. I wince when I recall the conversation now. How thoughtless and insensitive, how plain rude. It must have been something to do with the low centre of gravity he now had. The pull towards the depths was simply inescapable.

'Do you regret Lizzy never really making it in America?' I asked him, out of the blue.

He turned his sad face towards me and smiled. 'Yer, but dat's like saying you regret not fookin' Kate Bush . . .'

I nodded. Fair point.

'What about Live Aid, though?' It must have been a bummer not being included. Especially as Geldof had been running the show. Weren't the two of them supposed to be friends?

He looked me over.

'It would have meant getting Lizzy back, and I didn't want that,' he lied.

When I heard of his death just a few weeks later, I was amazed. I knew he was still fucked up, still on the gear, the same death trip he'd been on for years. And yet . . . cats like Phil Lynott didn't die just like that, did they? Unless it was an OD. But the papers said it wasn't an OD, that it was multiple organ failure, brought on by years of bad living. I thought of my bad living through some of those years and still didn't get it. Could it be that Phil had lived a life even badder than the baddest of us?

Apparently it could. And that's when it dawned on me that I'd never really known Lynott at all. That perhaps none of us had. I wanted to find out more yet knew this was not the time. That those who knew the real Phil Lynott would be unwilling to share that information. Maybe one day, but not now . . .

Cut to twenty years later.

I was talking to Gary Moore, the guitarist who had joined and left Thin Lizzy three times. Now middle-aged and over ourselves, Gary and I had nothing left to hide about those long ago days. We had both moved far enough away from the traumas of the past to finally talk about them honestly. I was asking him about the young Philip Lynott he'd first known in Dublin in the late sixties.

Phil was the twenty-year-old lead singer in Skid Row, seventeen-year-old Gary's first professional group: 'He used to get up so early in those days. He was always up at eight o'clock, down the market buying clothes. He was always incredibly driven.'

He recalled Phil taking him for his first ever Chinese meal at a restaurant on Grafton Street, where he got him to try sweet and sour pork for the first time. 'I hated it so he ate mine and his, and that kind of set the tone for our relationship.' He chuckled at the memory. 'He was a real hustler, Phil, and a very crafty sort of a fellow.'

When Phil got chucked out of Skid Row he and Gary formed a trio with a drummer named Johnny Doohan, sharing one room in a flat in Donnybrook. 'Phil was like our mum, he'd cook breakfast for us every morning. I was only seventeen at the time, and he'd be like, "Right, yer fookin' breakfast's ready and you ain't going anywhere till you eat it!" He was so on the case in those days.'

Gary recalled the young Phil being 'more into lyrics and poetry than anybody I knew. I didn't give a shit. I was just into guitar. He loved all the old Irish poets and he was really into Van Morrison. The contemporary rock artists he was into were all people who were very into lyrics.

'He'd spend more time on the words than the music because he found the music not that difficult. They were very simple songs, you know? He'd play you "Dancing In The Moonlight" on the acoustic guitar and you'd go, "Is that it?" Then you'd hear the finished thing and understand what he'd been so enthusiastic about, because he was hearing it as the finished thing in his head.'

It was Phil's untiring work ethic that finally propelled Thin Lizzy into the charts for the first time in 1973 with 'Whiskey In The Jar', Gary said. 'In the studio he'd be the first guy in and the last guy out. He'd stay there all night getting it right. He was such a workaholic you wouldn't believe it.'

This was the Phil Lynott that Scott Gorham met when he was one of two guitarists brought in, in 1974, to replace Moore (the other being Brian Robertson).

'He had this real presence going for him. I thought, "Shit, man, this guy is interesting, real charismatic." He had that real authority thing. I felt it coming off him: "I know what I'm talking about, I'm the business, listen to me . . ."'

Scott had been through rehab and quit heroin long before Phil had died. He was one of the last sober people to see Phil alive, to try to talk him down from the ledge he had been standing on.

At the height of Thin Lizzy's success, said Scott, 'Phil had been so fucking on top of it. Music, clothes, where you stood on stage, everything . . . he was fucking driven. He always put on a show. But, of course, he was also the party guy. He could screw more chicks, drink more drinks, take more drugs, stay up more nights in a row than anybody I ever met before.'

The success that followed 'The Boys Are Back In Town', said Scott, 'brought that out even more. You get a little more money and a lot more friends . . .'

He had that romantic idea of the rock and roller, living outside the law, I said.

'Well, we kinda were,' he smiled. 'I know that's how Phil felt about it, absolutely. Up to a point, he felt he was a law unto himself. He wanted to make all the important decisions about everything. Even if the record company had the most fantastic idea ever, he didn't want to hear it. Like, we're not gonna take any advice and, "By the way, get the fuck out of our dressing room." After a while I stopped having that attitude but Phil kept it up.'

Phil also had this big thing about being Irish. It was something he and I had talked about when I first knew him and he found out my parents were both from the old country, as he put it. When he found out that Wall was my mother's name, that she had never been married to my father, he had grinned. 'So we're both bastards. I knew we had something in common . . .'

It all changed, though, after the smack came into it. As it always does.

According to Gary, 'By the time of *Black Rose* [in 1979] the drugs had definitely kicked in and I saw a big change in him. He had lost a lot of his energy and it was very difficult. I left the band [again] basically because of all that shit. I just couldn't stand it any more.'

Lizzy being the gang they were, once Phil and Scott got heavily into it, most of the road crew did too. Gary recalled their tour manager, Big Charlie, bragging about 'putting a line of smack out for the big fella'. It seemed to me, from the outside, that the Lizzy tours never really came to an end, they just carried on at Phil's place. It just turned into this continual over the top party situation – he lost control at that point.

It took a while for the rest of us to figure that out, though. Meanwhile, Phil and Lizzy appeared to go from strength to strength, from hit to hit. Phil's picture always in the paper, always on TV . . . being a judge at Miss World, turning into Rod Stewart . . .

Scott said he thought that 'what happened to Phil was probably a direct result of that: "Jeez, I gotta keep my shit together. I gotta find inspiration. I gotta keep up, man. Hey, chop me out a line of that coke . . ." Then next time it would be two lines. And that's basically what happened. We needed that fucking joy juice, man, just to get us up to keep us working. We figured the drugs were the only things that were saving us. Now that's a crazy way to think, but that's the way it was back then.'

I recall being in the studio for Phil's first solo album in 1980, *Solo In Soho*, and the place being packed with people off their faces. Phil and Lizzy had always been magnets for the party people, me included, but this was turning into something else. There weren't many joy bangers left in that crowd, not even many females. Mainly, it was just the dark knights of smack flocking like vultures to the scene of the crime, living for the next brown line or bloody fix. I was no different to the rest. I wasn't interested in the fact that Phil was now the father of two little girls, never questioned that he had a wife waiting at home who wasn't prepared to put up with Phil's fucking around. I just wanted to hang, man. We all did – Phil, included, only he was the one in charge, the one who was supposed to know what was *really* going on; the one actually responsible for all the hits. When word got back that his wife, Caroline, had finally split with the kids, I don't recall anybody batting an eye. Not anybody that still wanted to hang and get fucked up with the Great Philip, anyway.

When Lizzy also broke up around the same time, Scott went back to California and cleaned up. After not seeing Phil for a year he returned to London and went to visit him in his Kew house. 'One of the sacrifices I had to make was to lose Phil and to lose that whole crowd,' he later told me. 'But I'd been in Los Angeles, I'd done some recordings and I really wanted to see Phil. I really wanted to get his opinion. I mean, I was glowing at this point, the skin was great, I'd gained weight back, it was all looking real good for me. But as soon as I spoke to him on the phone I could hear the wheezing. You could always tell when Phil was doing smack because his asthma would attack him in a big way.'

Gary, who had dragged Phil out of his rut and back into the studio for what became the last ever hit, 'Out In The Fields', in the summer of 1985, recalled him being 'very depressed' at the time, 'very down. And that wasn't like him at all.' They ended up spending a lot of time together that summer, promoting 'Out In The Fields', and trying to record more material: 'Losing Thin Lizzy had a huge impact on him because that was like his family, his gang. He spent more time with those guys than he did with his own family. And he'd lost his wife and his kids and he was living on his own in this big house out in Kew with a bunch of leeches and really not very nice people hanging around the place – a bunch of dealers and smackheads. And I think he was a very lonely guy by then.'

Gary had taken Phil to a studio he had in his garage where they did the demos for 'Out In The Fields'. Gary tried working with him there on other things, but 'you couldn't get him out of bed before two in the afternoon. Then he'd come down with a glass of whiskey and a spliff, one in each hand. And that was how the day would start. So he must have been feeling terrible all the time.'

They did a few TV shows to promote the hit: 'But he wasn't in good shape. It was really hard just to get him anywhere on time, just to get him out of bed and into the car. Then he would drink quite a lot while he was with you. He was just not on top of it at all any more, and it was really sad.'

Gary related an awful story about the last time they had tried to work together: 'I was in the studio with Phil one day and this guy, who was a dealer, he came over to West Side Studios, and the whole thing had just gotten so fucking seedy and disgusting he'd brought this little girl, she was about three years old, and he took her in the toilet with him and Phil to do a deal. I was fucking *so* appalled. I don't mean to be the moralist but it was sick . . .

'Then this guy apparently was up at Phil's funeral . . . But he got put away, I think. But all this vermin . . . you know, if you get into that world you are going to hang out with a bunch of scum, there's no doubt about it. Because you don't actually care who you're hanging out with. In the old days Phil wouldn't have walked down the same side of the street as some of those guys. Not the Phil I knew . . .'

Scott Gorham had been to pay Phil a visit at his house in Kew a few weeks before he died: 'Soon as he opened up the door I saw he was just a mess. He was puffed out, bloated, the eyes were real bloodshot. He was still pulling at the hair trying to get that afro just perfect.

'We sat around and I know that he was looking at me thinking, "Shit, man, this guy looks fucking great." 'Cos he even said a couple of times, "You know, I'm gonna get my shit together, get rid of all this drug thing. I'm really gonna go for it. Try to get myself better, I'm really up for it this time." He actually sounded convincing, to the point where he whipped out the acoustic guitars and showed me some of the songs he'd just written.

'He was even talking about how he and I should get back together and start writing songs again and even get the band back together. And I'm looking at him, and we've just been talking about how hard it is out on the road even when you're in great shape – I'm looking at him, thinking, "Phil, you're not gonna make it, man. You've got to get your shit together and then we can do this thing." But I'm saying, "Yeah, yeah, it sounds good to me."

'So we left it at that, me thinking that he's gonna try to get better, try to get some help. Because at least he was talking about it, which is always the first step. And that was literally the last time I saw him. Three weeks later I got the call – massive heart attack, intensive care, emergency hospital, pipes coming out of everywhere . . .'

I was sitting at home one morning in January 1986, rolling a joint and looking ahead to my day at the *Kerrang!* office when someone rang me with the news. Phil was dead. What? Phil was dead. He had died at the hospital the day before. But of what? OD? No, nothing as simple as that. Something else, something harder to brush off. Phil had died of what in earlier times they might simply have called old age. Yes, he'd OD'ed on a fix. But that wasn't what killed him. It was all the hundreds and thousands of times before that, when he hadn't OD'ed but maybe should have, had he not been so cussed and Irish and black and fucking undeniable. His organs had finally given up. As they do for all of us, one way or another, eventually. Except in Phil's case it had happened when he was thirty-six.

You might say he had lived hard enough for two lives in that time, but that would be romantic hogwash. We all have only one life. And when you listen back now to the albums Phil made, with and without Thin Lizzy, you have to admit he really should have packed in a lot more than he did into those years. Most of it is patchy, brilliant one track, average the next. That, ultimately, Philip Lynott, friend to all us strays and throwaways, was unkindest to himself – and his family. He'd always longed to be a rock star, always dreamed of dying like one too. In the end he did both, neither. All of it and never enough. While those of us who lied, and thought of ourselves as Philip's friends, did nothing to help him. His heart, as he famously sang, like a promise, made to be broken.

18. Mr Big

Rock managers are a law unto themselves. The best tend to have egos often bigger than the artists they represent. When it's a guy like Peter Mensch, though, you have to respect it. Still probably the most successful manager in the world, overseeing the affairs in recent years of everyone from Led Zeppelin to Metallica and the Red Hot Chili Peppers, to name just three of dozens, Peter's a hard-ass who always acts like he doesn't know you. Or that he knows you too well. He doesn't play favours, though, and either you've got something to say he wants to hear or you might as well just fuck off and kill yourself. He's the real deal and I have always liked him, even though I very much doubt he would say the same about me.

Others, like Rod Smallwood, who despite managing several top-drawer acts over the years, has essentially devoted the lion's share of his career to managing Iron Maiden, plays on being the friendly dealer you can always rely on. In the years when I was Maiden's official biographer, Rod would continually assure me that I was 'part of the family'. As such, I would be sent laminated all-areas passes for every tour, and gold records for award-winning UK album sales. When my mother died in 1986 Rod even sent a wreath, with all the band members' names on it – and Rod's too, of course. It guaranteed my loyalty for a long, long time.

The legendary managers, though, are the ones who came before. The ones the rest all learned from; the evolutionary progenitors who paved the way, drew the maps, and wrote the rules of the road as most rock bands still live them today. It was through my connection with Sharon Osbourne that I got to know one of the really big beasts of music-biz rock management – her notorious father, Don Arden.

Like everybody else who ever knew him, I'd heard about Don long before I ever met him. He was the Al Capone of pop, as the tabloids had anointed him in the seventies (and as he adored to be known); the music-biz gangster who'd hung fellow pop impresario Robert Stigwood by his legs from a balcony window for daring to cross swords with him; the Small Faces manager who, they later claimed, kept all their money for himself; the gun-toting former manager of Gene Vincent, Little Richard, Black Sabbath and many others including, most lucratively of all, the Electric Light Orchestra, whose phenomenal record sales in the seventies allowed Don to purchase Howard Hughes' old Hollywood mansion for $8 million (the equivalent of around $30 million today) – in cash.

When his daughter, Sharon – well-known then as the wife and manager of Ozzy; much more famous now as the glamorous if foul-mouthed matriarch of *The Osbournes*, *The X Factor* and *America's Got Talent* – rang late one night and asked if I'd consider working with Don on his memoirs, I was taken aback. Having known Sharon and Ozzy for over twenty years, I'd been made painfully aware of the antipathy that existed between her and her father. Once a knee-sitting daddy's girl who'd learned everything about the music business from working for Don, the two had fallen out so badly that they'd effectively waged war on each other ever since: Sharon throwing soup over the woman Don had begun a serious extramarital relationship with in Hollywood in the early eighties (leaving Sharon's mother to live alone in England) and once even trying to run Don over in her car (as Ozzy had cowered in the passenger seat).

For his part, Don had sued Sharon for millions when she took Ozzy away from his record label, Jet, and threatened her with the same chilling retribution that had long been his calling card.

'There were times when I was on the floor crying and shaking because he'd threatened to come over to the house and kill me,' Sharon told me. 'He's an evil old bastard and I can't wait for him to die.'

Indeed, as far as Sharon's and Ozzy's three kids – Aimee, Kelly and Jack – were concerned, their grandfather was already dead.

'I told them that because I didn't want him anywhere near them, and I certainly didn't want them seeing him,' she said. Once, as they all watched from the car baffled as Sharon screamed obscenities at her father in the street, she told them the white-haired old man she was yelling at was Tony Curtis (a friend of Don's and 'just the first name that came into my head').

Now, though, Sharon said, she had been reflecting a great deal on her life. She and Ozzy had been in New York the day the twin towers were attacked and felled, an event that had affected her deeply. Then when her brother, and Don's right-hand man for many years, David Arden, had called her with news that Don, now in his mid-seventies, had been diagnosed as being in the early stages of Alzheimer's disease, she had decided the time was right for reconciliation – that is, if the old man would agree to meet with her without threatening violence, something he had steadfastly refused to do for nearly two decades.

When Don agreed, 'Everyone was very nervous,' David told me. 'But as soon as the two of them were together in the same room again the bad feelings just melted away and they were father and daughter again.'

Determined to do something for her ailing father, Sharon encouraged Don to finish his memoirs, a project he had been working on sporadically for five years. But he needed a writer to work with. Sharon recommended me.

We would meet a couple of times a week at the luxury Park Lane apartment he was renting while he was in London working with me on the book. Don was old, and he could be painfully funny, and I certainly enjoyed my time with him. It wasn't every day, after all, that one got to hang out with a genuine mafiosi-connected throwback to the time when the music biz really did resemble the Wild West.

Don, however, was still quite frightening when he wanted to be. He no longer actively hung people out of windows or placed a loaded gun against their heads. ('Sometimes I would just lay it on the table at meetings,' he told me. 'It had a wonderful way of focusing everybody's minds.') But he was always quick to suggest he still knew people who did. How much of this was simple bravado and how much real, I couldn't gauge. I sensed it was probably the former, but not enough to put it to the test. Not when he was continually telling me stories of all the different people he had 'sorted out' over the sixty years he had been in the business – like the stage manager he'd beaten up and 'rolled down the stairs like a bundle of rags' in his days as a young song-and-dance man, whose crime was, 'Fucking up the lights during my act, then not even apologising!' Then there were the bootleggers and drug pushers he'd broken the arms and legs of during his days as a tour promoter – 'The scum of the earth, I'd leave them unconscious in the gutter'. And the rival managers he'd 'given a kick up the arse to' like Robert Stigwood and, less famously but even more brutally, Clifford Davis, who'd had the misfortune to challenge Don over management of sixties' hit makers The Move.

Don recounted with typical relish the day he turned up unannounced at Clifford's office: 'He had a big cigar in his mouth and he said, "I know where you live, Don." I said, "Take that fucking cigar out of your mouth, I can't hear what you're saying."'

At which point, according to Don, he held the unfortunate Clifford in a headlock then ground the lit end of the cigar into his face, 'Right between the eyes.'

What did Clifford do? I asked, in shock.

'Oh, he cried out and all that. He struggled at first then his body went all limp. I felt so good afterwards I dismissed my driver and walked home . . .'

Other times, he'd tell me old music hall jokes and sing me funny little Yiddisher songs 'from the old days' when he was a variety star, headlining the London Palladium or appearing on TV in the 1950s as one of the original Black and White Minstrels.

One day, I turned around and he was wearing my jacket. It was a worn old thing purchased from a charity shop on a whim, because it looked vaguely foppish, I thought, in a post-modern kind of not-bad-for-a-fiver sort of way.

'What the fuck is this?' he roared, prancing around the room in it. 'If you're gonna be hanging round with me we're gonna have to get you to my tailor!' I smiled weakly. 'We don't want people thinking I associate with a fucking *tramp*!'

People used to ask me what he was like. 'He's great,' I'd say. 'I really like him. I'm really glad I didn't know him when he was younger, though.'

Don Arden was born Harry Levy in Cheetham, Manchester, in 1926, the son of émigré Jews from Russia and Poland. He grew up 'in the ghetto' in a house with no electricity and one cold-water tap. 'We used to queue up to wash every morning, my father first 'cos he had to go to work.'

Singing in the synagogue, he and his mother were obsessed with the music hall and would attend shows weekly. He lied about his age in order to get his first professional stage job at fourteen, and became obsessed with Hollywood gangster movies – his hero was James Cagney, whom he would practise impersonating in front of the mirror. 'Years later,' he told me, 'I used the same techniques before I went into meetings.'

And, of course, he was a great storyteller – about the time in the 1950s when he first brought American rock 'n' rollers to Britain, like Jerry Lee Lewis ('a redneck racist'), Little Richard ('a pervert but I loved him') and Gene Vincent ('a fucking lunatic, much worse than Ozzy or anybody you've got now'). Or when he ran the Star Club in Hamburg ('any trouble at all and I would knock 'em out and have 'em thrown unconscious into the gutter') where he also encountered The Beatles ('I didn't think much of 'em, not compared to Richard or Gene').

Clearly, his musical judgement wasn't always failsafe, but he learned quickly and when The Beatles changed the music business overnight Don was ready to change with it, signing first The Animals then the Small Faces, the Nashville Teens and The Move.

'None of them had a clue what to do till I came along,' he boasted. And there was some truth in that. It was Don who paid for The Animals to leave Newcastle and tour the country on the back of a recording he had financed, for a song called 'House Of The Rising Sun'. And despite the band's later claims that he ripped them off, it was Don who paid for the large London house the Small Faces lived in, along with the chauffeur-driven Jag and accounts at all the smart Carnaby Street clothes shops.

It was also Don who handpicked their breakthrough hit, 'Sha-La-La-Lee'. 'I wanted something like "Do Wah Diddy Diddy", which was then Number One, so I went to my mate Kenny Lynch to write it. The band hated it but it brought them massive success. Then they were all kissing my feet.' He added that he had actually pulled his gun on them and threatened to shoot them if they didn't record the song, but I had learned by then that Don liked to embellish his stories a little. Just for the sheer hell of it.

Then there were the stories that clearly didn't need any embellishment. By the mid-seventies Don was managing Black Sabbath, which is how Sharon met Ozzy; had started his own record label, Jet; and had helped manoeuvre the split of The Move into two of the most successful acts of the decade: Electric Light Orchestra (ELO) and Wizzard. While the latter would become famous in Britain for hits like 'See My Baby Jive' and 'I Wish It Could Be Christmas Every Day', it was the former who would turn Don into a multimillionaire, as ELO became one of the biggest-selling acts in America, releasing a string of multi-platinum hits.

By the end of the seventies Don and his family were living in the Hughes mansion in Hollywood, throwing lavish celebrity-filled parties in the atrium. When the fellow multimillionaire who owned the mansion next door complained at the noise, Don told me, 'I went round there with a briefcase full of cash and told him, "Here, fucking take it! I'll buy your shitty house!" But the guy said no, he didn't want to sell. So I showed him my gun and told him again, "I said I want to buy your house. Now, are you gonna take the cash or what?" He took the cash!'

Don's best friends now included Cary Grant and Tony Curtis. Harvey Weinstein, who would go on to form the mega-successful Miramax film company, was another acolyte ('like a son to me'). Through Cary Grant, Don told me, he also became involved with the Republican Party of Ronald Reagan, invited to fund-raisers and later, when Reagan became president, to the White House itself.

But it was also during this period that the seeds of destruction for Don and his business were first sown, when he became close friends of Joe Pagano, head of one of the five big Mafia families in New York. 'Decent, family people,' Don called them. Maybe so, but they were a clan reportedly connected to more than 150 'contract' killings – which, it was clear from our conversations, had only enamoured Don to them more. Like him, they always carried guns. And, of course, he had routinely beaten and threatened anyone who stood in his way for most of his life too.

Now, rich beyond his wildest imaginings, and drunk on the power of being 'connected' to the Mafia, Don began to think of himself as almost omnipotent. Hubris was around the corner. The first chink in his armour came with the exposé Roger Cook did for BBC Radio Four's *Checkpoint* programme in 1979. Although Don laughed it off at the time, and was heard on-air threatening the broadcaster ('Just remember, legs do break, Mr Cook'), he was still incandescent with rage more than twenty years later when I broached the subject with him: 'I'd still kill him if ever I met him, yes,' he said, not a trace of mirth in his voice. 'Kill him slowly, with his wife watching, if I could . . .'

But worse was to follow when, in the early eighties, Don discovered one of his accountants had been siphoning off cash from his various businesses. Don went wild, had him abducted and brought to his home, where he beat and tortured him. The result was an Old Bailey court case that effectively finished Don off. While he was miraculously cleared on charges of assault, kidnapping, blackmail and torture, his son David was sentenced to two years' imprisonment for his part in proceedings.

'It broke my fucking heart,' Don told me, 'because David was always the good guy and had nothing to do with the case. They just went after him on trumped-up charges when they realised they weren't going to get me.'

With ELO past their peak and winding down, Ozzy now a solo artist managed by Sharon, whom he had disowned, and David in prison, an innocent victim of his father's crimes, Don sold Jet and all its assets off to CBS for $40 million and went into semi-retirement. Professionally battered but personally un-bowed, by the time I met him he seemed happy enough with his lot. As he said, 'I still get my suits made by the same tailor as Frank Sinatra. I still eat a good breakfast every day.'

Despite Sharon insisting she and her father had put their troubles behind them, it still rankled the old man. 'People go on now about how Sharon turned Ozzy into a star,' he grumbled one time. 'Absolute rubbish! I was his manager! I was the one who took him into my house, gave him somewhere to clean himself up and sort himself out – she was just the day-to-day run-around for him. By the time he started again he was on $5,000 a night; by the end of it he was making $100,000 a night. Who did that for him? My daughter? Don't make me laugh. Oh, she did a good job in the years after that, I'll grant you, but people forget he was already a star by then. And who made him that way? Me, that's who! Me!'

He even claimed it was he – and not Sharon – who was respon-sible for the career-defining moment when Ozzy bit the heads off the doves at the CBS Records convention in 1981. 'I was the one pulling out all the stops, trying to get everyone in America interested in him – not Sharon! It was me who organised the get-together with the heads of all the various departments at CBS in Los Angeles. It was even me who wrote the little speech for him to give – some old bollocks about how he did it all for love, not money. It was at the end of that he was supposed to pull out the doves and release them into the air. I thought every-body would go, "Coo! How wonderful!" Except he'd polished off a bottle of brandy in the car on the way over there and went mad.' He shook his head. 'And who turned it round when it all went wrong? No, not Sharon! Me! Everyone else just did what they were told – including my daughter.'

All he wanted to do now, though, he said, once he'd quieted down, was get his book out, and he would have 'a whole new career, kid. That's my aim.'

He planned to do a one-man show, he said, based on the book, which we called *Mr Big*. But by the end of our time together, with the Alzheimer's becoming worse, it was hard to see how that might be possible. There was also talk of his other 'son', Harvey Weinstein, commissioning a biopic based on the book for Miramax – a possibility that seemed much more likely, especially when he and David sat down one day and began questioning me earnestly about what I really wanted from the book.

My deal meant I would have been entitled to 25 per cent of any advance for film rights Don was given, but with Miramax talking in the region of $3 million it was clear neither Don nor David was happy with that arrangement any more. David did the soft talking while Don merely sat there, staring at me with dead fish eyes, as though he didn't know me suddenly. It was the first – and thankfully the last, as Miramax pulled out of the deal not long after – time I had ever experienced Don in 'negotiating' mode. The first time I'd really had an inkling of what it must have been like to deal with the old boy in his terrifying heyday.

Mostly, though, we had a laugh together. He was fond of berating me for my clothes. And he was always giving me advice on how to conduct myself. 'All that stuff about "sticks and stones" and "words may never hurt me" it's all bollocks,' he assured me. 'The thought of violence is much more of a deterrent than the actual deed. By the time you come to actually hurt someone, it's too late for them, it's over. But the *thought* of what you might do to them keeps them right where you want them. Always let your reputation precede you.'

I promised I'd give it a go.

Once, chatting over breakfast, I mentioned in passing some small trouble I was having with someone in the magazine publishing world. 'You want me to make a call, kid?' he asked me, apparently seriously. 'Say the word. We'll straighten the fucker out.'

'No, thank you, Don,' I told him. I didn't like the person I'd mentioned but I didn't want anything to, you know, *happen* to him.

The last time I saw Don was at Sharon and Ozzy's palatial mansion in Buckinghamshire in early 2003. He had quit the Park Lane apartment and, as he became more ill by the day, was going off to live in the same Hollywood mansion then seen regularly on TV in *The Osbournes*. All that was left was for him to say a few goodbyes but, again, he seemed to have trouble remembering who I actually was – not through any tough-guy act this time, but because he really couldn't remember. The fog of Alzheimer's had finally descended too far.

I noticed someone I hadn't met before at the house too. A young woman in her late twenties, not unattractive but dressed very casually in gym pants and trainers, with a young child in tow.

'Who's that?' I whispered to David.

'Don's girlfriend,' he sighed.

I don't know what happened to her, but I presume she never saw the old man again after that day either.

Unfortunately, the story didn't quite end there. When Don's memoirs, *Mr Big*, were finally published in 2004, for reasons I can only guess at, Sharon took umbrage and had her 'people' contact my agent, accusing us of 'taking advantage of a sick old man' and misusing her family name to sell books.

Yet it was Sharon who had personally asked me to take on the job; and Sharon to whom we had arranged a special sneak-peek of the manuscript over a year before publication to check there wasn't anything there she was unduly uncomfortable with. (She did ask for a couple of minor changes, which I was happy to make.)

But then, as David once explained to me, 'Sharon is Don in a skirt. You don't wanna fuck with her.'

Or as Don himself said, as we sat in a pub around the corner from his apartment, fellow lunchtime pub dwellers shifting uneasily in their seats while his voice boomed around the room, 'It ain't about who's right or who's wrong, kid. It's about who *wins*. And I was always a winner, whatever anyone says about me. *Always*. Anyone ever tries to tell you any different, send 'em to me. I'll soon fucking put them straight!'

Then he laughed again.

19. **One Nervous Cat**

It takes one to know one, they say, and, like all clichés, it's true.

Steve Clark and I were drawn to each other like cheap magnets. I don't know what they call it these days down at the detox centre – 'mutual dependence syndrome' or some such – but it was one of those. The same age, the same space and time, the same confused search for love and approval through the bottom of a glass or the length of a badly rolled dollar . . . I was the presenter of what had become the hottest TV rock show in Europe – twenty-three countries kissing my ring three times a week – and he was the guitarist of Def Leppard, whose fourth album, *Hysteria*, was No. 1 all over the world. Major motherfuckers in our own mutually dependent backyards, what a double-act we should have been. Surrounded by cocksuckers jostling to light our cigarettes, chased by chicks who belonged to other guys, we should have been out there somewhere, having a so-called good time.

Instead, we were sat in a hotel room, always a hotel room, hiding from the crowd, our heads bowed over the glass coffee table, ignoring the reflections that hovered in it like ghosts, staring back at us from behind the thin, white bars of their cell windows.

You ask me now, years later, what it was like, what it was for, or even why . . . and I don't know how to answer. The questions are simply not the right ones. N/A. In my mind, it's like one long, interminable 'session' – as he called it. Days and nights flashing by like the forlorn lights of a passing train, rumbling ominously by the window, making your insides quiver ... Steve's trembling hand reaching again for the litre bottle of vodka ... the encouraging tap-tap-tap of blade on glass ... the red message light on the phone blinking ... night on day ... one on one ... for-ev-er ...

Steve was beautiful, he really was: gentle, kind, generous, and as easy to read as an open book. Steve's face could hide nothing; he would have made a very poor poker player. And he was surprisingly shy. Unnervingly so if all you knew was the razzed-up rocker on stage with Leppard; the skinny fucker with the guitar slung low to his knees, lit cigarette jutting from the corner of his mouth, peeling out the face-slapping riffs with the unabashed glee of a dog burying a bone.

Off stage, though, he was a completely different sort of cat. The sleek, feral tom who prowled the stage was just an illusion, a raffish projection of the kind of guitarist Steve thought he should be – the kind he'd admired since he was a kid; truly devilish dudes like Zeppelin's Jimmy Page. But that wasn't who Steve really was. Who Steve really was, even he didn't know, of course. But the person he was when he came off stage, at least, was the old man pulling the levers behind the big scary screen in *The Wizard of Oz* – frightened, alone, with no more clue as to how it all worked than the next guy. Same as a lot of rock stars, in fact. But in Steve's case, certainly by the time we began knocking about together in 1987, the faking it part had begun to take on weird, new dimensions. The couple of hours on stage every night was all right, he said. It was the other twenty-two hours on the clock he found hard to handle.

Off stage was where the real fakery occurred. The most glamorous member of the hottest young rock band in America, he shuddered and turned his back when a video for their latest hit 'Armageddon It' came on in a hotel bar in Colorado we were drinking in one night on the *Hysteria* tour. His American model girlfriend, Lorelei, who was also with us, told him off: 'Why do you *do* that? Aren't you *proud* of what you've done, who you *are*?'

He turned and looked at me with that same thoroughly defeated expression I recognised from all our conversations about the band. He didn't expect her to get it but he assumed, at least, that I did. I would smile and try to be reassuring but the truth was, I was as baffled as Lorelei.

Being embarrassed, even frightened, of being recognised in public was something anyone could relate to. But, it soon became clear, there was more to it than that for Steve. Fundamentally, he had no problem with fame; that was what being a successful rock star was all about, one of the luxuries he had dreamed of as a kid. What it came down to, I eventually realised, was that he didn't think he *deserved* the attention. It made him feel like even more of a fake. 'That video, those . . . records,' I remember him stuttering. 'That's not . . . me.'

It was a question of self-esteem; something Steve seemed to have run out of long before either his girlfriend or I had shown up. But it took me a while to figure that one out and until then I had assumed, like everybody else, that Steve's problems stemmed, in the main, from his over-involvement with booze and drugs. He'd been lying to the rest of the band about his off-stage habits for years. Now he had begun lying about it to himself.

'It's not like . . . like . . . I *have* to . . .' he'd say, pouring himself another large vodka and cranberry juice (the cranberry to kill the breath). 'It's . . . I *want* to. Fuck . . . you know? I'm out here . . . *we're* out here . . . the road . . . months . . . I mean, it's good, but . . . you know?'

Steve had a sideways kind of way of talking, skipping certain words, leaving you to fill in the blanks. But I knew, all right . . . getting up just as the sun goes down, fumbling blindly for the Tylenol, searching for your head among the ruins of your room, trying to put it all back together and failing . . . ah, God, the pain, the sickness, the regret . . . the overpowering stench of your own mortality clogging up the room. Then staggering to the bathroom, cowering in the shower . . . gagging as you brush your teeth . . . anything to try to clear away the poisonous shadows that hover over everything like a cloud of flies. Collapsing exhausted back on the bed, staring at the silver room-service tray . . . swamped by thoughts of death, thoughts of home, thoughts of fakery . . . thoughts of all the things you didn't do yesterday that deep down inside you know you won't be doing again today.

Deep down inside . . . what a terrible place to wake up to each day on the road. It was bad enough for officially sanctioned freeloaders like me, there just for a few days at a time to write a story or shoot a TV clip. But for Steve, there not only for the long haul but also as *a principle member of the team*, the pain and the guilt must have been overwhelming. And the worse he felt, the more quickly he moved to kill the pain with vodka and cocaine and anything else he could get his shaky hands on. Which just fed the guilt more. What a rotten wheel to be trapped on. What a death trip. I couldn't figure it. Why didn't he just stop? Even just for a little while, until he had it together again? Or just slow down? What was his fucking hurry anyway?

But whenever I suggested it, even just casually, he'd shake his long, blond tresses impatiently. 'I *do* . . . do that . . . but then . . . I dunno. I mean . . . What else is there?'

He had me there.

'I never really ... drink. Never ... anything ... before I go on,' he lied. 'I always *try* to do the gig straight.' That part I did believe. 'It's just ... after. What's the ... I mean ... few drinks ... whatever ... What's wrong with that?'

He made it sound so reasonable. If only the reality had been as straightforward. By the time I got to know Steve well enough for him to talk to me about this stuff – the first time, as I recall, after a Leppard gig in Milan, in the spring of '88, when some chick from the Italian record company slipped a couple of grams in his hand – he was, it transpired, already on a round-the-clock regime of vodka, schnapps, beer, cocaine, painkillers, antidepressants, sleeping tablets and various other party-favour tranquillisers. A strong, fit man would have buckled under the weight of that medicine chest. Steve was neither a strong nor a fit man and the wonder was that he was still able to get up on that stage each night and run around like he did. Even without the added extras, he was smoking maybe forty cigarettes a day, would go limp at the very mention of the word 'exercise', and hardly ever hit the sack before daybreak.

In retrospect then, you might say he was an accident waiting to happen; that somebody should have done something to stop him before it was too late. As one of those possible somebodies, I would say this: the Steve Clark I knew looked and talked like a man for whom the tragedy had already occurred. That maybe it was already too late to help him.

Maybe. I was hardly the right guy for Steve to bring something like this to. It had never occurred to me back then that getting shit-faced after a gig was anything other than perfectly acceptable behaviour. The normal perk of a pleasingly abnormal job. The first few times we'd met – casually, for magazine interviews – I had assumed Steve was living the dream: the skinny dude with the axe dangling round his knees and the coke spoon hanging from his neck. The one the chicks *and* the guys dug deep.

But then I came from the seventies, where love was free, drugs were enlightening and rock 'n' roll was for gen-u-wine outlaws. Steve, too. To me, he was just riding high. No lows allowed. But because of his band's astonishing success – he was just twenty-one when Leppard's second album, *High 'N' Dry*, went gold in America – he had been thrust early into the new, eighties milieu of moneyed-up, no-shit materialism.

It didn't suit him. Not at all. And while he made what he did with Leppard appear almost effortless, the second nature of a real-deal rock 'n' roller, it was Steve, perhaps more than any of the band, who, in his own frazzled, permanently freaked-out way, truly understood what the real cost of the whole enterprise had been. Not in terms of money but in terms of the mounting debt of human pain and emotional sacrifice that had been made to get them to where they now stood in 1988. Top of the world, ma!

Cue fatal explosion . . .

I would get the story in bits, half-truths and late-night remembrances; booze-soliloquies only vaguely listened to but repeated so often I came to know them off by heart; rock 'n' roll nursery rhymes we would sing together like lonely children. One of our favourites was 'Don't Tell The Others'.

'Don't tell the others,' he'd start as he dabbed at the specks of coke left on the table. 'I know they . . . *care* . . . I know that . . . I just . . . I just don't want . . .'

The sentence would be left dangling.

'Don't tell the others,' I'd say, joining in. 'If they know you've been in my room again . . .'

In the end, there were so many things we didn't want to tell the others we would act as though we hardly knew each other whenever the rest of the band was around. Not just because Steve wanted to keep secret the fact that he was so out of it all the time, but because he had started talking about things that really mattered to him. Stuff he didn't like being reminded of the next day.

Like the time he said: 'Don't tell the others but . . . like . . . I'm not saying I didn't . . . you know . . . didn't *play* on the album . . . it's just . . .'

What? Did he say he didn't play on *Hysteria*?

'No. I didn't say . . . that. It's just . . .'

At first, I assumed it was just more space-talk – words missing, timeline all fucked, the true meaning left unrevealed. But slowly, over maybe a dozen different, mostly clandestine encounters during that fifteen-month world tour, I got enough pieces to see a picture.

Sometimes, about three in the morning, skiing down another icy slope, he'd get paranoid. 'Listen, I . . . I don't mean to . . . uh . . . you know . . . but you're not . . . like, you're not . . .'

'Taping this?' I'd say, hoping he didn't mean that, 'cos that would mean he still thought of me as a media-goon, an interloper, someone who *didn't get it*. Something I thought we'd left behind a long way back down the road.

'Uh . . . yeah.'

'Fuck's sake, Steve! What, you think I want to listen back to this bullshit the next day? You're off your fuckin' head!'

He smiled that tight, worried smile, his nervous, fretful eyes hiding behind that hair.

'No, I know you wouldn't . . . It's just . . . I don't like . . . like this . . . you know . . . normally.'

Of course not. Nevertheless, the words, some of them, still stay with me. They meant so little at the time, on their own, all broken down like that, but now, seen all together like this. Well . . .

Born on 23 April 1960 – right on the cusp of Aries the fiery leader and Taurus the stubborn bull – Stephen Maynard Clark grew up in the poor, broken-down Hillsborough district of Sheffield, in England's grim industrial north. The son of a cab driver, at school he did well without excelling. Or, as he told me: 'Lessons bored me shitless.'

When he was eleven, Steve sweet-talked his parents into giving him a guitar on the promise that he would also take classical lessons. Good as his word, for the first year, he studiously divided his time between the sheet music of the old masters and prancing around in front of his bedroom mirror to Led Zeppelin and Thin Lizzy.

He left school as soon as he legally could, at sixteen, and took a factory job as an apprentice lathe-operator. Part of his course included day trips to college, where he met another young apprentice by the name of Pete Willis. Pete also played guitar but was way ahead of Steve: Pete was actually in a band. They were called Def Leppard, in imitation of the equally nonsensical but enigmatic Led Zeppelin.

The next bit is now part of the well-told Leppard legend, beginning with the story of Steve's first jam with the band in the small garage they rehearsed in, in January 1978. Leppard at that time consisted of Pete, singer Joe Elliott, bassist Rick Savage and drummer Tony Kenning – soon to be replaced by fifteen-year-old schoolboy Rick Allen. They were good, exceptional even for teenagers, but they were about to get better.

They had not been looking for a second guitarist, but after Steve lit into an impassioned, almost note-perfect rendition of the impossibly extravagant solo from Lynyrd Skynyrd's 'Free Bird', the sheer explosive weight of his performance forced them to reconsider; thereby introducing the classic twin-guitar shape that was to become Def Leppard's platinum-embossed signature over the next decade.

The rest of the fairytale went like this: little more than a year after their first performance together, at Wakefield School in Sheffield, in July 1978, the band were signed to Phonogram Records, the London division of the largest, most powerful record company in the world. By the time their first album, *On Through the Night*, was released in 1980, the name Def Leppard was already a familiar one in the UK rock press and the album shot straight into the Top 30.

But if their swift rise to prominence in their home country was commendable, more impressive still was how quickly they also achieved recognition in America, where their second album, *High 'N' Dry*, eventually went platinum. Partly taken by how unusually young the band were and partly, by contrast, how astonishingly mature their records sounded, by the time Leppard's third album, *Pyromania*, hit the racks in 1983 they were the biggest-selling rock band in America. Only Michael Jackson's *Thriller* kept *Pyromania* from No. 1 in America that year, where it sold over six million copies by the time the follow-up, *Hysteria*, was finally released four years later.

I wasn't there for Leppard's crazy, early years. The days when they were opening for bands they still had pictures of on their bedroom walls, before blowing them away with the flame-on arrogance of youth. And I wasn't there for those triumphant end-of-tour shows in Los Angeles at the climax of the *Pyromania* tour, in December 1983, when Queen guitarist Brian May stood on stage next to Steve for a full-on blast through the old Zep war-horse, 'Rock And Roll'. By all accounts, I missed some good shit.

I was there, however, for Steve's last gig with Def Leppard, at the Memorial Arena in Tacoma, Washington, in October

1988, almost ten years exactly after his first. If Steve's eighteen-year-old self could have seen his twenty-eight-year-old self on stage that night – witnessed the smiling, upturned faces of the thousands of over-excited, mainly female fans – and if he could have seen, too, that his latest album had gone to No. 1 and that his personal bank account had long since achieved seven-figure status, how happy and fulfilled his younger self would have assumed his twenty-eight-year-old self to be. And how wrong he would have been.

The question remains: why? To hear Joe Elliott tell it, the band had survived their travails and emerged stronger, more together than ever before. For Joe, being in Def Leppard was to live a life not without its sadness and frustration, but nevertheless a life fulfilled. A tall, outgoing Yorkshireman and a natural bandleader, he found it hard to understand why someone like Steve, who appeared to have so much going for him, should crumple so easily under the pressure of being in the band. All he knew for sure, he told me, was that 'Steve only makes things worse for himself'. And, of course, he was right, though not, perhaps, entirely for the reasons we suspected.

Steve, for his part, seemed to view Joe's lack of understanding as a personal betrayal. He pined for the days when he, Joe and the others got drunk and fucked-up together on a regular, as he put it, 'more normal', basis. But that had been back in the care-free days before *Pyromania* turned the band into a zillion-dollar industry. In order to sustain that level of success, Leppard had been forced to grow up quickly. Inevitably, there were casualties along the way. Steve, in a chillingly prophetic way, seemed to accept that he would be next to fall by the wayside.

The band had already demonstrated just how hard-nosed they could be when it came to career decisions. The first skin to be shed was that of the small-town management team who had steered them out of the garage and towards a record deal – left for dead after the band allowed themselves to be snaffled up by AC/DC's former American manager Peter Mensch. Tough though it was on the poor saps they left behind to dream of what might have been, it was a shrewd business decision which proved, right from the start, that while the band might have been unfeasibly young they weren't stoopid.

More ruthless, if equally prudent, was the decision, in 1982, to fire Pete Willis, the guitarist whom Joe had actually founded the band with. Like everyone else back then, Pete enjoyed party-ing to excess. By the end of the *High 'N' Dry* tour, though, Pete's nasty habits were having such a deleterious effect on his person-ality his position in the band had become seriously undermined.

'Pete underwent a sort of personality change when he got out of it,' Joe told me. 'He could become quite . . . nasty.'

Then later, hearing it from Steve, who used to room with Pete on tour, it sounded like Pete had merely fallen for the same trap-pings they had once admired back in the days when they still believed what they read in the rock press. 'It all just kind of . . . went to his head,' said Steve. 'He could be a real . . . ego monster. Really, really . . . *hard* to be around. None of us was perfect, though . . .' Sacking him, said Steve, was 'probably the right thing', but he never looked quite sure when he said it. Pete had 'a drinking problem', said Steve, avoiding my eyes. 'It started to affect his playing . . .'

'Oh,' I said, feeling suddenly thirsty.

But if Steve's feelings were understandably mixed about the manner of Pete's departure – Steve thought they could have given Pete 'some time to get straight' but there had been pressure to get another album out and 'we didn't want to wait' – what really troubled him was the impact Pete's replacement, Phil Collen, had had on the band – and Steve's place in it.

To begin with, Steve and Phil had been great mates. The former musical linchpin in Girl – the London glam rock band whose singer, Phil Lewis, would also later find brief fame in America with LA Guns – not only was Phil a technically far more adept guitarist than Pete, like Steve he was a hard-drinking, hell-raiser in the finest English rock tradition. By the time the *Pyromania* tour was in full swing, the pair had been dubbed the Terror Twins. Steve often recalled how, on sunny days, they would ride bicycles to the gig together. 'It was great,' Steve shrugged. 'We were . . . close.'

Things changed dramatically, though, when Phil woke up one morning in 1984 to find a $10,000 watch strapped to his wrist that he had absolutely no recollection of buying. He decided right then that his drinking days were over. A decision he has stuck to remarkably well, considering his day job, ever since. 'It had been in the back of my mind for a while anyway, I think,' Phil told me later. 'The Leppard thing had gotten so huge, the tours so long . . . I'd already more or less decided I had to do something about keeping myself in shape. And then the watch thing happened and that just sort of sparked a whole thing for me.'

By the time Leppard lit out on the opening British leg of the *Hysteria* tour, in August 1987, Phil had been off the sauce for almost three years. He had also become a vegetarian and a devotee of the gym. He had, in short, become everything Steve was not: clean, fit and sober.

Steve had not taken the news well. It shouldn't have mattered, he knew that. But somehow it did. Not so much at first, he said, while the band were still writing the songs for *Hysteria* – but later, after Rick had returned from the car accident which ripped off his left arm and things had gotten super deadly serious; when all the important guitar work during the recording of the album appeared to be offered only to the newly sober Phil.

'I'm not saying I didn't . . . play . . . on the album. It's just . . .'

The band may have been formed by Joe and Pete, but Steve was always a doer more than a thinker. It was Steve who'd famously threatened to quit in the early days if they didn't get off their asses and start playing proper gigs; and it was Steve's low-slung Les Paul that had provided the musical muscle behind early crowd-pleasers like 'Another Hit And Run', 'High 'N' Dry (Saturday Night)', 'Rock! Rock! (Till You Drop)', 'Photograph', 'Rock of Ages' – all of them built on bona fide Steamin' Steve Clark chord changes and licks.

Now that position had subtly altered. It had not been intentional, but once the band had returned to work with Svengali producer 'Mutt' Lange, it was, perhaps, inevitable. The reclusive wizard who had worked the studio magic on AC/DC's *Highway to Hell* and *Back in Black* albums, before repeating the trick for Def Leppard with *High 'n' Dry* and *Pyromania*, Lange was a legendary perfectionist whose intricate studio methods were far ahead of their time. For most producers back then, recording a rock album was merely a case of reproducing the sound of the band live. Lange, who was not concerned with live music, brought a far more cerebral approach to the task.

'Working with "Mutt" is a totally different thing,' Phil Collen once explained. 'He'll break down the sound of each chord into separate strings and record them one at a time, then put them all together later. And he'll make you do that again and again, until he's got what he wants. Which is how he always gets that incredibly powerful sound out of the guitars.'

That was just one of a panoply of party tricks Lange brought with him to the studio, it was also one of the reasons recording *Hysteria* took so long (over a year to complete) and proved so expensive (over a million dollars). Little wonder then that he often preferred to work on the guitar tracks with the more technically concise Phil. As a guitarist, Steve's speciality was improvisation: one-take wonders. 'Mutt' never did one take of anything.

It was after the second of two Leppard shows in Worcester, Massachusetts, and, as usual, we had slunk away from the small after-show gathering in the hotel bar and returned to my room. That was the first time I remember him talking about it seriously.

It had to be my room because, by then, in an effort to curb his behaviour, Steve had agreed to have two round-the-clock 'AA buddies' on the road with him, and rule number one was that Steve was not to be left alone with any guests in his room at night. But they were easy to fool, he said. 'I just say I'm going to a band meeting . . .'

He sat there chopping them out. 'I'm not saying I didn't . . . play . . . on the album,' he said. But there was 'a lot of . . . waiting around . . . nothing to do. I drank out of boredom.'

And the more Steve drank, the more Lange was likely to turn to the other guitarist in the band to provide the sober technical runs needed to satisfy his feverishly precise demands. Steve knew it, everybody knew it. But he felt helpless to stop it, he said. It became a rut; a well of fear and loathing he had dug for himself. He talked of one occasion when he had been 'hanging round for *days* . . . sober . . . waiting for "Mutt" to call . . . for this . . . *thing* I was supposed to do. But it never happened . . . never happened . . . eventually, I'm like, *fuck* . . . you know? I'm going home . . .'

He'd owned an apartment in Paris at the time; a train ride from where the band were recording in Amsterdam.

'I swear . . . I'm home, like, two hours . . . the phone rings. It's the studio . . . like, "Where are you? 'Mutt' wants you!" I'm like . . . fuck! You know? It was like a . . . a *game*. I couldn't get my head round it . . .'

By the time the *Hysteria* world tour was in full swing, the contrast between the two guitarists in Def Leppard could not have
been more striking; whatever guilt Steve was feeling was am-
plified a thousand times over by the fact that his guitar-slinging
partner on the other side of the stage never put a foot wrong
any more. Although he gave a good impersonation on stage of
someone enjoying himself, Steve felt sick at heart, he said. He
felt he was 'losing the band, letting 'em . . . down.'

I listened. I sympathised. I thought, 'Fuck the band, he's letting
himself down.' And what, say, was Phil supposed to do anyway?
Start getting as fucked-up as Steve again? What were any of us
who looked on helplessly, as Clarky began to disintegrate out on
the road, supposed to do?

His periods of drying out at various rehab joints around the
world (many paid for by the band, he confessed) and his mostly
forced participation in several alcohol-recovery programmes
didn't seem to make a dent. Not even Aerosmith's manager, Tim
Collins – who had somehow brought Steven Tyler and Joe Perry
back from the brink and had, I later found out, offered Clark
his assistance – could help. One doctor, Steve told me almost
proudly, had even gone so far as to diagnose his problem, whatever it really was, as 'incurable'.

Of course, even purgatory has its lighter moments – even if,
recalling them now, they come cloaked in portend. After one
particularly heavy night on that tour, who knows where, when I
finally came to the following afternoon, I turned over in bed to
find Steve lying next to me, snoring like a bum. *What the fuck?*
Then it started to come back to me. He had blacked-out on
my bed and I had not been able to wake him. 'He's dead to the
world,' I'd said to myself. Which had made me think of something else. Shit, what if he did die? Right now, in *my* fucking
bed! Jesus Christ . . .

I'd pulled myself together. 'Don't be ridiculous,' I'd told myself. 'He's not going to die. Of what? A little after-hours partying? Bullshit!' The guy was only twenty-eight. Nevertheless, I had read enough Hendrix books to force myself into the routine of taking off his shoes and unbuckling his belt. He was already lying on his side, so that was OK. I just emptied a trash basket out on to the floor and placed it by his side of the bed, in case the fucker started puking. Then I dragged my aching aura on to the other side of the bed, grabbed what I could of the duvet and turned out the overhead light . . .

That was then. This was now. I lay there staring at his back. He didn't look like he'd moved an inch, sweat sticking his dyed yellow hair to the pillow like cold eggs on a plate. I wondered fearfully what time it was. What if it was late and the others had been searching for him? Today wasn't a travel day, thank God, but I had a vague recollection of talk the night before of an afternoon soundcheck. What if they had gone down to the gig without him, cursing him for being the eternal fuck-up? And what would they say when they found out it was because he was with me?

Fuck . . .

I lay there, staring at his back, trying to decide how to play it. Then the phone rang. In the heavy, unnatural quiet of the still smoky room, it was like the sound of gunshot coming through the window.

Steve, until that moment still completely and utterly gone, sat bolt upright. The phone was by his side of the bed, but I was too thunderstruck to say anything before he could pick it up.

He grunted unintelligibly a couple of times and hung up, then lay back down again, his back to me. I could hear a low groan building from somewhere inside him.

'Who was it?' I asked.

His body shot up again. He spun round and looked at me, the shock mounting.

He screamed. '*Aarrrgghhh!! Aaarrrrggghhhh!!!*'

I thought he was going to hit me. 'Steve! Steve! It's me! OK? It's me! Everything's all right!'

He stopped screaming and sat there looking at me, completely aghast. He put his hands up to his face.

'Christ,' he gasped. 'What are you ... what ... in my room?'

'Steve,' I said, gently. 'It's not your room, it's mine . . .'

He let go another anguished howl. '*Nooo!* Jesus!' He looked at me, his head not right at all.

'You crashed out,' I said. 'I couldn't wake you.'

I waited for him to see the funny side but he was too far gone. He leapt out of bed. 'Gotta go,' he said. He practically ran to the door. I didn't get it. What was to know? He'd crashed out, what was I supposed to do? Call the fire department?

I lay back in bed and concentrated on my own hangover, the nausea washing over me like waves. I still didn't know what time it was or who had phoned. I still didn't know if this meant trouble or not.

Then a fierce banging on the door. 'Christ,' I muttered. 'Here we go.'

I made it to the door and opened it a crack. It was Steve.

'Uh . . . my shoes,' he said, embarrassed. 'Are they . . . ?'

'Oh, yes,' I went to get them. He didn't follow me in.

I came back and gave him the shoes. He looked at them. 'Uh . . . last night. I mean, uh . . . nothing like . . . uh, nothing sort of . . . uh . . .'

'Fuck off!' I said. 'In your dreams!'

At last he managed a small, wan smile. He was gone but not entirely forgotten. Not yet. He slunk off to his room and

I crawled back to bed. If it meant anything, neither of us knew what. We never spoke of it again.

The only time I really saw him with a smile on his pinched, little face was the time he talked of a recent tour-break vacation he and Lorelei had spent together in Antigua, where Steve had gotten to know Keith Richards, who owned a house there. 'He was just great,' Steve beamed. 'Exactly how you imagine him . . . really *funky* . . . We jammed together and . . . everything.'

You bet. He showed me pictures of the two of them sitting around playing guitars together by Keith's swimming pool, along with Squeeze singer Glenn Tilbrook, who also happened to be there and appeared to be wearing ladies' underwear on his head – all of them mugging for the camera in huge, expensive-looking sunglasses. Steve and Keith had even, he admitted somewhat bashfully, written 'a sort of . . . song . . . together.' He made it sound like nothing ('just a jam') but when, a few months later, I gave him my review copy of Keith's then still unreleased *Talk is Cheap* album, he immediately checked the track listing. Not because he really thought for a minute that it would be on there (it wasn't) but 'just in case . . .'

It was sad and strangely touching. I had never seen him so up about anything; never had a glimpse before of the innocent fan who still apparently lurked somewhere within. But then hanging out with Keith Richards was both another boyhood fantasy fulfilled and, best of all, a chance to get away from the meticulously manicured role Leppard's music now demanded of him. As he said, 'It was great just to hang out and . . . play stuff . . . let rip . . . so cool, so . . . different.'

During the quiet moments, around dawn, when we talked of things other than Def Leppard, he would admit that Joe was right: that he was his own worst enemy; that there were millions of people out there who would give more than was theirs to give to trade places with him. But instead of helping him shake off his self-doubt, to ease his inner loathing, knowing these things only made him feel even more of a fake, he said; even *less* deserving of respect.

At such times, his self-pity could be suffocating, and even I would grow impatient. When, on one occasion, he offered to 'lend' me $50,000, I nearly lost it.

'No big deal,' he had said cheerily. 'Just like if you ever . . . you know . . . *need* . . . you know? Like fifty grand . . . you know?'

I didn't like that. It smelled of something. I got to my feet unsteadily and looked at him.

'WHADDAYA THINK I AM?' I yelled. 'SOME SORT OF *FUCKING GROUPIE?*'

'No!' he stuttered. 'No! No! It's just . . . all I'm saying . . . just . . .'

'YOU THINK I'M HERE 'COS YOU'RE SOME FUCKING MILLIONAIRE?' I roared, unable to stop now I'd started.

'No!' he bleated. 'It's just . . .'

'*I DON'T NEED YOUR FUCKING MONEY, MAN!*'

He stood up and faced me, the tears welling in his eyes. 'No . . . no . . . no . . .' He reached for me, arms whirring like an out-of-control robot's. 'No, man . . . I didn't mean . . . no . . .'

I held him there like a baby, his face sobbing on my shoulder, and I realised then that he wasn't really talking about money. It wasn't money Steve wanted to give to me; to share. It was . . . something else.

That final night of the *Hysteria* tour, they threw a party in some big, empty room backstage at the venue. Being in the middle of nowhere – rule of the road: if it ain't NY or LA, baby, then it's nowhere – it was a strangely dismal occasion. Apart from the band, their management and roadies, various girlfriends and wives, and a sprinkling of media buds like myself, it was a party to which no one outside the tour had actually been invited, and despite the free beer and nibbles, nobody seemed much in the mood for it. The tour had taken fifteen months to complete and now everybody was in too much of a hurry to get home to bother with one more party.

I sat at a table chatting to Steve and Lorelei, but it was clear Steve's mind was elsewhere. He'd confided in me the night before that he'd just pocketed a tour-bonus cheque for around a million bucks. 'Thing is . . . I dunno what, like . . . you *do* with it.' By then, I knew him well enough to know this was code for: 'I don't deserve this money.' Instead of seeing it as his reward for the long months away from home, he saw it as yet more proof that he'd fooled them all again; that he was a bad man, soon for the chop.

But knowing what was going on in his head no longer made me particularly sympathetic. Fifty grand was one thing, but a man who doesn't know what to do with a million dollars is in serious fucking trouble. Even I knew that.

I left him there at the table, staring balefully into space, while Lorelei chatted away regardless, like everything just made sense. I paused at the door and looked back at them – her all chatty and sweet, him as silent as the grave – and I wondered idly how long it would be before she woke up one morning and realised this wasn't fun any more and that maybe it was time to find herself a real go-getter.

Because we left on different flights the next day, I never got a chance to say goodbye to Steve properly. We had already swapped numbers, so it didn't really matter. We would catch up with each other later, somewhere else down the road.

Sure enough, we did run into each other a few more times, the last occasion at a Queensrÿche show in London, maybe a year later. He was the same. A little less frayed around the edges

maybe, but as soon as we got to have a quiet word alone together at the bar it became clear nothing had really changed.

If anything, he appeared even more forlorn. Much as touring
drove him crazy, sitting around having nothing to do was even
worse, it seemed. Lorelei was gone – replaced by someone he
didn't even bother to introduce me to, and who I felt sorry for,
and who was trying in vain to get him to leave the bar and go
and watch the show. 'In a minute,' he kept saying. 'I'm just . . .
this . . .' Until she gave up and went off on her own.

We stayed in the bar all night drinking, of course, interspersed
with little bumps when we thought no one was looking. He had
this little brown bottle with a tiny silver spoon attached to the
inside of the cap. It was neat. But at the end, when he invited
me back to his pad in Chelsea for 'a nightcap' I found myself
making some excuse. Some stories just go on too long, I guess,
and you grow bored.

'How about . . . fishing, then?' he asked, as we stood on the
street.

'What?'

'Fishing . . . you know? I've been thinking about it. Just getting away . . . you know? Like, *totally* away . . . And I thought
. . . "Fishing!"'

At first I thought he was joking. I had never been fishing in
my life. Who the fuck would want to? But then I looked into his
eyes, noticed the tiniest glimmer of something very much resem-
bling hope lurking somewhere at the back there in the darkness,
and realised once again that it wasn't really fishing or money or
drugs or even the band Steve was ever talking about.

'I'd love to,' I said.

'Great,' he said. 'It'll be great. We'll just take off! Grab some
fishing poles, couple of beers . . . nothing . . . heavy . . . you
know? It'll be great. Just fucking forget about everything . . .'

'Yeah,' I said. 'It'll be great.'

'I'll get it sussed out and call you,' he said as we parted.

It was the last I ever heard from him.

I found out he'd died when the *Daily Mail* called me at home to ask for a quote. 'On what?' I asked, confused. 'On the death of Def Leppard guitarist Steve Clark,' the girl said casually. 'He was found dead at his apartment in Chelsea last night,' she added in reporter-speak.

I felt the ground move beneath me. Not metaphorically – I actually felt it give. The walls leaned towards me at a sickening angle, my legs lost strength, and I found myself sitting on the floor. My free hand grabbed at the carpet for support but none was forthcoming.

The story, such as it was, was an entirely predictable one. His unconscious body had been discovered by his girlfriend, whoever that was by then, who had called the emergency services after failing to rouse him. Too late. Steve had already passed away sometime during the early hours of the morning. But that didn't lessen the shock. What did they mean 'he'd died'? Of what?

It was 8 January 1991. Steve was eighteen months younger than me, and I still didn't quite get it. Seven weeks later, I had my answer in cold black and white. Westminster Coroner's Court recorded the official cause of death as 'respiratory failure due to a compression of the brain stem, resulting from excess quantities of alcohol mixed with antidepressants and painkillers.' The coroner added that there were no suspicious circumstances surrounding the 'accident'. Other than the fact that he was only thirty years old, of course.

Booze, trancs and smack-substitutes . . . in other words, any other boring night for Steve. What a strangely banal way for a thirty-year-old man to go: dead not so much of drugs but of something more complicated than that. This wasn't an OD so much as a kind of throwing in the towel.

I wept after I put the phone down. Not in the hugely emotional, end-of-the-world way I did when my pet German Shepherd dog died. But in a quiet, sorry-for-myself kind of way. I realised then that for all the time we had spent together, I'd never really known Steve. The same as Phil Lynott. The same as all of them, that was the truth, I now began to see. Never really cared for him any more than he'd ever really cared for me. We were on the road and all I'd wanted to do was rock. Well, we all wanted that . . .

20. The King of Speed

It was a cold November afternoon at the White House hotel, late last century. Lemmy liked to stay there because it was just around the corner from his favourite shop in London, Blunderbuss Antiques, where you could buy genuine World War I military gear: a regimental officer's sword, perhaps, or a copperplate pistol. And – Lemmy's big favourite – authentic Nazi regalia.

Being a big collector of Nazi memorabilia did not, he insisted, make Lemmy a Nazi sympathiser: 'I'm just fascinated with the whole phenomenon. Hitler was the first rock star.'

I had first met Lemmy nearly twenty years before, when he formed Motörhead. He was still living in Ladbroke Grove and I was still working off Portobello Road for Step Forward. You would see him strolling up to the bar of the pub, asking the land-lord to cash him a cheque. Looking as he did – like a Hell's Angel with a broken wing – any other pub in London would have re-fused him. But this was Ladbroke Grove in the late seventies and if the pubs didn't look after the odd-bods and screwballs, the freaks and the fruits, the punks and the hippies, they wouldn't have had any clientele at all.

I'd been warned: don't ever lend him any money. His real name was Ian and 'Lemmy' was short for 'lend-me-a-fiver'. As the years passed, though, I would occasionally cash a cheque for him, and it would never bounce. Lemmy was a man of his word.

He had his own system of morality going on, and he never deviated from it. Right was right. Wrong was wrong. Lemmy was Lemmy.

You always knew where you stood with him, a quality so rare as to be almost non-existent in other rock stars. I admired him for that. He was also very fraternal, always happy to give a leg up to other, younger bands. When Twisted Sister played their first UK gig, opening for Motörhead at Wrexham football ground in 1982, they were so nervous, Lemmy told me, 'There were all these huge geezers backstage dressed as women freaking out, you know? And I went up to [singer] Dee Snider and asked him if he would like me to introduce them. He said, "Oh, fuck, yeah, man, would you?" So I went on and introduced them. I announced them as, "My friends Twisted Sister," and they got a rousing ovation as soon as they hit the stage.'

Around the same time, I had been on tour with Motörhead when another young band, Tank, supported them. Sure enough, Lemmy was at the side of the stage every night watching them do their thing. Whenever any of the kids in the audience spotted him lurking in the wings he would give them the Lemmy thumbs-up and they would respond by cheering and waving madly. A huge bolster to Tank's confidence and the best sort of endorsement they could have had.

Lemmy had also been warm and supportive in my own career. He sidled up to me at a gig once and told me how much he liked my *Monsters of Rock* show. 'You've really got something,' he said, in that charred voice we were all now more familiar with from his frequent and comic TV appearances. 'It's not fake like all the other fuckers you see on telly. Just one thing: grow a bit of facial hair. Otherwise you look like a ponce. Give it a bit of facial hair, dirty it up a bit. You'll see it will work wonders.'

I thought about it, looked at the videotapes, and realised he was right. I needed to look like I did in so-called real life. To go as myself. Just like Lemmy, in fact.

The other thing he did which really moved me was come up and say a few words when he'd heard my mother had just died. It was at another gig – me and Lemmy were the sort of people that were *always* at gigs in the eighties – and he spotted me at the bar, laughing along at somebody's unfunny joke.

'You don't need to do that, you know,' he said.

'Do what?'

'Pretend.'

I stared at him.

'I heard about your mother. I was sorry to hear that. This,' he said, glancing around, 'must be hell for you right now.'

Was he saying I should quit it and go home, do my mourning in private?

'Well, you can if you want to,' he said. 'If that's what will make you feel better.' He paused. 'Or you can hang out with me tonight, for a bit, if you like.' He tapped the zipped breast pocket of his leather jacket, and sniffed. 'See if we can pull a couple of chicks too. That'll take your mind off it.'

I wasn't quite ready for all of that, not that night. But the fact he went out of his way meant the world to me back then. Nobody else had a clue what to do with me. Lemmy had a good idea, though.

More than ten years later, we were meeting again for a similarly abject reason, though I didn't let on I knew. A mutual friend had tipped me off that Lemmy was ill. Seriously ill. That his time may nearly be over. For a short spell in the mid-nineties I had worked back in PR, lured by an offer of working with Motörhead, Yes and Willie Nelson, among others. As such, I had become fully reacquainted with Lemmy's habit of not just burning the candle at both ends, but blowing up the middle too.

But then, as Lemmy famously sang in his personal mission statement, 'Ace Of Spades': '*You know I'm born to lose/'Cos gambling's for fools/But that's the way I like it, baby/I don't want to live for ever!*'

Lemmy was then fifty-three. To be told he might have finally overdone it and be on his way out was not really a shock. It was a tragedy, though. You only get to meet one Lemmy per lifetime, and only then if you are very, very lucky. I had just returned to writing for magazines again, primarily *Mojo* at the time, and took it upon myself to try to allow Lemmy a final word before . . . well, you know . . .

The first thing he said, though, was, 'Before we start let's get one thing straight. I am *not* fucking dying.'

Oh. Are you sure?

'Fuck off!'

It's just I heard . . .

'I know what you heard and they're wrong, OK? It's true I was in hospital for a bit, in Germany. But I'm fine now. Right?'

Right.

'Well, then.'

We sat down.

I was still at the stage where I brought my little brass hash pipe everywhere with me. Lemmy was still at the stage he was born and will one day die in: eating little hash pipes for break-fast, lunching on expensive whiskey, getting his evenings off to the right start with some high-grade methamphetamine. Plus forty cigarettes a day, minimum.

But let Lemmy give you a glimpse into what I'm talking about. I had asked him to recall the famous occasion when Hawkwind recorded their original version of 'Silver Machine', on stage at the Greasy Truckers Party at the Roundhouse in London in February 1972. The same recording – with Lemmy's lead vocal overdubbed in a studio later – that became their one and only hit single. He passed me back my pipe, blew smoke in my face and remembered it like this: 'Me and Dik Mik had been up for four days straight already on Dexedrine Spansules, so we were pretty well bent by then anyway, you see.'

Yes?

'But we had this gig at the Roundhouse – the one where we re-corded 'Silver Machine' – so we had a couple of Mandrax each to calm us down. Then we got to the Roundhouse and somebody came in with a lot of bombers and we took ten each. That's a lot of bombers. We were getting very twisted up by now, and so we had at least three more Mandrax each to calm us down again. Then somebody came up with some cocaine, fucking big bags of it, and so we thought we'd have some of that. And all this time in the dressing room there is constant smoking, you know, so we were all blasted out of our heads from smoking dope as well. And acid. People were producing acid and mescaline. So we all had some of that, too . . .' He paused as he refilled his glass.

How the fuck had they managed to play anything if he was like that?

'Well, by the time we came to go on stage, me and Dik Mik were stiff as boards. I said, "I can't move, Dik Mik, can you?" He went, "No. It's great, isn't it?" I said, "What are we gonna do when we can't fucking play?" He said, "They'll think of some-thing . . ."'

This last delivered with such Keaton-esque deadpan I nearly choked with laughter.

One arm moved up to a zipped pocket and he pulled out a small white envelope. He looked at me. He didn't need to ask. Not this time.

I wasn't sure if he was lying to me about dying. So I carried on with trying to wheedle the story out of him. He told me lots of things I didn't know until then. Like the fact that he had been born on Christmas Eve. It was 1945, and young Ian Kilmister's family lived in Burslem, Stoke-on-Trent, a town known then for its coal and steel industry and its pottery. None of which interested the young Ian Kilmister one bit.

His father, a former RAF *padre*, had 'done a bunk' when he was three months old and his mother, a librarian, took the family to North Wales, where she later remarried. 'It would never have worked out between us anyway. He was a vicar. A horrible little bald fucker. Good riddance.'

Brought up in North Wales, he knew he wanted to play guitar 'the first time I saw *Oh Boy!*. It was supposed to be like children's TV, but it was all chicks in hot pants, all screaming at the bands. I thought, "That looks like a good idea."'

Expelled from school for 'whacking the headmaster round the head with his own cane' he had worked, briefly, at the local riding stables ('I was very big into horses') and at the local Hotpoint factory. But by then, 'I'd heard Little Richard and it was all over. I fucking loved Little Richard, didn't know he was black, didn't know anything except how it made me feel. I was quite introverted, actually, until I got to my teens, always on the outside – the Watcher! But that rock 'n' roll don't half bring you out of yourself . . .'

The first record he ever bought was Tommy Steele's 'Knee Deep In The Blues'. With the aid of Bert Weedon's *Play in a Day* book and his mother's old Hawaiian guitar, he learned to play 'well enough to impersonate Ricky Nelson'.

Lemmy's parents did not react well to this metamorphosis. 'My mother was most disapproving. I remember when I got my first Teddy Boy jacket. It was powder blue with a very thin red stripe, double-breasted, one button, you know. Very hot. She hated that. But everybody who ever became individualistic, in any way, has got a lot of flak from their parents. 'Cos it isn't like what they did themselves and they hate that. It means you've left the nest . . .'

Deciding to 'strike out for the big city' at seventeen, Lemmy and a friend hitchhiked to Manchester, where he got his first professional gig playing guitar in the Rocking Vicars and 'for the next two years lived the life of bleeding Riley. It was the era of Billy Fury and Johnny Kidd & The Pirates. Then they all became has-beens overnight when The Beatles came along.'

Part covers band, part cabaret act, The Vicars 'were one of those bands nobody down south ever heard of but who were huge up north on the ballroom circuit. We all had Jags. I had a Zephyr 6, which was big news in them days.'

It was also while living in Manchester that Lemmy discovered drugs. 'In about 1962. There was plenty of dope around in them days. You just had to be in a big city. We used to call it "shit" and sometimes it was. It was just part of the scene – different from getting pissed, but that's all it was, different. It wasn't worse or better.'

What about the drug that would become most closely associated with Lemmy, personally and musically? When did that relationship begin in earnest?

'Again, when I was in Manchester. When I was in the Rocking Vicars. "Pep pills", they called them. But I was into all sorts by then. The psychedelic era had begun and I'd seen Hendrix on a bill with the Walker Brothers, Engelbert Humperdinck and Cat Stevens. It was like, follow *that*, you know?'

Frustrated, eventually, by The Vicars' lack of ambition, Lemmy came to London in 1967, where he worked for £10 a week as a roadie for Jimi Hendrix. 'I went to stay at [Rolling

Stones guitarist] Ron Wood's mum's house. Then I got the gig with Hendrix, just humping gear and scoring acid for him. I used to score acid for him. I'd get ten hits and he'd take seven and give me three. My first tour was a co-headline with The Move, plus Syd Barrett's Pink Floyd, Keith Emerson's The Nice, and some others. It was like the Rocking Vicars to the power of twelve. I mean it was fucking *madness!* They say acid doesn't work two days in a row. But if you double the dose it does.'

But when Jimi left for America, Lemmy was laid off. He was 'dealing dope in Kensington Market' when he first met Dik Mik – real name, Michael Davis – and 'discovered we had this mutual interest in how long the human body can be made to jump about without stopping'.

It was 1971. Dik Mik was Hawkwind's 'audio generator' player (a customised ring modulator which Dik Mik liked to claim he'd made from the parts of an old vacuum cleaner). When the band, whose line-up could never be described as 'stable', found themselves in urgent need of a bass player, Dik Mik suggested his new pal. It didn't matter that Lemmy didn't actually play bass.

History has tended to look on Hawkwind as the runt of the psychedelic litter, but for Lemmy, 'They were unique. For me, they were better than the Floyd.'

Featuring a vast and colourful cast of in-house eccentrics – including writers Robert Calvert and Michael Moorcock; lighting wizard Jonathan Smeeton (aka Liquid Len); stage designer Barney Bubbles; and not least the gorgeous Stacia, whose naked 'Amazonian' dancing was always a highlight – Lemmy still managed to somehow stick out.

At the time Lemmy joined them, Hawkwind were already renowned – if that's the right word – in London for their free gigs with the likes of the Pink Fairies, playing every Saturday under the arches in Portobello Road. They had also gained a foothold on the UK charts when their second album, *In Search of Space*, got as high as No. 18. ('The band's claim that it is specifically aimed at dope freaks certainly seems to be valid,' reckoned *Melody Maker* in its review.)

It was 'Silver Machine', though, released six months after Lemmy joined, that sealed Hawkwind's fate for ever. Mixed straight off the desk at the Roundhouse by future Stiff Records supremo Dave Robinson, and originally featuring the certifiably mad Robert Calvert, who wrote the lyrics, on 'spoken-word' vocals, the recording only came to life when the band's manager, Doug Smith, later took Lemmy into the studio to re-record the vocals and remix it himself.

'Lemmy just had the best voice for it,' Doug would later tell me, during my time as Hawkwind's PR in the late seventies. 'But, of course, Bob was *not* pleased when he found out.' In fact, Bob, who had just been sectioned for twenty-eight days, had no say in the matter. 'My decision, I'm afraid,' said Doug.

Almost everybody with the exception of Doug and Lemmy were stunned when 'Silver Machine' actually became a hit, reaching No. 3 in the UK in July 1972. 'It just reverberated everywhere and we had a hit in virtually every country in the world.'

According to Lemmy, the rest of the band 'hated it' when 'Silver Machine' became a hit with his vocals. 'They tried *everybody* else in the band before me: Nik Turner, Bob Calvert, Dave Brock . . . there was only me and the drummer left. So they tried me and I sang it very, very well the first time. And they fucking couldn't stand it! And then it was a hit and they *really* couldn't stand it! My picture on the front of the *NME* without them – the one who took them filthy speed drugs.'

'Silver Machine' was also a turning point in other ways. 'Everybody became very serious suddenly,' he scowled. 'Hawk-wind were dangerous, man. We used to give people epileptic fits. We used to lock all the doors in the hall and we used to have the strobes pointed out at the crowd. Five strobes from the stage all slow – wocka-wocka-wocka. We used to fuck people up good, man.'

Certainly that was the feeling I got at the Rainbow in 1972 when the crowd broke down the doors to allow the ticketless in. The police arrived but there was nothing they could do and the crowd cheered as the outnumbered 'pigs' were forced to with-draw, realising they would have a riot on their hands if they tried to throw even one person out.

The band headed at warp-speed for America, where word had now spread of the new 'space rock' band from England. By April '74, they were headlining 7,000-seater arenas like the Chicago Auditorium; Stevie Wonder and Alice Cooper both attended their show at Stein's Academy of Music, in New York.

And, of course, America was also the home of more familiar pastimes. 'We got spiked once, in Cleveland, with angel dust by two separate bunches of hippies,' Lemmy told me, 'and we were out there on stage going, "OK, I'm Superman! No, I'm not. I'm a piece of wood!" Those were the days.'

And so they might have continued had the band not been ... well, Hawkwind. Lemmy made two more albums with Hawkwind, *Hall of the Mountain Grill*, named after a café in Ladbroke Grove, and *Warrior on the Edge of Time*. Then Lemmy got busted on the Canadian border, *en route* to a show in Toronto, in May 1975, and his world collapsed. Charged with possession of cocaine (a felony later downgraded to a fine when it turned out it was amphetamine sulphate he was carrying, not then actually illegal in Canada), over twenty years later Lemmy still insisted the bust 'was just an excuse to get rid of me'. According to Lemmy, 'The band was split into the speed camp and the psychedelic camp. Me and Dik Mik were the untouchables because we liked speed.'

Lemmy, the hard man with the biker mutton chops and the Iron Cross about his neck, was devastated. 'He rang me in tears,' Doug would later tell me. 'Because, in his own way, Lemmy's a free spirit. Life came and life went for Lemmy. You didn't question the fact that sometimes he was a pain in the arse, and sometimes he was late, or rude, or wicked, or just a nuisance. Everybody had their own foibles that were just appalling on some occasions.'

There was, of course, a silver lining. As Lemmy pointed out, 'I would never have left Hawkwind if they hadn't fired me.' And not forgetting that, 'When I got back from America after being sacked I went round and fucked all their old ladies. As revenge.'

Lemmy originally wanted to call his new band Bastard, but Doug Smith simply refused, taking it upon himself to give them the name Motörhead – American slang for speed freak, and the title of the last recording Lemmy made with Hawkwind, released as the B-side to the 1975 single, 'Kings Of Speed'.

Lemmy wasn't having any of it, though, when we spoke. 'It's one of the best names of any rock 'n' roll band ever. I wrote the song, I agreed to the name, so the decision to name the band was mine.'

It hardly mattered at the time. In their first review in the *NME*, star writer Nick Kent labelled them 'the worst band in the world'. Lemmy, meanwhile, recalled, 'Incredible poverty, living in squats. This bird we knew called Aeroplane Gaye used to work under a furniture store in Chelsea, and if anyone quit early we'd all dash down there and rehearse. We were struggling for a long time with no bread.' He lit another fag and added, 'I was just gonna be the bass player. I wanted to get a singer in but of course we couldn't find one. And it was cheaper for me to do it, 'cos I was already there.'

Their first, self-titled album came out in 1977 – and did nothing. 'You had the punks on one side, but we didn't have short spiky hair like them. And you had the hippies on the other, but we were just too fast and in your face for them, so no one knew what to think of us.' The band, though, had their own take on their emerging musical identity. 'If we move in next door to you, your lawn will die,' Lemmy memorably told *Sounds*. And for a while it seemed like it might be true.

Over the next four years, Motörhead released the albums that established them as legends, beginning with *Bomber* in 1979, and climaxing with the live *No Sleep 'Til Hammersmith*, in 1981, which went straight into the charts at No. 1. 'The whole thing just went whammo!,' said Lemmy. 'But there was no plan to it. We didn't give a fuck, and that is the secret. Because if you start trying to please people, you *will* fuck up.'

By 1982, they were so successful they were able to offer leg-ups to other artists and embarked on a number of collaborations. The most memorable being the joint 'St Valentine's Day Massacre' EP they recorded with Bronze labelmates Girlschool; their most forgettable a ludicrous 'duet' with a leather-jacketed Nolan Sisters.

But even Lemmy couldn't defy the laws of gravity for ever, and when their next album, *Iron Fist*, a disappointing hotchpotch bashed out to meet a recording deadline, received poor reviews, the writing was on the wall. Plans for yet another headline-grabbing collaboration – a version of Tammy Wynette's 'Stand By Your Man' with ex-Plasmatics singer Wendy O Williams – proved to be the final straw for their guitarist, 'Fast' Eddie Clarke, who walked out in the middle of the sessions.

But if Clarke's departure was the first crack in the armour, the arrival of his replacement, ex-Thin Lizzy guitarist Brian Robertson, divided the band and its audience totally. Robbo's short red hair, pink shorts and penchant for playing the same song three times in a row made the loss of Eddie even more unbearable for Motörhead fans. Robbo's sacking after one tour was not a surprise. But when Taylor also left soon after, it seemed the band might founder.

But Lemmy soldiered on with new line-ups, and even better albums. By the early nineties, though, Lemmy had moved to Los Angeles, a city he had always loved: 'I think that if we hadn't have moved to America when we did we'd have been gone now. The last album went in at No. 79 and went out again. We had outstayed our welcome.' So he packed a bag, flew to LA, and checked into a hotel until he could find an apartment – which he duly did, a two-bed condo for $700 a month just a drunken stagger from the Strip, on a cross street virtually adjacent to the Rainbow Bar & Grill. 'I don't drive, you see. So I didn't want to live five miles from somewhere I like to go – a lot.' He emitted a suitably throaty chuckle. 'It compares very favourably with Fulham . . .'

No longer 'sleeping on different floors every night' in Ladbroke Grove, as he did back in Hawkwind, Lemmy still insisted, however, that it wasn't he that had changed. 'It's everybody else that's changed.'

Still living alone – 'I haven't found a bird that's stopped me chasing all the other ones' – I found it hard to hide my concern when he explained, with his usual bravado, how he would be having Christmas dinner that year, as per normal since he'd moved to LA, at his usual table at the Rainbow Bar & Grill on Sunset Strip. 'I'm a regular, you see,' he said, studying his nails. 'And 'cos they know me, they lay on a really nice spread . . .'

The move to America also coincided with the beginning of Motörhead as emblematic outlaw band-cum-national treasure. Fêted by a new generation of rock superstars like Metallica and Guns N' Roses, a Motörhead T-shirt looked cool on just about anybody who wanted to show they still retained some semblance of their wild, rebellious youth – including such rock rebels as Kate Moss, Ade Edmondson, Sporty Spice and that nice Art teacher who looks at your daughter funny.

Motörhead didn't actually sell many more records because of this but Lemmy's fame just grew. He also finally became rich when Ozzy Osbourne, who Lemmy had been pals with (inevitably) for years, used several of his lyrics on a series of multi-platinum albums. Lemmy, as always, affected not to care, but it was hard to believe he didn't gain some consoling satisfaction from the new-found recognition.

He disliked the idea, though, he said, of being seen purely as a rock star: 'Most of them seem to think they've descended from the son of heaven! Fucking walking around . . .' he adopted an airy fairy voice, '. . . "Nobody leaves this room until we find David's glove!" It's fucking terrifying! Like the second coming of Bathsheba or something. They seem to think they have a message for "the kids", you know? Mostly, they haven't. 'Cos if you think that, you obviously haven't got a message for anyone. Or the message is: "beware!"'

What really endeared Lemmy to me, though, were those un-expected shots of light he allowed to peek through his gruff demeanour, almost in spite of himself. At one point, when we were working together again, in the mid-nineties, he took to faxing me his poems. He was in LA by then, and writing ex-clusively in the small hours, so these fantastically long screeds, handwritten in Gothic script, would come snaking out of my fax machine in London just as I was having my breakfast. I wish I still had them so I could quote them now, but I do recall they tended to centre around men and beasts and great journeys over mountains, to and from the stars, a great deal of fighting, vengeance and bloodshed, but also deeper, more anguished cries of sorrow and even existential despair.

Inspired, I began faxing him back some poems of my own. These were not so Gothic and tended along the lines of a poor man's Charles Bukowski, which meant very poor indeed. At which point he promptly stopped faxing me any more of his poems. Must have been something I'd written. Or not written. Or the fact that, as he put it, 'I hate anything that smells of work. Like, I never wanted to be in an office. Fucking hate offices – your office, my office, any office, I hate to be in it. I wanna be in bed with a woman, or on stage playing, or on the bus doing the crossword puzzle, or whatever the fuck it is. I do *not* want to be in an office, at work.'

Trying to get him back on to the subject of his health, I drew his attention to the line in 'Ace Of Spades' where he sings, 'I don't want to live for ever'. At fifty-three, did he still feel that way?

'Of course! See, "I don't want to live for ever" is a long time. You could be 294 and not reach "for ever". But I think you'd be sick of it by then. I think anybody would be sick of it by then. Even me. And I like to stay up late, you know? Actually, I'd like to die the year *before* for ever. To avoid the rush . . .'

With the exception of the greying muzzle and the added girth every dedicated whiskeyman in their mid-fifties must come to accept, Lemmy looked almost unchanged from the twenty-six-year-old biker from hell who sang 'Silver Machine'. Though he may have updated his black leather jacket and battered Levi's more than once since then, he still wore the same silver Iron Cross around his neck that he had in 1972, as well as the same

I-know-something-you-don't-want-to-know smirk on his pale, wart-ridden, yet strangely handsome face.

What about the inside, though? Had that changed over the years?

'Not much, man. A few more scars, maybe. You get a bit more impatient a bit quicker as time goes by: I liked my life ten or fifteen years ago, and I don't see why I should change it, if I like it. I just lived my life how I lived it, and people can like it or lump it, you know? It's always that way if you want to be an individual. I was always like that. That's why I kept getting fired out of all the other bands I was in. I had to form me own band to stop getting fired.'

Being a legendary figure, there are a lot of funny stories that have circulated over the years about Lemmy. Like the one where he went to see the doctor because he wanted to stop taking speed, and the doctor told him not to because the shock to his system would be so great it would kill him. True?

'Yeah, it's true. It's partly apocryphal. It was when that Keith Richards thing broke, about his blood change. So [my manager] had this brainwave, he was gonna clean us all up and make us solid citizens. So he took me down to Harley Street, to a private doctor, and he took a blood test. We went back a week later for the results and he said, "Whatever you do don't give him whole blood, it will probably kill him!" My blood at the time had evolved into some sort of organic soup – all kinds of trace elements in it. But, I mean, it's probably a lot purer now than it was then. I haven't cut down so much as *centralised*, you know?'

Another thing about Lemmy, whether you dug his music or not, you just knew he didn't go home at night and take off the costume. That, like him or hate him, he was for real. That was the part I most admired.

'I'm not dressing up, no. What you see is what you get, man. I've only got one pair of pants and I've had them for twenty-five years, and nobody knows that. They think I get new pairs but I just paint the holes in my legs black.'

As the years have gone by, I have lost my personal connect with Lemmy. I had his email, then lost it. I had his phone number, then he got an answering service and simply stopped returning my calls. Did that mean he had, finally, succumbed to the rock star idyll, living so high up in the clouds of his own smoke he could no longer see the ground?

Good for him. He deserves it more than most and, besides, I haven't written a decent poem in years.

21. **Hollyweird**

If I had spent the late seventies and most of the eighties attempting to live out my own little rock 'n' roll fantasy, it seemed only fitting that I should end that journey – or at least, the part of it that revolved around cloning the so-called rock 'n' roll lifestyle and using what features of it I still thought I liked best to actually define myself – in its spiritual home, Jim Morrison's City Of Night.

I no longer felt like a visitor. I had my own room in my own place, right around the corner from the Roxy and the Rainbow. I did my own shopping, cooked my own food, and had my own bank account and social security number. I was a citizen in all but Green Card – these were the pre-9/11 days when a 'journalist' could virtually come and go as he pleased. I came but I no longer wished to go.

I began writing for American magazines, reading American newspapers and having American dreams. I became frenzied with the idea of reinventing myself, just like all the other one-time-visitors-now-neighbourhood-guys. But I became carried away. I was going to the gym so much and eating so many healthy salads I became buff and sex-crazed. I could no longer sit at my typewriter for more than half an hour without having to get up and masturbate. Then when I would sit down again the words would start to come in a stream. I got it into my head that I was performing some kind of sex-magick ritual to make the work better, and took to masturbating furiously over the typewriter, coming over the pages, sometimes, eight, nine times a story. The keys would become sticky, but I had the cure for that: just buy another typewriter! I could afford it, why not? My girlfriends started complaining that I wanked so much I never had anything left in me to give them. They were right, so I would make them masturbate over the typewriter too. Anything to keep the magic sparking.

At the same time as basking like a lizard in the sun, however, catching some of Diamond Dave's rays, smoking Dolly's weed, snorting Skinny Pete's coke and playing with Slash's snakes, I really did sense that this was the end times. That some great rapture was about to occur that would bring to an end all our devil dreams, lifting the good to heaven and leaving the rest of us where we belonged, face-down in the pool.

You could sense it musically, in new dicks on the block like the Red Hot Chili Peppers and Faith No More, crazy-ass young Californians who were mixing rock with funk, metal with rap, to come up with what the Chili's singer Anthony Kiedis called his 'psychedelic sex funk from heaven'. That was definitely the future, I decided. Someone else I knew, some streetwise kid from Orange County who'd only just started writing for the rock mags, told me there was this whole new scene in Seattle about to break out too, but he was only a kid, he was allowed to dream small. Seattle? I'd been there. It was like Manchester, very rainy. Nothing big was ever coming out of there, I was sure.

Mostly, I sensed it in the way the ground began to shift under my feet. The way the sun looked down disapprovingly most mornings. Maybe it was the weed, but I doubted it. Everyone I met then seemed affected by the heat. Lars Ulrich from Metallica dropped by one night and began telling me about his 'twelve-foot dick'! Lars was now married, or just about to be, or something. There was an English chick he'd been with for years – Debbie – but Lars couldn't help himself any more. He admitted he felt more like he was in Guns N' Roses now than Metallica. He even got a white leather jacket like the one Axl wore in the 'Paradise City' video. Everyone took the piss – Metallica's angry, uptight singer James Hetfield most of all – but Lars just didn't seem to notice. Or care. He was fucking more strippers than Mötley Crüe, riding around in limos bigger than the ones Zeppelin used to. Lars, who had never wanted to be anything other than the biggest rock star in the world, was on his own special LA trip – and if you didn't like it, well, fuck you very much.

We all were. That was what LA was for, baby! Right? I mean, right? Fuck, yeah, dude . . .

I became blasé, and when a promising young British group called Little Angels came to LA I hung out with them long enough to write a story about them then skipped their gig because David Coverdale had invited me out to dinner. I lied, told them I was ill. But they knew. Little Angels were a damn good young band, but I had always been more interested in the stories than the music. New bands bored me most of all – they simply didn't have the stories to tell yet. Of course, they were pissed off when they found out, and complained bitterly to the magazine, but by then I no longer cared. I didn't even read the magazines I wrote for any more.

Meanwhile, I was laughing my ass off in some Japanese restaurant where David regaled me with all sorts of stories you'd never have got in any normal interview situation. I got him on the subject of Deep Purple, whom he'd joined when he was just twenty-two and they were already one of the biggest bands in the world. Specifically, I asked him about his relationship with Purple guitarist Ritchie Blackmore. Blackmore was to Purple what Page was to Zeppelin. How did David find him in those years, in his black-with-everything plumage?

'From the start, it was master and disciple. The two people I learned most from were Jon [Lord] and Ritchie. How to be with people, through Jon, and, musically, it was really Ritchie. Ritchie was huge. I just thought Blackmore was amazing. I heard him play some shit, some freeform stuff, it just blew me away. I'm the Edith Piaf of rock, I don't have any regrets. But there are times when I go, "Fuck, what would I have been able to do with Ritchie had I had some more experience?" Because I was flying by the seat of my fucking loons, baby.'

More! More!

He laughed. He said the first time he sang 'Strange Kind Of Woman', 'Ritchie walked up to me and kind of softly said, "That's how I heard it when I wrote it," and walked off. Yeah, so, of course, I got a bit of a boner. Ritchie's a clever man. Now, most of the times I'm asked about Purple and their offshoots is when I'm in Europe. Most of the media are so uninformed in the States they have no idea that I was ever with Deep Purple.'

What about Glenn Hughes, who had joined Purple at the same time? Glenn with the voice of an angel and the drug habits of a demon . . .

'We were pretty close in Deep Purple because we were both the new kids on the block. Ritchie came into that first rehearsal with two German Wolfhounds. He was kind of standing off to the side. I'm having involuntary bowel movements with nerves when suddenly these swing-doors open and Glenn Hughes falls in! Like, all Medusa curls, with his Rickenbacker bass and a shoulder bag and those *Easy Rider* sunglasses hanging off his nose. It was hilarious and it lightened my mood immensely.'

And what about Tommy Bolin, who came in later after Ritchie left and was even more far out than Glenn?

'Tommy Bolin I loved dearly. I was responsible for bringing him to Deep Purple's attention. I got on great with him, but he had a love affair with very many questionable things. He was a beautiful soul, a beautiful spirit and one of those people [who] tend to think they're immortal . . . There was a character weakness there with Tommy, which he filled with [the drugs] that ultimately cost him his life. I worked beautifully with Tommy, I found him extremely inspiring, until it became a downward spiral. And that was one of the reasons that I actually left Deep Purple: I didn't want to be part of dragging it down. At the Liverpool Empire [the final Purple show with Bolin] I was totally upset. I turned round and I saw Jon Lord playing with his head down, Ian Paice playing with his head down, and thought, "Somebody's got to do something about this." And that was it. I had three extraordinary years and I was done.'

We would all be done soon. I felt it so strongly I gave up even questioning it. When it was arranged for me to have lunch and interview Dave Mustaine, formerly of Metallica, now leader of his own multi-platinum selling nouveau metal band, Megadeth, I jumped at the chance. Dave had been a hopeless smack addict for most of the time I'd known him. But now he was clean – been through rehab, found God, and finally had something real to say. Something that maybe I needed to hear, I thought. Maybe.

It was another typically scorching hot day in LA, in the summer of 1990. I'd always liked Dave. We were sitting in a Thai restaurant in West Hollywood, Dave's record company were paying, and neither of us was drinking. Dave was off everything: not just smack and coke but weed, wine, and women. No, strike that last part. Dave would never be able to give up the women.

The only reason I wasn't drinking was because he wasn't. Otherwise I'd have been going for it as usual. I didn't want to freak him out, though, put temptation his way, and all that. So for the time being we were both on the green tea and mineral water.

Now that he didn't have the drugs to get him off, Dave's new passion was sky-diving, he told me, getting his kicks from jumping out of aeroplanes and allowing himself to fall several hundred feet before finally letting the parachute out. He was still a maniac, even without the drugs. 'You gotta try it,' he grinned, between mouthfuls of special fried noodles.

'Fuck that,' I said, reaching for the jungle curry.

There was only one thing left we both wanted to talk about. That was when he started to tell me about what he called 'the sex hex'.

He said he had known a white witch and that when he was young she had taught him many magic spells, including the sex hex. It sounded useful. He listed the things you needed: virgin parchment; hair of a cat (or dog), or maybe a broom; something from the object of your desire (more hair, or maybe just a cigarette butt they had smoked); some other stuff.

Then you took the virgin parchment and drew a vagina on it along with her name and a penis (erect) with your name. Then you wrapped all the goodies up in it and burned it, all the time concentrating really hard on the person you were hexing. Then you sat back and waited.

'I guarantee you, within twenty-four hours that person will be banging at your door, begging to be let in,' he chuckled darkly.

'And then?'

'And then, my friend, she will fuck your brains out.'

'Cool,' I said.

I thought about it. 'What about the next day, though?'

'The next day?' replied Dave. 'The next day you're in fucking trouble!' he cackled. "Cos unless that person really wanted to fuck you anyway they're gonna hate themselves for doing what they did. Then they're gonna start wondering why and the next thing you know they're gonna blame you. They won't know *how* you did it, they'll just know it was *you* – or at the very least, that you shouldn't have let them do it. Either way, it will be your fault.'

I thought some more. 'And you've tried this yourself?'

'Sure.'

'And it works?'

'Fuck, yeah!'

'Wait,' I said. 'Tell me again. I want to write this down . . .'

I produced a notepad I had taken from the hotel and he very patiently wrote it all down for me, drawing the vagina and the erect penis and indicating where you put the names. When he had finished, he handed it to me and I sat there looking at it, wondering. He must have seen the look in my eye because he added another proviso. 'Don't forget, this fucking works, OK? So you gotta be real careful who you do it on.'

'I know, you said.'

'Not just that. I mean, you might upset more than just the girl.'

'How do you mean?'

'Well, don't go doing it on Princess Di,' he smirked. 'You might wind up dead.'

I took his point and mentally crossed her name off my list. Then I carefully folded up the piece of paper and put it in my wallet and we went back to our noodles and green tea.

'So,' I said. 'Do you still do any magic?'

'Naw,' he said. 'That shit's too fucked up. I'd have to really hate someone to do that, and I try not to hate anybody any more. Anyway,' he shrugged, 'I got more than enough to deal with, with the band and everything.'

It was true. Megadeth were big now and getting bigger every day. Soon their new album, *Rust in Peace*, would be out and everybody felt sure it would go platinum. (It did.)

We finished our meal and I said goodbye, in a hurry to get back to the hotel for a beer.

'Well,' he said, as I got up to go, 'You gonna use it?'

'What, the sex hex? I don't know. Maybe . . .'

He just looked at me and grinned.

When I got back to my room that night I pulled out the piece of paper and studied it. *The Sex Hex*, it said at the top of the page. I thought about it: who would I try it on? I couldn't think of anybody. Or rather, I could, but I couldn't be arsed to try to find some virgin parchment and cat hairs and the rest. Maybe one day I would feel differently, though, I realised. So I carefully folded the piece of paper up again and put it back in my wallet, where it stayed for years. Until one day, when I looked and it was gone. I don't know what happened to it, but I never did get around to using it. Whether that was a good thing or a bad thing, I still haven't decided.

When Stevie Nicks invited me to her dream tower in the hills overlooking Hollywood I don't know if I even brought a tape-recorder with me. There wasn't anything left any rock star could tell me I hadn't already heard a thousand times before.

She was only forty-two and the extra weight still looked good on her, squeezed into a little black cocktail dress, the innocent-looking face still like that of a messed-up china doll. Every time she sat down or leaned over I got an eyeful of her pants, front and back, sideways and full-on. There was plenty to see. She didn't seem to mind. It was just the LA way. All the same, being simple man-meat, I couldn't help wonder if . . .

But I was ten years and several lifetimes younger, and when she gave me a tour of her house that ended in her bedroom, suddenly I felt like I had at nineteen when that other older lady friend had plied me cocaine then ordered me to be a good boy and pull my trousers down. I'm not saying Stevie had any ideas like that, I'm saying I would have run a mile this time. She was still very sexy, but all I could think of were all those brave warriors who had crossed those mountain peaks before me.

For some reason we ended up back in her lounge surrounded by thousands of lit candles all sucking up the night air, while she read from one of her old journals. By now, I had no idea what was going on or what I was supposed to make of the pressed flowers and teenage poems written to some poor love lost. In fact, I could hardly keep my eyes open . . . until . . .

I woke up with my head buried in her chest, my hair stuck to her neck with saliva.

'Oh, you're awake again,' she said nonplussed, 'that's good.'

I sat up trying to put it all together, as I had done a hundred times before when I'd simply zoned out, unable to keep up the fake interest any longer. She just carried on reading, the candles flickering about her like tiny landing lights, as you looked on and radioed in for permission to land . . .

Even women I'd known back in England seemed to relate differently once we were all in LA. I remember having lunch with Sharon Osbourne, sitting at a table by the pool at the Sunset Marquis. I had always liked Sharon, she was such a hoot! Told the filthiest stories you'd ever heard. Sharon had been a *habitué* of LA since the seventies, knew the nitty-gritty behind every mover and shaker who'd ever strolled down the Boulevard. To sit there with Sharon and have her go on a roll about some 'perverted old freak' who only signed bands 'who have sucked his filthy cock first' was to feel like a proper Hollyweird A-lister.

Or the one about the ageing Lothario singer, new in town, whose fiancée was well known back in her Hollywood High groupie days for 'fucking Alsatians'; the girl singer who only shacked up with guys who knew how to 'give her a black eye'; the time on tour when Sharon woke up in the middle of the night to find Ozzy had brought a groupie back to their hotel room and put her in the bed next to where she was sleeping. 'What did you do?' I gasped. 'I fucking whacked her round the head!' she roared with laughter. 'It was no use blaming Ozzy. He was too fucking out of it to know what he was doing. She should have known better, though – actually climbing into the bed next to me!'

Of course, there was a lot more to Sharon than knowing who was fucking who – there was a big brain working overtime and a mouth that could maim at will. Once I had witnessed her, as she put it, 'tearing a new arsehole' into a photographer friend who had committed the heinous crime of repeating rumours we had all heard and repeated to each other – that Sharon had had a fling with a certain musician – but which only the hapless photographer had been unfortunate enough to have Sharon find out about. We were backstage at Irvine Meadows, a specially designated area where all the VIP guests could mingle, when Sharon lit into him.

'You fucking piece of shit!' she screamed into his face. 'You dirty motherfucker! How *dare* you spread fucking rumours and lies about me!'

'But, Sharon,' he wailed desperately. 'I swear on my child's life, it wasn't me!'

'Fuck your child!' she spat, pushing her face right into his. 'I hope it fucking dies of cancer!'

No one knew where to look. Weeks later, however, when his name came up over lunch, Sharon merely smiled and said how much she liked working with him. 'But . . . what about what happened the last time you saw him?'

'Oh, that,' she giggled. 'That's over, done with. I said my piece and now it's all forgotten as far as I'm concerned. No, if he wants to come and do some shots of Ozzy that's absolutely fine.'

One wondered what Ozzy made of it all. Ask him and you'd get a different answer every time. 'She saved my life,' he'd tell you, that far away look in his eye. Other times, he'd complain, 'I can't stand it. She's driving me fucking nuts!'

She knew I still scored weed for Ozzy sometimes, knew I'd never say no to a furtive line or two with him, but she didn't give a fuck. As long as I kept churning out the suds, telling the world what a wonder of the rocking world her old man was, that was just beautiful. Sharon knew better than anyone alive who Ozzy was, what he was. She wasn't going to be fazed by some silly little twat from England coming in and out of the picture occasionally.

And yet . . . whenever I see Sharon now on TV doing her nice act, or her queen evil turn, or just ratcheting up the gore-score on some easily shocked TV chat show, it makes me wonder. Where did she go? The woman I used to know in LA who seemed so confident and in control of things? The one that would never have dreamed of having her face out front, not when she had Ozzy to do it for her? Had the gothic LA sky crowded in on her too, finally, then? To the point where she was now the real star of the show, Ozzy merely the chorus?

She would give me advice, the best of which was, 'Once you've got a name in this business, baby, you're *never* dead. Not if you just hang on in there long enough.'

Words that would come back to haunt me over the coming years, as all I did was try to hang on in there. Until I just gave up. Which felt better.

It was only the early nineties but it was already the end of an era. Exactly seven days after Guns N' Roses went insane and released *two* double albums *simultaneously*, in September 1991, one of those nothing little bands from Seattle my young pal had been yawing about called Nirvana, released their album, *Nevermind*, and suddenly the rock world that I knew vanished virtually overnight.

Mötley Crüe, Bon Jovi, Def Leppard, Poison, Whitesnake, David Lee Roth ... all shot in the head, one by one, and left to die in the gutter, their hair still sticking up from all the back-combing. Even Guns N' Roses, who remained commercially successful, now looked bloated and beyond the pale, compared to the leaner, meaner, more real musical mien Nirvana had re-introduced to rock, along with the inevitable wave of copycat bands that instantly followed them into the charts: Pearl Jam, Soundgarden, Alice In Chains, Hole, Smashing Pumpkins ... on and on until the grunge pity pot was over-spilling with suicide acts doing it right on the stage.

In the end, there were no survivors. Big mainstream rock acts like Bon Jovi and Def Leppard would cut their hair and swap their designer glam threads for the designer thrift-store look, crafting Top 40 pop hits while MTV still deigned to show their videos. But it was like seeing Dad walking round in shorts and shades. The classic rock crowd still dug them, but the kids had stopped relating long ago.

My luck was also out. Just as Nirvana were having their moment in the midnight sun, I had decided to go into rock management, after discovering what I foolishly believed was the 'new' Def Leppard. I thought I was getting out of rock journalism at just the right time, while I was still on top. Besides, wasn't it time for me to make some real money, too? I'd supped with enough boneheaded millionaires to feel I could outsmart all of them. I hadn't counted on karma, though, and when the Big One hit the coast in 1992 – the year the deal went down and

Kurt Cobain decided, as David Lee Roth put it, 'that fun wasn't fun any more' – I returned to a London that now laughed at my cowboy boots, made fun of my mullet hair, and had no interest in the old, filthy rich Def Leppard, let alone my new, still penniless version.

In what proved to be the final killing joke, my long-suffering girlfriend, the uptight English rose whose name I never bothered to remember on all my travels, who I'd never really loved but now found myself strangely dependent on now I was dangling like one of Don Arden's victims from my own suicidal career-window, left me for some goateed garage mechanic in Seattle who played in a grunge band. As karma goes, that was a doozy.

I'd seen the end coming since the start. Now it was here I was suddenly bereft, not knowing how or if I even should try to begin again. Rock, finally, it seemed, really was dead. My kind of rock anyway. The kind that liked to look at itself in the mirror while it was doing it. The kind I had used as my horse with no name to get me through the desert these past fifteen years. The kind that lay in bed all day and partied all night, that lived for snorting coke off the bellies of *Playboy* models, and to hell with whatever those gormless little strips of humanity on the *NME* or the stiffs at Radio 1 thought about it.

The clownish, tits-first, balls-out kind that had somehow come to define a world gone wrong long before would-be bad-asses with names like Axl or Ozzy or Lemmy tried to reclaim it.

The kind of rock that was born to die and would consequently live for ever. Or until the day before for ever, like Lemmy said.